The Software Optimization Cookbook

High-performance Recipes for the Intel®
Architecture

Richard Gerber

**INTEL
PRESS**

Charles Corydon

ISBN 0-9712887-1-2

This publication is designed to provide accurate and authoritative information in regard to the subject matter covered. It is sold with the understanding that the publisher is not engaged in professional services. If professional advice or other expert assistance is required, the services of a competent professional person should be sought.

Intel Corporation may have patents or pending patent applications, trademarks, copyrights, or other intellectual property rights that relate to the presented subject matter. The furnishing of documents and other materials and information does not provide any license, express or implied, by estoppel or otherwise, to any such patents, trademarks, copyrights, or other intellectual property rights.

Intel may make changes to specifications, product descriptions, and plans at any time, without notice.

Intel products are not intended for use in medical, life saving, life sustaining, critical control or safety systems, or in nuclear facility applications.

Intel, Pentium, Intel Xeon, Intel NetBurst, MMX, VTune, Intel386, and Intel486 are trademarks or registered trademarks of Intel Corporation or its subsidiaries in the United States and other countries.

† Other names and brands may be claimed as the property of others.

Recipes used with permission are: "Chicken Monterey" from *The Silver Palate Cookbook*, Julee Rosso and Sheila Lukins, Workman Publishing Company, Inc.; and "Balinese Grilled Bananas In Coconut Milk Caramel" from *The Barbecue! Bible*, Steven Raichlen, Workman Publishing Company, Inc. Our version of "Winter Squash and Apple Soup" was inspired by one in T*he Good Housekeeping Step-by-Step Cookbook*, Susan Westmoreland (editor), Hearst Books and is used with permission.

This book is printed on acid-free paper. ∞

Publisher: Rich Bowles
Editor: David Spencer
Content Manager: Stuart Goldstein
Text Design & Composition: Marianne Phelps
Graphic Art: Donna Lawless (illustrations), Ted Cyrek (cover)

Library of Congress Cataloging in Publication Data:

Printed in the United States of America

10 9 8 7 6 5 4 3 2

For my wife Marni-for her encouragement, editing skills, and love.

Contents

Preface   xiii

Part I Performance Tools and Concepts   1

Chapter 1 Introduction   3

   Building an Application   4
   Optimization Pitfalls   4
   The Software Optimization Process   6
   Key Point   7

Chapter 2 The Benchmark   9

   The Attributes of the Benchmark   10
      Repeatable (Required)   10
      Representative (Required)   11
      Easy to Run (Required)   11
      Verifiable (Required)   12
      Measure Elapsed Time (Optional)   12
      Complete Coverage (Situation-dependent)   12
      Precision (Situation-dependent)   12
      Quality Assurance and Testing (Desirable, but Optional)   13
   Automobile Fuel Economy   13
   Key Points   15

Chapter 3 Performance Tools   17

Timing Tools   17
Optimizing Compilers   19
    Using the Intel® C++ Compiler   19
    Optimizing for Specific Processors   21
    Writing Functions Specific to One Processor   22
    Using SIMD Instructions   23
    Automatic Vectorization   24
    C++ Class Libraries for SIMD Operations   24
    Intrinsics   26
    Inline Assembly Language   26
    Other Compiler Optimizations   27
Types of Software Profilers   28
Performance Monitor   28
VTune™ Performance Analyzer   29
    Sampling   29
    Call Graph Profiling   31
    Source Code Analysis   33
Microsoft Visual C++ Profiler   34
Sampling Versus Instrumentation   35
Human Brain: Trial and Error, Common Sense, and Patience   36
Key Points   37

Chapter 4 The Hotspot   39

What Causes Hotspots and Cold-spots?   40
More Than Just Time   41
Uniform Execution and No Hotspots   43
Key Points   45

Chapter 5 Processor Architecture   47

Functional Blocks   48
    Two Cheeseburgers Please!   49
    Instruction Fetch and Decode   52
    Instruction Execution   53
    Retirement   55
Memory   55
Key Points   57

Part II Performance Issues   59

Chapter 6 Algorithms   61

Computational Complexity   61
Choice of Instructions   62
Data Dependencies and Instruction Parallelism   66
Memory Requirements   68
Detecting Algorithm Issues   69
Key Points   71

Chapter 7 Branching   73

Finding the Critical Mis-predicted Branches   76
    Step 1: Find the Mis-predicted Branches   76
    Step 2: Find the Time-consuming Hotspots   77
    Step 3: Determine the Percentage of Mis-predicted Branches   78
    Final Sanity Check   79
The Different Types of Branches   80
Removing Branches with CMOV   82
Removing Branches with Masks   83
Removing Branches with Min/Max Instructions   84
Removing Branches By Doing Extra Work   85
Improving Branches   86
Key Points   87

Chapter 8 Memory   89

Memory Overview   90
    Main Memory and Virtual Memory   91
    Processor Caches   91
    L1 Cache Details   93
    Software Prefetch   94
    Writing Data Without the Cache: Non-temporal Writes   96
Issues Affecting Memory Performance   97
    Cache Compulsory Loads   98
    Cache Capacity Loads   98
    Cache Conflict Loads   99
    Cache Efficiency   100
    Data Alignment   100
    Compilers and Data Alignment   102

Detecting Memory Issues   102
  Finding Page Misses   103
  Finding L1 Cache Misses   106
  Understanding Potential Improvement   107
Fixing Memory Problems   109
Key Points   115

Chapter 9 Loops   117
Common Loop Problems   118
Loop Unrolling   119
Loop Invariant Work   123
Loop Invariant Branches   124
Iteration Dependencies   125
Memory Address Dependencies   126
Key Points   127

Chapter 10 Slow Operations   129
Slow Instructions   130
Lookup Tables   131
System Calls   134
System Idle Process   137
Key Points   141

Chapter 11 Floating Point   143
Numeric Exceptions   144
Flush-to-Zero and Denormals are Zero   147
Precision   148
Scalar-SIMD Floating Point   152
Float-to-Integer Conversions, Rounding   152
  Using the Intel C++ Compiler's Round Instead of Truncate
    Switch   154
  Assembly Language   154
  SIMD Convert with Truncation Instructions   157
  Direct Bit Manipulation   157
Floating-Point Manipulation Tricks   158
  Square Root   158
  Reciprocal Square Root   158
Key Points   159

Chapter 12 SIMD   161

Using the SIMD Instructions   162
SIMD Instruction Issues   164
   Data Alignment   164
   Compatibility of SIMD and x87 FPU Floating-Point
      Calculations   165
   Data Simplifying Buffer Lengths/Padding   166
Integer SIMD   166
Single-Precision Floating-Point SIMD   167
Reciprocal Approximations Accuracy   168
Double-Precision Floating-Point SIMD   168
SIMD Data Organization   169
Determining Where to Use SIMD   176
Key Points   177

Chapter 13 Processor-Specific Optimizations   179

32-bit Intel Architectures   179
The Pentium III Processor   182
L1 Instruction Cache   182
Instruction Decoding   183
Instruction Latencies   184
Instruction Set   185
Floating-Point Control Register   185
L1 Data Cache   186
Memory Prefetch   186
Processor Events   187
Partial Register Stalls   187
Partial Flag Stall   189
Pause Instruction   189
Key Points   189

Chapter 14 Introduction to Multiprocessing   191

Parallel Programming   192
Thread Management   193
   Low-level Thread Libraries   194
   High-Level Thread Management with OpenMP   194
Threading Goals   197
Threading Issues   198
Tools   202
Key Points   203

Part III DESIGN AND APPLICATION OPTIMIZATION   205

Chapter 15 Design For Performance   207

Data Movement   208
Performance Experiments for Design   210
Algorithms   211
Key Points   213

Chapter 16 Putting It Together: Basic Optimizations   215

The Sample Application   215
Quick Review of the Algorithms   220
    Bilinear Pixel Interpolation   220
    Alpha Blending   222
    Image Rotation   223
Let The Optimizations Begin   224
Compilation   224
The Benchmark   225
Locate the Hotspots   228
Removing Calls To _ftol   229
Algorithm Issues   233
Investigation and Thought   234
Performance Experiments   236
Removing Work   237
Calling Functions Differently   238
Summary of Optimizations   239
Key Points   241

Chapter 17 Putting It Together: More Optimizations   243

Additional Analysis   243
Writing a Specialized Merged Function   247
Using SIMD Technology   250
More Analysis, Reduce MemCopyRect   254
Pick a Different Algorithm   256
Improving the Algorithm   257
Pre-calculating Values   259
Write-Combining Memory   260
More Analysis, Remove Multiplies   263
Knowing When to Stop Optimizing   265
Summary of Optimizations   266
Key Points   266

References   267

Index   269

Preface

At a dinner one night, my friend Tony said, "I hear that you are writing a software optimization book. What is that?"

To which I replied, "It is the process that a software engineer goes through to make a program run faster."

"You mean like buying a new computer? That makes programs run faster, right?"

"Well, yes, a faster computer typically makes programs run faster, but that is not what the book is about. It is about rewriting the software to make it run faster on the same computer."

"Oh, I get it," he said knowing very well that he still had no idea what I was talking about.

After spending a few minutes thinking about an easy way to answer Tony's question, I came up with the following analogy, based upon the ubiquitous spell checker, to explain what software optimization is.

"Tony, How do you think spell checkers work?"

"Well, Rich. They probably have a list of all the words in a dictionary, and when a word needs to be checked, the computer can search for it in the list. If the spell checker finds a match, the word is correct; otherwise, the program tells the user that the word is misspelled."

Obviously, this approach is very slow and many improvements are possible, such as using a sorted list of words in the dictionary then to stop testing when there is a match or at a place where due to the alphabetical order, the word cannot be later in the dictionary. Additional improvements might be splitting the dictionary into 26 parts, one for each letter of the alphabet, allowing the search to start at least at the correct first letter. These optimizations are all about testing fewer words and will greatly improve performance.

Many other optimization techniques can make a program run faster while performing exactly the same task on exactly the same computer, and that is exactly what this book is about.

Acknowledgements

I would like to thank the following people who helped make this book understandable and accurate: Tim Mattson, William E. Damon III, Eric Moore, Dean Macri, Pete Baker, Paul Peterson, Koby Gottlieb, Michael A. Julier, Ronen Zohar, Sara Sarmiento, Stuart Goldstein, and Davi dB. Spencer.

Part I
Performance Tools and Concepts

Appetizers

Winter Squash and Apple Soup

Inspired by The Good Housekeeping Step-by-Step Cookbook

Ingredients

1 medium Golden Delicious apple peeled and cored
1-3 pound butternut squash or other winter squash like pumpkin or acorn
1-14 ounce can vegetable broth
honey and water to adjust taste and texture

Directions

1. Preheat oven to 350°F. Cut the squash in half, remove the seeds, and place on a baking sheet cut side down in oven for 40 - 60 minutes until a fork can be easily inserted into the squash. Cool.
2. Cut the peeled and cored apple into small chunks.
3. When squash has cooled, spoon out the flesh into a blender, add the apple pieces, and vegetable broth and blend until smooth. This step will have to be done in batches unless you have a very large blender.
4. Place the blended mixture in a pot, and simmer for about 10 minutes adding water if too thick and honey if not sweet enough.

Chapter 1

Introduction

In 1981, IBM started selling the first personal computer. It used the Intel® 8088 microprocessor running at 4.77 MHz. Twenty years later, a 2-gigahertz Intel® Pentium® 4 processor powers the fastest personal computers-a speed increase of over 400 times. In other words, something that took over 6 minutes in 1981 would now take less than a second. So why do we still need software optimization?

Today's software is more complex and is packed with more features than the twenty-year old simple text-based applications. From games and educational software to databases and operating systems, everything uses more computing resources than before and today's software is still hungry for more. Software performance can vary dramatically depending upon how the programmer chooses to solve a problem or implement a feature. Highly optimized applications can run tens of times faster than poorly written ones. A combination of using efficient algorithms and well-designed implementations leads to great high performance applications.

This book is about how to make an application run faster on the same computer with the same hardware and operating system. The first section of the book discusses the tools, concepts, and techniques used to analyze an application to determine what portions need improvement. The second section discusses key performance issues, how to detect them and how to improve them. The final section discusses how to design an application from the beginning for high performance and reviews the entire optimization process by optimizing a sample application to gain a 20-times improvement.

Building an Application

The first thing that comes to mind when discussing a new product is the feature set- how many compelling features can be incorporated into the product so that people will want to buy it. Unfortunately, performance is frequently overlooked. An article in *PC Magazine*[1] compared three compression utilities in a table, showing the amount of compression for each utility, but execution time was completely ignored. Customers surely want good and fast compression; small files alone are not enough.

Commonly, software optimization is done at the end of the software development process with whatever time remains, which is usually very little. Waiting to the end to start optimizing an application makes it much more difficult to get great performance improvements. Just like the implementation of features and detection of bugs, the earlier an issue is addressed, the easier it is to fix and the better the solution can be. Patches and software hacks are not good optimization techniques.

To help make sure that your application is complete and runs with the expected performance, you should treat performance just like any other feature. That means the performance of an application should be specified in design documents so that engineers know the goals before they start programming. Performance should be designed into the application from the start instead of fixing issues at the end, and quality assurance should test the performance of the application as it is being built, along with all the other functional tests.

Optimization Pitfalls

Software optimization is not without its potential pitfalls and misunderstandings. Here are eight of them.

Trap 1: Application performance cannot be improved before it runs. Trying to do so is like testing the product for the first time after it has been completely finished. Can you imagine how hard it would be to find a bug this way? The same goes for performance. Continual performance experiments, monitoring, and improvements make it easy and efficient to find and improve performance. Wait to the end, and it becomes more difficult and time consuming.

---

[1] PC Magazine, June 22, 2001, "Performance Tests: Compression Comparison". Compared uncompressed, LZH, RAR, and ZIP.

Trap 2: Build the application then see what machine it runs on. Well what happens if it doesn't run on any computer or only the most expensive ones? This approach leaves too much to chance. Planning, evaluation, and optimization before, during, and after application development results in high performance applications with the least amount of effort.

Trap 3: Optimize by removing features, if they run too slowly. An ongoing trend is to have software dials that lower quality or remove features to improve speed. This is most common in games where knobs can turn off realistic lighting or fancy audio effects. This is generally a good idea because doing less work is always a good optimization technique. However, this can be a trap. Instead of spending the time optimizing the program, time is spent adding another button to turn more features off. Make sure to understand where the biggest return on investment is- either turning off features or making them faster.

Trap 4: Runs great on my computer. Developers typically have fast new computers that do not exhibit the same performance characteristics as their customers. Two simple ways to fix this problem: give the engineers slower more typical computers and make sure that the quality assurance department is up and running early doing performance tests on a wide range of computers and reporting the results.

Trap 5: Debug versus release builds. While software is being developed, the compiler optimization settings are sometimes kept off to make debugging easier. Unfortunately, without the use of an optimizing compiler, no performance analysis or monitoring can be done. It is critical that an optimizing compiler with the optimization switches turned on be used throughout the application development process. This helps to identify performance issues early and, as a bonus, any functional bugs that may arise when using compiler optimizations.

Trap 6: Performance requires assembly language programming. Assembly language programming is frequently used to improve performance but is not required, anymore. In the past, compilers did not have support for new instructions and did not do a great job at optimizations. It was therefore fairly easy to beat the compiler with hand-coded assembly language. However, processors and compilers have come a long way. Now optimizations can deal with algorithm design, memory access patterns, and helping the compiler generate efficient code instead of hand-coding assembly language. Assembly language is occasionally still used, but mostly to examine the compiler's optimizations or lack of them.

Beating the compiler with assembly language almost certainly involves using assumptions and shortcuts that the compiler is not. Before jumping to assembly language, try to get the compiler to generate better code.

Trap 7: Code features first then optimize if there is time leftover. Unfortunately, this is a common problem and there always seems to be very little time left at the end. Remember that speed sells and should be one of the main features. Optimizing performance throughout the application development process takes less time and produces better results than waiting until the end.

Trap 8: Optimizations require a processor architect. Most processor architects know a whole bunch of details about small portions of the processor. But since they don't write software for a living (they are off designing processors), they are not always the best at optimizing an application. All the micro-architectural information that is needed to optimize a program is well documented in Intel's technical manuals available at Intel® Developer's Web site and in this book.

The Software Optimization Process

The typical software optimization process starts with the development of a benchmark that is used to objectively measure the performance of the whole application or whatever portion or algorithm is being optimized. With the benchmark in hand, optimizations can begin. The first step is to find the hotspots or the areas of the application that are consuming the majority of time; it's very similar to finding the weakest link in a chain. An investigation is then conducted on a hotspot to determine its cause; slow memory accesses, inefficient algorithms, high loop counts, branch prediction problems, and slow instructions are just some of the possibilities. Once you know the cause of the hotspot, a solution can be designed and implemented. Since not all changes result in performance improvements, the benchmark is used to verify that performance was improved as a result of the implemented changes. Figure 1.1 summarizes these steps.

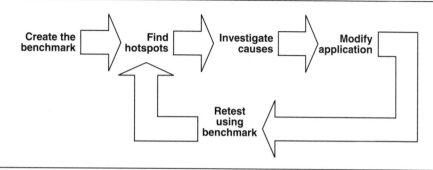

Figure 1.1 The Software Optimization Process

This book is divided into three sections to make it easy to skip around. If you are already familiar with performance analysis tools like optimizing compilers or the VTune™ Performance Analyzer, and with concepts like hotspots, you can skip directly to Section II: "The Performance Issues." If you have some optimization experience already, you might want to skim Section II then jump to Section III: "Design and Application Optimization," where the techniques described in this book are used to optimize a sample application.

The examples provided throughout this book are not meant to test your knowledge, but instead, they are designed to teach an optimization technique in the simplest possible manner-through an example. The best place to test your knowledge is on your own applications and algorithms. Just write a benchmark and start practicing those optimization skills! Your benchmark will tell you if you made a successful optimization, and remember, there is no such thing as the fastest possible code.

Key Point

Software optimization does not begin when coding ends-it is an ongoing process that starts at the design stage and continues all the way through development.

Patriotic Potato and Bean Salad

Ingredients

2 pounds new potatoes, blend of red, white, and blue
1 16 ounce can red kidney beans, washed and dried
1 16 ounce can white kidney beans, washed and dried
1 pint sweet cherry tomatoes, halved
1 clove garlic, minced
¾ cup best quality olive oil
¼ cup red wine vinegar

Directions

1. Shake vigorously, in a water-tight jar, the olive oil, garlic, and vinegar. Adjust taste with salt, freshly ground pepper and more olive oil or vinegar.
2. Cut potatoes in half or quarters to obtain bite-sized pieces. Cook potatoes in boiling salted water for about 5 minutes until tender. Drain potatoes.
3. Add ½ of the dressing to the hot potatoes and let them soak up the dressing.
4. Add beans and tomatoes. Toss. Add remaining dressing.

Chapter 2

The Benchmark

The *benchmark* is the program or process used to:

- Objectively evaluate the performance of an application.
- Provide a repeatable application behavior for use with performance analysis tools.

The benchmark is run before and after optimizations are made to detect changes in performance. If an optimization attempt fails and performance gets worse, the programmer can back-out the failed optimizations and try something different. When performance improves, the amount of improvement can be compared with the expected results to verify a successful optimization. Ideally, performance would constantly improve with each optimization attempt, but unfortunately, that is not always the case. It is the function of the benchmark to detect performance improvements and regressions so that it is easy to avoid changes that make the application run slower.

The benchmark is also used in combination with performance analysis tools. Performance tools work best when the application can be run multiple times in exactly the same manner, thus exercising the same pieces of code. Since performance analysis tools only launch and analyze applications, it's the programmer's responsibility to make sure that the program runs the same way each time, which is exactly what the benchmark is designed to do. One or multiple benchmarks can be used for both performance measurement and analysis tools purposes- it simply depends upon what works best and is easiest to use.

Benchmarks can be either off-the-shelf programs or new programs written specifically to test your application. Since writing your own benchmark means doing additional work, it is a good idea to see if you can use any existing programs. Many industry standard benchmark programs exist, such as TPC-C[1] and 3D WinBench[2]. These industry standard benchmarks measure the performance of some amount of software or hardware, and they produce a representative number or set of numbers that can be used to detect performance changes. Using an industry standard benchmark has an added benefit: usually you can compare your application's performance to a competitor's for marketing purposes. But sometimes the industry standard benchmarks can be a little too general, too cumbersome to install, or time consuming, making the custom-built situation-specific benchmark a better choice. Whatever combination of custom and industry standard benchmarks you use, make sure to keep the process of running the benchmark quick and easy so that it can be run often without much hassle.

The Attributes of the Benchmark

Consider the following attributes of benchmarks when determining which ones to use or create.

Repeatable (Required)

A benchmark that produces different results each time it is run is not very useful. Shutting down all other applications like virus checkers, e-mail programs, and fax drivers helps to produce more consistent results, but transient issues such as the cache state, temporary files, and pre-computed values and indexes still could cause the application to run differently on successive runs. Furthermore, things outside the control of the user and the application, such as hard drive caching controllers, operating system background tasks, and different hardware also affect system performance and almost certainly could lead to different performance numbers.

---

[1] TPC-C is a benchmark written by the Transaction Processing Performance Council. See http://www.tpc.org for more information

[2] WinBench is written by Ziff Davis Media. See http://www.zdnet.com for more information.

Averaging a few runs sometimes helps to produce a more consistent measurement, but this solution is not ideal because it can include things that are not part of your application like the incoming fax- assuming that you are not writing a fax driver. A better choice might be to use the minimum performance number of a few runs as opposed to the average or maximum. The minimum number avoids the fax problem but hides things like cache warm-up effects that are real and should possibly be included. The best choice is to understand the transient effects and to create a benchmark that includes the things that you want to optimize.

Representative (Required)

The benchmark needs to cause the execution of a typical code path in the application, so that common situations are analyzed and therefore optimized. Analyzing error conditions, degenerate cases, or atypical cases generates misleading performance numbers, subsequent analysis, and worthless optimization attempts. The best benchmarks mimic how customers use the application, because only then can you be certain that you are optimizing cases that make a difference.

Sometimes, a temptation might be to use the quality assurance test suite. But beware, quality assurance tests usually evaluate edge cases, error conditions, or otherwise irregular cases that are most likely not the things that users typically do and are therefore not worth optimizing. Quality assurance tests typically are used to evaluate software functionality, not software performance, thus making them poor benchmarks.

Easy to Run (Required)

Easy to run means at least easy to install, easy to operate, runs in a short period of time, and produces simple to interpret results. The goal is to make it as quick and hassle free as possible to run the benchmark and accurately interpret the results. The easier it is to run, the more times it will be run by more people providing more chance to detect performance issues sooner.

Verifiable (Required)

It must be possible to verify the accuracy of what the benchmark is testing and the results it produces. Basically, you need a quality assurance check for the benchmark. It is extremely frustrating to spend time unsuccessfully optimizing a portion of the application only to find out later that the benchmark was defective, leading you to optimize the incorrect portion of the application or the wrong performance issue in it.

Measure Elapsed Time (Optional)

Measuring elapsed time, although very common, is not the only possible benchmark number. Other numbers can be used to represent software performance. The amount of memory used, the milliseconds per frame, the vertices per second, or the maximum number of users that can be supported by a system- any of such measurement might work perfectly well as a benchmark. Any number that represents your application's software performance is valid. Sometimes numbers like vertices per second or other industry reported numbers serve your purpose better than elapsed time because direct comparisons to competitor's products are possible and they can also be used to market your application.

Complete Coverage (Situation-dependent)

A benchmark should only exercise the typical code paths or, more importantly, the code paths that should be optimized. It is a waste of time to use or create a benchmark that tests error conditions or other non-performance sensitive code. Sometimes, in the case of some drivers and small performance prototype applications, the whole application is performance sensitive, in which case, complete coverage would be desired.

Precision (Situation-dependent)

Optimizations are only kept when they result in satisfactory performance improvement, so benchmarks only need be accurate enough to detect satisfactory performance gains. Usually detecting a percent or two improvement is sufficient and desirable because too much accuracy can lead to confusion. Saying something takes between 18,001,119,464 to 18,784,514,894 clocks is not nearly as useful as saying about 12.2 seconds.

Quality Assurance and Testing (Desirable, but Optional)

Using the benchmark to test for functional accuracy can be very helpful, too, especially when approximating values and performing algorithmic tricks to gain performance. Remember a fast application that produces incorrect results is not useful.

Automobile Fuel Economy

Let's suppose you are an automobile engineer assigned to improve fuel economy. The first thing that you need to do is to find a way to objectively measure the fuel consumption so that you can tell whether you are making progress. To start, you need to determine what to measure. You might use an industry standard number like miles per gallon (mpg) or liters per 100 kilometers (ltr/100km), or maybe you prefer to make up one of your own like minutes to consume 1 gallon. Let's suppose you select mpg because it is common, easily understood, can be used to compare to other cars, and can be used for marketing.

Now you need to make sure that you can reliably and consistently obtain an accurate number. You start by specifying the type of fuel, weather conditions, traffic conditions, road conditions, the driver, age of the car, oil, tire pressure, etc... Real quick you can see that the list would be endless and it would still be hard to get consistent results from each test. A solution might be to use a city and highway benchmark, average it over a period of time, and state, "your mileage may vary." You should see that mpg is a benchmark that is best used for marketing brochures and Web sites, not for performance optimizations. There must be an easier way to get an accurate number!

Automobile engineers probably test a modified car with a very accurate gas meter and measure something like how many seconds to consume 10 milliliters of gas at various engine speeds. This test would be repeatable, roughly representative, and easy to run. Using a laboratory benchmark like this one, small performance improvements can be detected and detailed analysis while running the benchmark is possible. The benchmark of number of seconds to consume 10 milliliters is not useful to consumers, but that doesn't matter because benchmarks are used for performance instead of marketing.

Example 2.1 Create a Benchmark

Sometimes, the benchmark can be as simple as using a stopwatch to measure the execution time of your application while processing a few different data sets and recording the results in a table. Don't pass up an opportunity to keep the benchmark extra simple.

Problem

Create a benchmark for the HUFF.EXE sample program located on the CD. HUFF.EXE uses the technique of Huffman Encoding to compress a file.

Solution

The first step is to determine what should be measured. Elapsed time and amount of compression seem like two great choices. To make the benchmark representative of a typical usage, files of different lengths and compression difficulty should be used. To record the benchmark results, use the table shown in Table 2.1.

Table 2.1   Sample Table for Reporting Benchmark Numbers for HUFF.EXE

	Version 1	Version 2	Version 3
JPEG file: **Mars.jpg** **510,272 bytes**	4.5 seconds 484,777 bytes		
Text file: **Constitution5.txt** **559,140 bytes**	2.1 seconds 339,969 bytes		

After running the tests multiple times in a row, the timings are very similar meaning that the results contain very few, if any, transient issues. Just in case an unexpected fax comes in, you should specify that the benchmark should be run twice on each file, and if the results are not similar, additional tests should be done until the results are similar.

Key Points

Keep these characteristics of the benchmark in mind when you start to optimize performance:

- The benchmark is the program or process that is used to measure application performance and conduct performance analysis.

- The benchmark has to be at least repeatable, representative, and easy to run.

- Benchmarks already exist for some types of applications like databases and 3D libraries. For other applications, one or more custom benchmarks may need to be written.

Crab-licious Crab Cakes

Ingredients

1 pound lump crabmeat, picked over without breaking lumps
to remove any shells
2 teaspoons chopped basil
2 teaspoons chopped dill
½ teaspoon dried mustard
4 tablespoons Panko flakes, Japanese style bread crumbs
1 egg
4 tablespoons vegetable oil
1 lemon
1 cup chili sauce (find near the ketchup in the market)
Fresh horseradish root, grated

Directions

1. Gently mix crabmeat, basil, dill, mustard, half of the Panko, egg, and 1 tablespoon of vegetable oil. Add more crumbs, if necessary, until the mixture kind of sticks together.
2. Divide mixture into four cakes and refrigerate covered for at least 2 hours to help them stick together when cooking.
3. Mix chili sauce and freshly grated horseradish root to taste to make the cocktail sauce.
4. Heat remaining 3 tablespoons oil over medium-high heat in a nonstick skillet and pan-fry cakes on each side for about 4 minutes until crisp. Serve immediately with lemon wedges and cocktail sauce.

Chapter 3

Performance Tools

The three fundamental performance tools are:

- Timing mechanisms
- An optimizing compiler
- A software profiler

The human brain is the power that makes these tools work: without trial and error, common sense, and patience, you are unlikely to get optimum results for any tool set.

Timing Tools

A stopwatch is the simplest timing tool. Stopwatches can either be the physical type or software-based, such as the UNIX † command-line utility time[1]. A command-line time program called timeC.exe has been included on the CD; it displays elapsed CPU clocks and milliseconds. A sample output of the timeC.exe program follows.

---

[1] The program time in Microsoft Windows displays and adjusts the current time unlike the UNIX version that displays the elapsed time of an application.

```
C:\dev\huff> timeC huff.exe constitution.txt
Huffman Coding          'constitution.txt'
Compressed file         'constitution.txt.huff'

Elapsed CPU clocks: 301165274, 210 ms
```

Software-based stopwatch programs like timeC.exe work well for measuring programs that run longer than a few seconds. Anything shorter, and the overhead of using this kind of stopwatch style program becomes a significant portion of the total execution time. When additional accuracy is required, adding timer functions calls directly into the application is required.

Table 3.1 shows the common types of timers and their attributes.

Table 3.1 Timing Function Used to Measure Performance

Timer	Accuracy	Code Sample

C runtime function	73 years ±1 sec	`time_t StartTime, ElapsedTime;`
		`StartTime = time(NULL);`
		`<… your code …>`
		`ElapsedTime = time(NULL) - StartTime;`
		`printf ("Time in sec %d", ElapsedTime);`

Windows[†] multimedia timer	~49 days ±10 ms	`DWORD StartTime, ElapsedTime;`
		`StartTime = timeGetTime();`
		`<… your code …>`
		`ElapsedTime = timeGetTime() - StartTime;`
		`printf ("Time in ms %d", ElapsedTime);`

CPU clocks 32 bits	4.29 sec ±0.001 µsec* (1 GHz processor) * Is affected by power management and out-of-order execution.	`DWORD StartTime, ElapsedTime;`
		`_asm {`
		`  RDTSC`
		`  mov StartTime, eax`
		`}`
		`<… your code …>`
		`_asm {`
		`  RDTSC`
		`  sub eax, StartTime`
		`  mov ElapsedTime, eax`
		`}`
		`printf ("Time in CPU clocks %d",`
		`     ElapsedTime);`

CPU clocks 64 bits	~580 years ±0.001 µsec* (1 GHz processor) * Is affected by power management and out-of-order execution.	`__int64 StartTime, EndTime;`
		`_asm {`
		`  RDTSC`
		`  mov DWORD PTR StartTime, eax`
		`  mov DWORD PTR StartTime+4, edx`
		`}`
		`<… your code …>`
		`_asm {`
		`  RDTSC`
		`  mov DWORD PTR EndTime, eax`
		`  mov DWORD PTR EndTime+4, edx`
		`}`
		`printf ("Time in CPU clocks %I64d",`
		`     EndTime - StartTime);`

Timing functions can be used to measure the whole application or any portion of the application because you can place them anywhere in your code and call them as many times as you like. These functions are most commonly used for timing things such as initialization, key algorithms, and wait times. In the Huffman Encoding example from Chapter 2, a timing function could have recorded how long it took to read the file, to build the frequency array, to generate the priority queue, and so forth. Having the extra timing information is helpful during performance analysis.

Optimizing Compilers

The quickest and easiest way to improve performance is to use an optimizing compiler. Optimizing compilers have come a long way in recent years, and a good one can help you take advantage of the latest processor features and optimization strategies automatically, without ever needing to open a processor manual.

To maximize performance, always keep the compiler optimizations enabled. This optional setting helps find compiler optimization issues early, when they are easier to find and fix, and it also keeps a watch on performance. Only when necessary for debugging, should you disable compiler optimizations.

Since compilers are continually updated and improved, it is important to thoroughly read the compiler's documentation so you understand all possible optimization switches, pragmas, and performance features.

Using the Intel® C++ Compiler

The Intel® C++ Compiler has a whole range of optimization features that take advantage of the newest processor features and optimization strategies. Within the Microsoft Visual C++† development environment, the Intel C++ Compiler can be used as a total replacement for the Microsoft compiler by using the Compiler Selection Tool shown in Figure 3.1 or on a file-by-file basis by defining the _USE_INTEL_COMPILER macro or the _USE_NON_INTEL_COMPILER, as shown in Figure 3.2. A version of the Intel C++ Compiler is also available for Linux† and has the same features as the Windows compiler. See the Intel Software Development Products Web site for details on the Intel C++ Compiler and the Intel® Fortran compilers for Microsoft Windows and Linux.

Figure 3.1 Compiler Selection Tool Used to Specify the Default Compiler

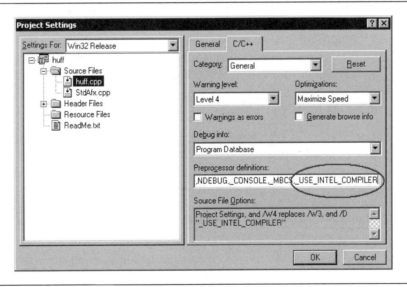

Figure 3.2 Use of the _USE_INTEL_COMPILER in Microsoft Visual C++

Optimizing for Specific Processors

The Intel C++ Compiler supports new processors by using their new instructions and code scheduling rules. When using instructions specific to a processor, like the Streaming SIMD Extensions 2 (SSE2) that are only available on the Pentium® 4 processor and subsequent processors, the compiler can be instructed to produce an additional, generic code path that will be executed on older processors. This output makes it possible to obtain maximum performance on new processors while still running on all older processors. Table 3.2 lists the processor-specific command-line switches for the Intel C++ Compiler.

Table 3.2   List of Compiler Switches to Target Specific Processors

Optimizations favor this processor but code works on all processors	
Pentium processor, Pentium processor with MMX™ technology	-G5
Pentium Pro, Pentium II, and Pentium III processors	-G6
Pentium 4 processor	-G7

Code will only work on this processor and newer	
Pentium Pro and Pentium II processors (CMOV, FCMOV)	-Qxi
Pentium processor with MMX technology	-QxM
Pentium III processor with Streaming SIMD Extensions	-QxK
Pentium 4 processor with Streaming SIMD Extensions 2	-QxW

Multiple code paths are generated, one specific to a processor and one general for all other processors	
Pentium Pro and Pentium II processors (CMOV, FCMOV)	-Qaxi
Pentium processor with MMX technology	-QaxM
Pentium III processor with Streaming SIMD Extensions	-QaxK
Pentium 4 processor with Streaming SIMD Extensions 2	-QaxW

The compiler options can be combined. For example, to require Streaming SIMD Extensions but favor execution on the Pentium 4 processor, you would use the -G7 -QxK options together. These compiler options are added in the Project Settings dialog box in the Project Options edit box as shown in Figure 3.3.

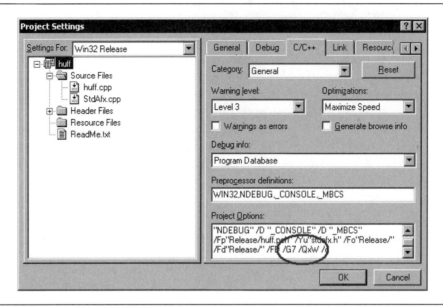

Figure 3.3 Intel C++ Compiler Optimization Options

Writing Functions Specific to One Processor

Sometimes you need to write a function using instructions, such as MMX technology, that are available only on certain processors, and when doing so, the compiler needs CPU detection code. The type of CPU can be determined by calling the assembly instruction CPUID with the value of the EAX register equal to one. (See the *Intel® Architecture Software Developer's Manual, Volume 2*: *Instruction Set Reference* and Application Note AP-485 *Intel® Processor Identification and the CPUID Instruction* for details on the CPUID instruction.) After executing the CPUID instruction, the registers will contain information identifying the current processor along with other information like feature information and the cache sizes. In your application, you could use this information to selectively call different functions on different processors.

An easier way to achieve the same goal is to use the Intel C++ Compiler's processor dispatch feature that automatically generates highly efficient CPU detection code that makes it easy to write a function specific to one processor or a group of processors without dealing with the details of the CPUID instruction. The cpu_dispatch and cpu_specific keywords modify the function declaration causing the compiler to call a specific function on the specified processor, as shown in the following code.

```
__declspec(cpu_specific(generic)) void fn(void)
{
    // Put generic code here
}

__declspec(cpu_specific(Pentium_4)) void fn(void)
{
    // Put code specific to the Pentium 4 processor
}

__declspec(cpu_dispatch(generic, Pentium_4)) void
fn(void)
{
    // Empty function body. Don't put anything here.
// The compiler will put the CPU-dispatch code here.
}
```

Using SIMD Instructions

Using SIMD instructions can result in large performance gains, but the definition of the C/C++ language does not include any direct way to use them. In the past, you had to write in assembly language to use the SIMD instructions, and that meant extra development, debug, and maintenance efforts. Fortunately, the Intel C++ Compiler has extensions that make use of the SIMD instructions easier right from the C/C++ language. The four methods for using the SIMD instructions with the Intel C++ Compiler are shown in Figure 3.4.

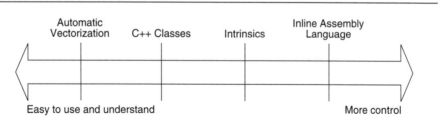

Figure 3.4 Four Methods for Using SIMD Instructions

With more control comes the possibility of more performance, but at the expense of extra engineering effort. When using automatic vectorization, you are letting the compiler make all the code scheduling optimizations that might or might not be as complete or efficient as you can do with assembly language. But, don't automatically assume that maximum performance requires assembly language because the compiler does a whole bunch of optimizations that you might miss. The best approach is to use the simplest technique that contains the desired functionality and determine with performance analysis whether additional optimizations or coding techniques are required.

Automatic Vectorization

The Intel C++ Compiler can analyze loops in an application and automatically use SIMD instructions. The command-line switch -Q[a]x{I|M|K|W} tells the compiler that it is safe to use the SIMD instructions. The following example shows the use of the -QxW switch to give the compiler permission to use the Pentium 4 processor instructions.

```
C:\dev\simd> icl -c -QxW simd.cpp
Intel(R) C++ Compiler for 32-bit applications, Version
5.0 Build 001120
Copyright (C) 1985-2000 Intel Corporation.  All rights
reserved.

simd.cpp
simd.cpp(8) : (col. 2) remark: LOOP WAS VECTORIZED.
simd.cpp(21) : (col. 2) remark: LOOP WAS VECTORIZED.
```

Many command-line switches and pragmas control automatic vectorization. Refer to the *Intel C++ Compiler User's Guide* for additional information available at the Intel Software Development Products Web site.

C++ Class Libraries for SIMD Operations

The Intel C++ Compiler contains C++ SIMD data types that directly use the SIMD instructions. You can use these data types in lieu of automatic vectorization for more control over the compiled code. Table 3.3 lists the possible data types.

Table 3.3   SIMD Data Types Using the Intel C++ Compiler Classes

Data Type	Size and Quantity	Keyword
Integer	8 bit x 8, 16 16 bit x 4, 8 32 bit x 2, 4 64 bit x 1, 2 128 bit x 1	I8vec8, I8vec16 I16vec4, I16vec8 I32vec2, I32vec4 I64vec1, I64vec2 I128vec1
Single precision floating point	32 bit x 1, 4	F32vec1, F32vec4
Double precision floating point	64 bit x 2	F64vec2

To use these data types, simply declare a variable with the desired data type then reduce the loop count by the number of elements processed at a time. The following example shows the conversion of a function to use the I32vec4 data type (four packed 32-bit integers).

```
// Original version using integers
void quarter (int array[], int len)
{
      int i;
      for (i=0; i<len; i++)
          array[i] = array[i] >> 2;
}
// Modified version using Is32vec4, 4 SIMD integers
void quarterVec(int array[], int len)
{
      // assumes len is a multiple of 4
      // assumes array is 16 byte aligned
      Is32vec4 *array4 = (Is32vec4 *)array;
      int i;
      for (i=0; i<len/4; i++)   // four at a time
          array4[i] = array4[i] >> 2;
}
```

Intrinsics

The Intel C++ Compiler supports the use of intrinsics that roughly map to the SIMD instructions and many other assembly instructions. The following example shows the same `quarter()` function coded using intrinsics, which are similar to assembly language except that they use C/C++ variables instead of registers. The intrinsics are documented in the *IA-32 Intel Architecture Software Developer's Manual, Volume 2: Instruction Set Reference* available on the CD and the *Intel C++ Compiler User's Guide and Reference* available on the Intel Developers' Web site.

```
void quarterIntrinsic(int array[], int len)
{
        // assumes len is a multiple of 4
        // assumes array is 16 byte aligned
        __m128i temp;
        __m128i *array4 = (__m128i *)array;
        int i;
        for (i=0; i<len/4; i++)
        {
                // arithmetic shift right by 2
                temp = _mm_srai_epi32(array4[i], 2);
                _mm_store_si128(array4[i], temp);
        }
}
```

Inline Assembly Language

Inline assembly language is supported for coding at the lowest possible level. The following example shows the same function using inline assembly language.

```
void quarterAsm(int array[], int len)
{
        _asm {
                mov esi, array ; esi = array pointer
                mov ecx, len   ; ecx = loop counter
                shr ecx, 2     ; 4 shifts per loop iteration
        theloop:
                movdqa xmm0, [esi] ; load 4 integers
                psrad xmm0, 2  ; shift right all 4 integers
                movdqa [esi], xmm0 ; aligned store
                add esi, 16        ; move array pointer
                sub ecx, 1         ; decrement loop counter
                jnz theloop
        }
}
```

Other Compiler Optimizations

In addition to automatic vectorization and the use of SIMD instructions, the Intel C++ Compiler is capable of doing many additional types of optimization, such as the ones listed in Table 3.4.

Table 3.4 Sample of the Intel C++ Compiler's Performance Features

Optimization Feature	Switch	Description
Loop Unrolling	–Qunroll[n]	Automatically unrolls loops a specified maximum number of times.
Use rounding for floating-point to integer conversions	–Qrcd	Alters the behavior of floating-point to integer casts. When using this option, the compiler performs casts using round-to-nearest instead of truncation, which improves performance, but could introduce some compatibility issues. This option is great for performance experiments.
Profile-Guided Optimizations	-Qprof_gen -Qprof_use	A three-step process of instrumented compilation, instrumented execution, and feedback compilation.
Interprocedural Optimizations	-Qip -Qipo -wp_ipo	A two-phase, automatic, compile-time optimization that uses multiple files or whole programs instead of just functions to look for better optimizations.

Detailed information on how to use these and other optimizations is located in the *Intel C++ Compiler User's Guide and Reference* available on the Internet at the Intel Developers' Web site.

Types of Software Profilers

In addition to a good optimizing compiler, a good full-featured software profiler is required for software optimization. You can choose between the two types of software profilers, sampling and instrumenting, according to your purpose:

- *Sampling* profilers work by periodically interrupting the system to record performance information, such as the processor's instruction pointer, thread ID, process ID, and event counters. By collecting the right amount of samples, you can get an accurate representation of what the software was doing during the sampling session. Sampling works best when collecting just enough samples to get an accurate representation, but not so many as to affect the system's performance. Collecting roughly 1000 samples per second keeps the overhead low (usually around 1%) and the accuracy high.

    Two very common sampling profilers are the Microsoft Performance Monitor (PERFMON.EXE) that comes with Microsoft Windows NT† and newer Microsoft operating systems and the Intel® VTune‖ Performance Analyzer.

- *Instrumenting* profilers use either direct binary instrumentation or the compiler to insert profiling code into the application. This instrumentation is similar to adding your own timing calls in your application, except that additional performance data is collected, such as the call tree, number of calls, and function elapsed time.

    Two common instrumentation profilers are the Microsoft Visual C++ Profiler and the Intel VTune Performance Analyzer.

Performance Monitor

The Performance Monitor (PERFMON.EXE) is a sampling profiler that uses the operating system timer interrupt to wake up and record the value of software counters- disk reads, percentage of processor time, and free memory, for example- making it perfect for finding system issues. The maximum sampling frequency with Performance Monitor is once per second, making it a low-resolution tool. A downside to using the Performance Monitor is that it cannot identify the exact piece of code that caused the events to occur. Figure 3.5 is a screen-shot of the performance analyzer.

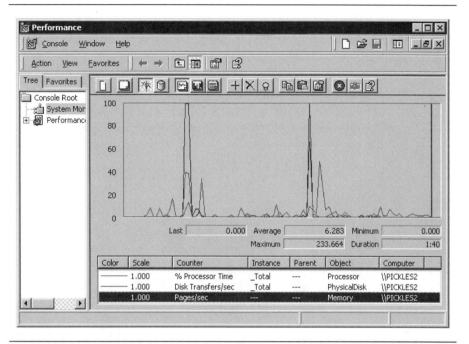

Figure 3.5 The Microsoft Performance Analyzer

VTune™ Performance Analyzer

The VTune Performance Analyzer is a full-featured software profiler that can analyze the whole system, an application, or a driver using both sampling and instrumentation. An evaluation version of the VTune Performance Analyzer is located on the Intel® Software Development Products Web site.

Sampling

The VTune analyzer performs system-wide sampling that uses as the interrupt trigger the operating system's timer, the event counters contained inside the processor, and other counters available in some hardware. When an interrupt occurs, the counter or counters are recorded along with the instruction pointer (EIP) so that the piece of code that caused the event can be located.

The most often used counter is `Clockticks` because it tracks time, making it possible to see which pieces of code take the longest to run. The samples can be sorted or grouped based upon process, thread, module, function, or EIP address.

Figure 3.6 is a screen shot of the VTune analyzer displaying the results of `Clockticks` sampling grouped by function.

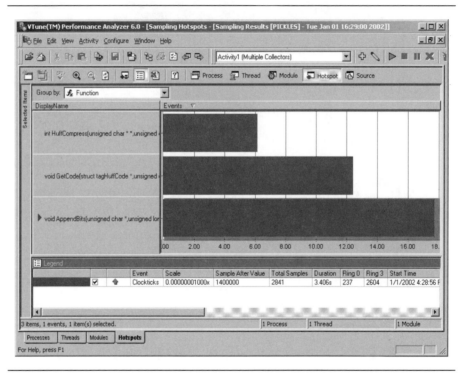

Figure 3.6 VTune Performance Analyzer Sampling on Clockticks for HUFF.EXE

The graph in Figure 3.6 shows that the function on the bottom, `AppendBits`, consumes the most time because it has the longest bar, and the `GetCode` and `HuffCompress` functions are the second and third highest consumers accordingly. Knowing which functions consume the most time tells you where to start optimizing the application.

The VTune analyzer can track about 50-100 processor events, depending upon the processor on which the application is running. One such common event is 1ˢᵗ Level Cache Load Misses Retired, which is shown in Figure 3.7.

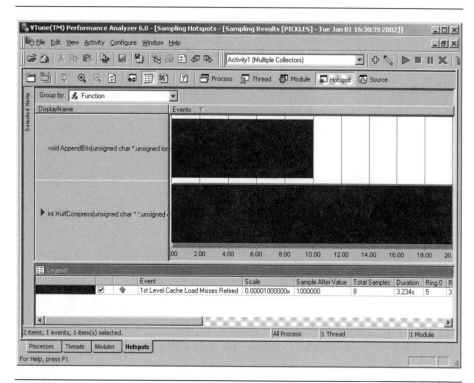

Figure 3.7 VTune Analyzer Sampling on L1 Cache Misses for HUFF.EXE

Here you can see that the function on the bottom, HuffCompress, contains the most samples and it therefore has the most L1 cache misses. It is interesting to note that HuffCompress is not the most time-consuming function, as shown in Figure 3.6. Combinations of the event counters help determine the reasons that a function is taking so much time.

Call Graph Profiling

Call graph profiling uses instrumentation to profile an application. It shows a function hierarchy, the time elapsed in the function and its descendants, and the number of calls. This type of information is most helpful for discovering algorithm issues and supplementing the sampling analysis. Figure 3.8 is a screen shot of call graph from the VTune analyzer.

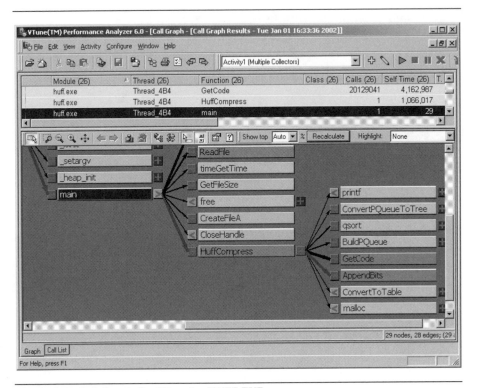

Figure 3.8 Call Graph Profiling for HUFF.EXE

The call graph picture shows that function `main` calls `HuffCompress` that calls `GetCode` and `AppendBits`. The bold red arrow drawn from the function `main` through `HuffCompress` and finally to `AppendBits` indicates the critical path or the path of functions that consume the most time.

Source Code Analysis

One of the major benefits of the VTune Performance Analyzer is its ability to perform analysis on the source code to detect compiler-related performance issues. Things like ignored return values, loop invariant statements, and integer type conversions can all affect performance, but these issues are hard to spot. Compilers, strictly limited by the C language specification, cannot perform some optimizations, even if the optimizations have extremely low chance of unwanted side effects in most situations. Using compiler technology, the VTune analyzer looks for these situations and reports them on the source window, as shown in Figure 3.9.

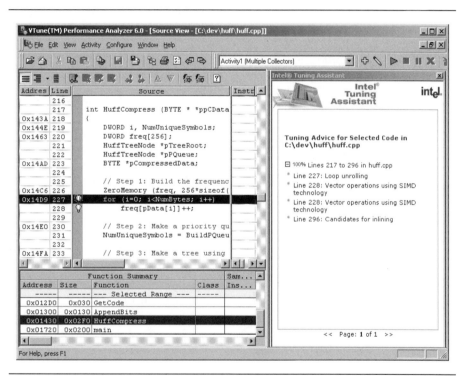

Figure 3.9 Intel® Tuning Assistant in the VTune Analyzer

Microsoft Visual C++ Profiler

The profiler that comes with Microsoft Visual C++/Visual Studio[†] uses instrumentation. It produces a text listing of the executed functions and the amount of time spent in each one, shown in Figure 3.10.

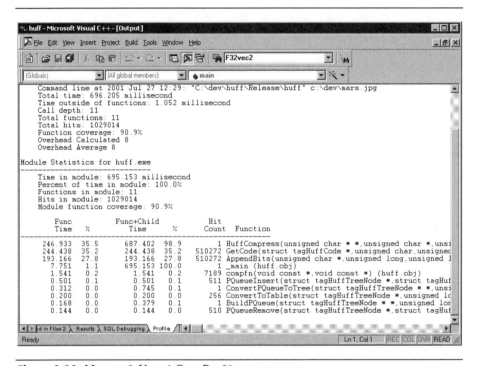

Figure 3.10 Microsoft Visual C++ Profiler

The Visual C++ profiler is best used for code coverage because it doesn't show any function relationship and has a high overhead.

Sampling Versus Instrumentation

Sampling and instrumentation are used as complementary performance analysis techniques. Typically, you begin profiling with sampling due to its low-overhead and system-wide analysis, then follow with call graph if additional information is required. Table 3.5 is a comparison of features and benefits.

Table 3.5 Sampling Versus Call Graph Profiling

	Sampling	Instrumentation
Overhead	Very low, typically ~1%.	Can be high, 10 - 500%.
System-wide profiling	Yes. Profiles everything—all applications, drivers, and operating system functions.	No, just the application, its call tree, and instrumented DLLs.
Detects unexpected events	Yes. Can detect other programs that are stealing system time, such as an incoming fax.	No, just tracks the applications and its call tree.
Setup	None.	Automatic insertion of data collection stubs required.
Data collected	Counter data, processor state, and operating system state.	Call graph, function hierarchy, call times, and critical path.
Data granularity	Identifies the assembly language instructions and source line that caused an event.	Identifies functions.
Detects algorithm issues	No. Limited to processes, thread, modules, functions and instructions.	Yes. Can see that an algorithm or a specific call path through the application is expensive.

Human Brain: Trial and Error, Common Sense, and Patience

All too often, optimization engineers get stuck in the low-level details of a performance issue and fail to address the larger problem. Ask yourself the following questions:

■ *Do the performance numbers make sense?* Sometimes due to processor architecture, power management, or background operating system tasks, performance numbers will be wrong. Think about what the numbers are telling you, what they mean, and do they make sense. If a program that uses a huge amount of memory has no cache misses, something is wrong. Make sure to compare results to expected values.

■ *What would the simple solution be?* Keeping optimizations simple and easy to understand make for long-lasting maintainable software. Always try to keep-it-simple- the processor, compiler, and your coworkers will be very happy. When optimizations get complicated and difficult to program, consider that better methods probably exist. Sit back for a little while and think about the goal of making the whole application faster and not just the one function.

■ *How can I test the performance of an algorithm before I finish writing it?* Test frameworks and prototype applications go a long way toward helping understand performance issues. A little time spent writing a short application that executes similar code can make it very quick and painless to try a bunch of solutions. Patience with trial and error tests goes a long way to making successful optimizations.

■ *Is this the fastest code?* Knowing when to stop is important. There is no such thing as the fastest code, only the fastest implementation of the day, so don't get stuck making one function a few percent faster for weeks at a time. Remember you are optimizing a whole application, not a single function- look at the big picture.

Key Points

Keep the following points in mind when using performance tools:

- Timing code placed directly in the application by the programmer is very beneficial because it can monitor algorithmic issues, not just instructions or functions that are monitored by other profiling tools.

- Always use the compiler optimization settings to build an optimized application for use with performance tools. Never try to analyze the performance of an un-optimized build; the profile is too different to provide a useful analysis.

- Understanding and using all the features of an optimizing compiler is required for maximum performance with the least amount of effort.

- Software profilers use either sampling or instrumentation to identify performance issues. They are complimentary techniques for performance analysis.

- Use your head.

Sandmans'
Sweet and Sour Meatballs

Ingredients for meatballs
- 1 pound ground beef (80% lean preferred)
- ¼ cup plain breadcrumbs
- 1 egg, beaten

Ingredients for sauce
- 1 15 ounce can ground/pureed tomatoes
- 8 ounce can jellied cranberry sauce
- ¼ red wine vinegar
- ¼ cup brown sugar
- 1 tablespoon lemon juice
- 2 teaspoons molasses
- 2 teaspoons mustard powder

Directions
1. In a large bowl, mix beef, egg, and breadcrumbs. Add salt and ground pepper to taste. Form into balls.
2. Over medium heat, sauté meatballs turning to brown evenly on all sides. Remove from pan and drain on paper towels.
3. Combine all the sauce ingredients in the order listed in a large saucepan. Over medium-high heat stir to combine cranberry sauce. When sauce comes to a low boil, lower heat to simmer and the add meatballs.
4. Cover and simmer for 1 hour stirring occasionally.
5. Serve over rice.

Chapter 4

The Hotspot

Knowing which portions of an application to optimize can be the single most important step in the software optimization process. Spending time optimizing the correct portions of the application will yield good results, and no matter how much time you spend optimizing the wrong parts, you will gain little or nothing. It's very similar to strengthening the weakest link of a chain. Strengthen the weakest link and the chain gets stronger, but strengthen an already strong link and nothing happens. Generally speaking, hotspots are the weakest links of an application and are therefore the areas to optimize first.

A *hotspot* is defined as an area of intense heat or activity. Figure 4.1 shows what hotspots look like on the Space Shuttle.

Figure 4.1 The Space Shuttle Has Hotspots   *Courtesy of FLIR Systems, Inc.*

NASA uses a thermal camera and space flight to determine the locations of the shuttle's hotspots. Software hotspots are located using a performance analyzer and a benchmark. The longer bars shown in Figure 4.2 are the hotspots in an application obtained using the VTune Performance Analyzer.

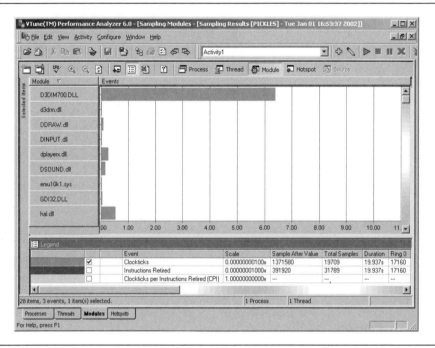

Figure 4.2 A Hotspot Identified Using the VTune Performance Analyzer

What Causes Hotspots and Cold-spots?

Software does not execute uniformly. Some parts of an application take little or no time to execute while other parts seem to take forever. The three primary reasons for inconsistent execution are:

■ Infrequent execution: some portions of an application such as initialization code and error handling are executed once or never. These areas tend to take very little time relative to the rest of the application and are therefore "cold spots," which are not worth optimizing.

- Slow execution: computationally demanding portions of an application can take a long time to execute. For example, the simulation of water flowing over a dam requires many computations and consumes a great deal of time. These areas are hotspots only when they consume a significant portion of time compared to the rest of the application.

- Frequent execution: many parts of an application are executed frequently. Redrawing the screen in a game or processing keystrokes in a word processor are just two common examples. Functions that are executed frequently are not automatically hotspots, only the ones that also consume a significant amount of time relative to the rest of the application.

Knowing whether or not a hotspot is caused by slow code, frequently executed code, or both helps you to determine what types of optimizations will work best.

More Than Just Time

Hotspots are areas of *any* intense activity, not just of heavy time consumption. In addition to time, hotspots can be found where things like cache misses, page misses, and mispredicted branches are plentiful. Since software optimization usually focuses on improving performance as measured by the user, time is almost always the priority. However, exceptions do exist. For example, it is sometimes more important for a driver to limit the number of cache lines used at the expense of a losing a little time because using less cache helps to preserve the state of the cache for the interrupted application.

Figure 4.3 shows hotspots for time, mispredicted branches, and L1 data cache misses for the same application. You can see that the hotspots for each event are located in different functions. For example, the function on the bottom consumes the least amount of time, contains the fewest mispredicted branches, but has the most L1 cache misses. Information like this helps you to focus the optimizations on certain types of operations within the functions, such as memory accesses or branching.

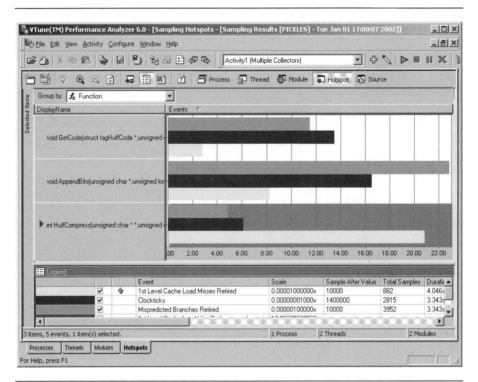

Figure 4.3 Cache Misses, Mis-predicted Branches, and Time-based Hotspots

Uniform Execution and No Hotspots

An interesting problem arises when sampling does not show any clear
hotspots, as in the graph shown in Figure 4.4. Unfortunately, this result
does not mean that the application is completely optimized. All it means
is that detecting hotspots using time-based sampling didn't meet the goal
of finding the place to start optimizing.

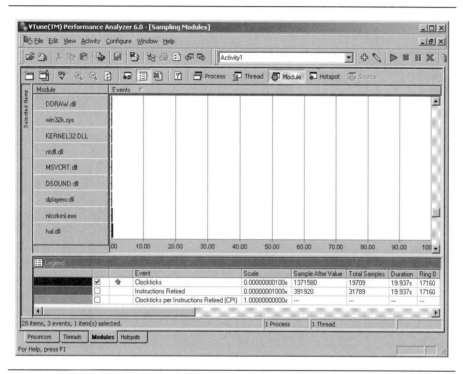

Figure 4.4 Sampling Produced No Significant Hotspots

At some level, the program always contains a hotspot; finding it just requires looking in different places or with different tools. Sometimes hotspots only appear at the function or application level, which could indicate algorithms, data structures, and architectural issues are to blame. In these cases, you can use call graph analysis to find hotspots. Figure 4.5 is a call graph analysis that shows function HuffCompress and its children are the hotspot. In these cases, you need to think about how you can improve the algorithm instead of those smaller blocks of code within the individual functions.

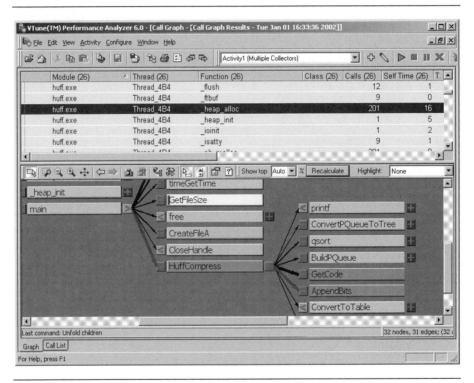

Figure 4.5 Finding Hotspots Using Call Graph

Sampling on memory events is another technique that can help find things to optimize. Cache misses and page misses mean that the code uses main memory instead of the faster cache memory, which is suboptimal. This type of analysis can identify data structures and memory buffers that are accessed inefficiently. See Chapter 8, "Memory," for a detailed discussion of how to optimize memory issues.

Key Points

Keep the following guidelines in mind when searching for hotspots:

- Hotspots are the areas of the application that have intense activity.

- Intense activity usually refers to time, but the definition can include anything, mis-predicted branches or cache misses, for example.

- Hotspots indicate the areas to start optimizing.

- Hotspots can be detected using sampling, instrumentation, or both.

Cheese and Basil Risotto

Ingredients

1 quart canned chicken broth
2 tablespoons unsalted butter
1 red onion, peeled and finely chopped
1½ cups risotto rice
¾ cup dry sherry
1 head celery, center white part only including leaves
1 garlic clove, diced
10-12 large fresh basil leaves, coarsely chopped
2 tablespoons lemon juice
¼ cup freshly grated Parmesan
4 tablespoons mascarpone cheese

Directions

1. In small pot, warm the chicken broth on medium-low heat.
2. Melt the butter in a heavy-bottomed saucepan. Lightly fry the onion and celery until soft. Add the garlic, stir, add the rice, stir, add the sherry, and stir.
3. Reduce heat to low. Allow liquid to bubble and reduce, then add the warm stock ½ cup at a time. Stir constantly and allow liquid to be absorbed before adding another.
4. When the rice is al dente, after about 20 - 30 minutes, stir in basil, lemon juice, and cheeses. The texture will be creamy.
5. Serve with fresh grated Parmesan.

Chapter 5

Processor Architecture

A basic understanding of processor architecture helps to provide some insight as to what optimizations might work and why. A few universal concepts are present in most processors and understanding them will provide you with a solid foundation for deciding how to optimize your application for the Pentium 4 processor and beyond.

The Pentium 4 processor uses 42 million transistors to execute instructions. Trying to understand what every transistor does is like trying to understand every line of code in an operating system; it's not the best way to learn and it would take forever. A much better way to understand the differences between processor architectures is to focus on the major functional blocks.

The original Pentium processor had a five-stage execution pipeline, as shown in Figure 5.1.

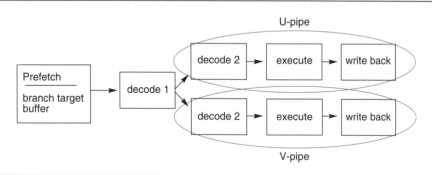

Figure 5.1 Pentium Processor Integer Pipeline

The last three stages are duplicated, allowing the Pentium processor to execute two instructions at the same time. Optimizing for the Pentium processor deals with selecting instructions that can be "U-V paired" or executed at the same time. U-V pairing is a tedious, time- consuming job, and you have to start over every time you make a change to the code. On the bright side, U-V pairing is easy to understand and it works very well.

The days of U-V pairing to gain performance improvements are long over. Processors now use multiple multi-stage pipelines to execute instructions simultaneously. Furthermore, instructions no longer are executed in program order, so you can't even be sure which instructions are going to be executed together. Starting with the Pentium Pro processor, you can use functional blocks instead of pipeline stages and high-level guidelines instead of U-V pairing rules to optimize an application. These high-level guidelines focus on making sure that the processor has multiple instructions available to execute on every clock.

Functional Blocks

The Pentium 4 processor executes instructions in three stages. Stage one, the front-end, fetches instructions from memory, decodes them in program order, and sends the decoded instructions to the instruction pool. Stage two, the execution stage, searches the instruction pool to find instructions that are ready to be executed and executes them in the fastest possible order, which could differ from the order of appearance in your program. Stage three, the back-end, removes the finished instructions from the instruction pool and retires them in the original program order. Figure 5.2 shows a block diagram of the Pentium 4 processor.

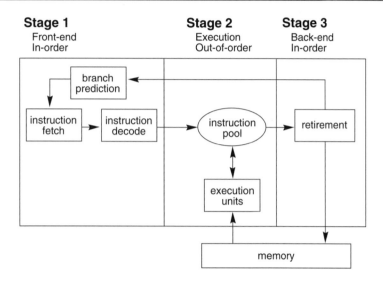

Figure 5.2 Simplified Block Diagram of the Pentium 4 Processor

Software optimizations are based upon keeping the three stages busy on every clock. An easy way to learn about the different stages is to compare them to a drive through window at a fast-food restaurant.

Two Cheeseburgers Please!

Drive-through fast-food restaurants use three stages to deliver your food: ordering, cooking, and delivery.

Ordering Stage

People drive up to the speaker and tell the cashier what they want. The cashier breaks down the order into individual items and passes the list to the cooks. To reduce the wait, a restaurant can make a few extra items ahead of time to have them ready.

Cooking Stage

The items are sent to the cooking stage where a few cooks, each with his own cooking station and specialties, begin preparing the food items that the manager assigned to them. Some cooks prepare only the fried items, like french-fries and onion rings, while other cooks make the burgers. When items are finished, the cooks place them in a holding area to wait for someone else to deliver them to the customer.

At this stage, someone is responsible for keeping the raw ingredients available, too. Raw ingredients can be either ready for use located in the food preparation area, on stand-by in the storage refrigerator located in the back, or mostly unavailable sitting in storage at the warehouse or regional distribution area. The farther away the ingredients are from the preparation area, the longer they take to retrieve. For example, ingredients in the refrigerator could take only a minute to get, but ordering from the warehouse might take a few days. It is therefore, very important for the restaurant to keep the ingredients on hand and ready to be used.

Delivery Stage

It is the job of the order delivery person to collect all the items that comprise a customer's order and to hand them to the correct customer. Since this delivery location is a drive up window, the correct customer is defined by the order in which each customer arrived.

Issues

Normally, these three stages work together to form an efficient fast-food restaurant, but sometimes things can go wrong.

- *Too many customers at once!* Customers need to arrive and order just fast enough to keep all the cooks busy, but not so fast as to overwhelm the system. If something causes a spike in orders, like a nearby baseball game finishing, the ordering stage becomes flooded and customers have to wait longer.

- *Too few customers!* During a lull in orders, employees will be sitting idle wasting time and money. Ideally, the restaurant wants to see an even and constant flow of customers arriving.

■ *Customers order just one item at a time?* The restaurant relies upon each car ordering a few items because it is much faster to take one order for multiple items than to take multiple orders for one item. A few items per order keeps everything running smoothly. If a whole bunch of cars order just one item, the efficiency of the ordering process goes down, and the cooks would have no instructions on what to make next.

■ *Same item repetitively ordered.* If suddenly every car ordered onion rings, the people making burgers would sit idle while the onion ring chef would be swamped. The restaurant designed its process to handle the preparation of a typical distribution of items. When too much of one item is ordered at one time, resources like the ovens or fryers will be swamped, unable to handle the spikes in demand, resulting in longer customer waits.

■ *Items going to waste.* To reduce the customer's wait, the restaurant cooks some items ahead of time, speculating that all or most of them will be sold. Most of the time, this works great- the items are still fresh and are delivered very quickly. When the item gets too old, it is thrown away, which wastes money and food but not necessarily time.

■ *Jumping line.* If a customer gets out of line, cuts the line, or in someway alters the order of the line, the items will be handed out to the wrong people. The order of the cars does not matter before they place their order or after they receive their food, only while they are waiting.

Now that we have a good understanding of how a fast-food restaurant works, lets compare its operation to the three stages of instruction execution performed by the Pentium 4 processor.

Instruction Fetch and Decode

Stage one is where the instructions enter the processor and are broken down into smaller sub-instructions, called micro-operations or μOps (pronounced you-ops), and deposited in the trace-cache buffer.[1] The trace-cache then sends the μOps to the instruction pool where they wait to be executed. Everything in this stage happens in the same order that the instructions are stored in memory with the exception of branching.

Branching requires the processor to be able to handle instructions that are not in order. The difficulty involves knowing what instruction should be fetched and decoded next, without actually waiting for the execution stage to calculate the actual branch result, as shown in Figure 5.3. If the instruction fetching stage waited until the execution stage finished executing the branch, valuable time would be lost.

```
if (a < 50)
    do_something () ;
else
    do_something_else () ;
```

Figure 5.3 What Happens When Branches are Encountered?

To avoid wasting time waiting for branches to be executed, stage one guesses what the next instruction is going to be and starts decoding it without delay. This is called *branch prediction*. When the guess is correct, everything runs smoothly and no time is lost. However, wrong guesses cause the processor to stop executing the incorrectly predicted instructions, discard them, fetch the correct instructions, and start decoding the correct ones. All this extra work hurts performance a little, usually two to ten clocks. However, the real performance penalty is the time wasted executing the wrong instructions instead of the real instructions.

[1] The trace-cache buffer is new on the Pentium 4 processor. It is just like the L1 instruction cache on the Pentium III processor except it holds μOps instead of assembly instructions.

Stage one is very similar to the ordering stage in the fast-food restaurant. Just as the restaurant tries to predict future orders and has a method to discard food not ordered, the processor tries to predict future instructions and can discard partially executed instructions. Branch history and some basic rules are used to make an educated prediction. The rules are designed so that most branches are predicted correctly. Only random branches cannot be predicted accurately and therefore should be avoided or reduced.

Instruction Execution

Stage two is where the instructions, actually μOps, are executed. μOps are removed from the instruction pool and sent to one of six execution ports, as shown in Figure 5.4.

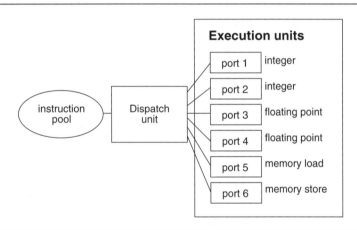

Figure 5.4 Stage Two: Instruction Execution

Each port executes a specific type of instruction. Two execute integer math, and two execute floating-point math. One loads memory, and one stores memory. On every clock, the dispatch unit scans the instruction pool and sends those μOps that are ready to an available execution unit to be executed. Instructions are ready when all their arguments are known. Let's take a closer look at instructions and when they are ready. Consider the following piece of code:

```
y = m * x + b
```

The μOps might be something like:

```
Load r0 = m
Load r1 = x
Execute r0 = r0 * r1
Load r2 = b
Execute r0 = r0 + r2
Store y = r0
```

To simplify things a bit, let's assume that all instructions take one clock to execute. On the first clock, only the load of variable m can occur because there is only 1 load port and none of the other instructions can execute because their arguments are not yet known. On the second clock, a second load for variable x can occur but the multiply operation still can't begin. On clock three, the multiply and the third load can be executed at the same time because the arguments for the multiply operation have been loaded and there are separate ports for loading memory and multiplying variables. On the forth clock, the add operation occurs and at clock five, the store. This sequence certainly would take longer than five clocks due to memory latencies and the speed of the instructions, but the idea is the same: arguments need to be ready before the operation can occur. The term *data dependencies* describes the condition where one operation is dependent upon the result of a previous operation. For example, in the previous equation, the addition of variable b is data dependent upon the multiplication of variables m and x. Data dependencies limit the performance of the execution stage by removing opportunities for our-of-order execution and parallel execution.

The same things limit the restaurant cooking stage. The cooks have to wait for the burger to finish cooking before adding the lettuce and tomato. Some operations- cooking a well-done burger, for instance- take longer than others, such as adding the pickles. Operations are delayed if the ingredients are not on-hand and need to be fetched from the refrigerator in the back. If too many orders for milkshakes come in at the same time, the milkshake maker might get backed up while other workers are doing nothing.

The execution stage runs efficiently when:

■ There is a good mix of instructions so that all six ports can be used at the same time.

■ Arguments are available from memory.

■ Data dependencies are low, keeping operations ready for execution.

Retirement

The retirement stage scans the instruction pool looking for finished µOps. It completes the execution of a µOp by updating the permanent machine state, notifying the rest of the processor if a branch prediction was incorrect, updating the branch prediction history buffer, storing memory if required, issuing exceptions (e.g. divide-by-zero), and then finally removing the µOp from the instruction pool. During this stage, all these activities occur in the same order in which instructions arrived in stage one.

The number of completed µOps in the instruction pool limits the efficiency of the retirement stage. If stage two is efficient and µOps are finishing on every clock, the retirement stage is kept busy. Optimizations for this stage focus on keeping the other two stages running smoothly.

In the restaurant, the order delivery person does something very similar. He delivers the food in the same order in which it was ordered and he is kept busy when all the previous stages are running smoothly.

Memory

Waiting for memory is probably the most common reason that applications run slowly. This delay is the same as the restaurant cooks running out of raw ingredients and having to spend time retrieving them from storage. µOps can only be executed when their arguments are ready, and only two things cause arguments not to be ready: data dependencies and memory.

Memory creates a big problem because processors- these are the cooks- are much faster at executing code than accessing main memory, the equivalent of retrieving food from the refrigerator or storage warehouse. Just as putting pickles on the burger is much faster than getting the pickles from storage, the processor can execute instructions much faster than accessing main memory. But, all hope is not lost! While the processor is waiting for memory, it can be doing other things, like decoding instructions, executing ready μOps, and retiring instructions. Unfortunately, the processor still could finish executing everything that it possibly can and have to wait for memory.

To improve memory access times, very fast small memories called *caches* are used to hold frequently used data. Figure 5.5 shows the memories used by the Pentium 4 processor.

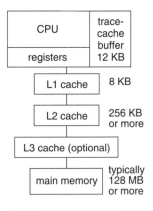

Figure 5.5 Simplified Memory Architecture for a Computer Based on a
Pentium 4 Processor

Memory that is further away from the CPU is larger and slower than memory that is closer. So main memory is the largest and slowest storage while the registers are the smallest and fastest. Memory architectures are built using main memory and caches to reduce cost. It would be prohibitively expensive to build a computer using only cache memory, and a performance gain would not be guaranteed. The good news is that you can write programs to take advantage of this memory architecture, avoiding the full performance issue associated with accessing main memory.

Key Points

To make effective use of the processor architecture, keep these points in mind:

- Processors are limited by data dependencies and the speed of instructions.
- A good blend of instructions keeps all the execution units busy at the same time.
- Waiting for memory with nothing else to execute is the most common reason for slow applications.
- The goals of software optimization are plenty of ready instructions, a good mix of instructions, and predictable branches.

Part II
Performance Issues

Entrées

Green Meatloaf

Ingredients

½ cup plain breadcrumbs
2 pounds ground turkey or ground beef
1 egg, lightly beaten
½ cup freshly grated Parmesan cheese
1 clove garlic, minced
1 small onion, minced
1 pound fresh spinach, washed, dried, and coarsely chopped
1 tablespoon Worcestershire sauce or more to taste

Directions

1. Preheat oven to 350°F.
2. In a skillet, cook chopped spinach until reduced by half. Let cool and drain.
3. Mix all the ingredients together, shape into a loaf and then place on a baking pan.
4. Bake 45 to 60 minutes until the internal temperature is 160°F and the outside is browned.

Chapter **6**

Algorithms

N othing is more important to software optimization than the use of a good algorithm. A good algorithm solves a problem in a fast and efficient manner, while a poor algorithm, no matter how well implemented, is never as fast.

You can get algorithms to solve just about any problem from the Internet, bookstores, coworkers, and journals. Determining which algorithm will be the best for your purpose is a little tricky. Computational complexity, memory usage, data dependencies, and the instructions used to implement the algorithm play a huge role in determining whether an algorithm is a performance superstar or a dud. Spending a little time up front experimenting with different prototype algorithms can save lots of time later on.

Computational Complexity

Algorithm performance can be judged by using the computer science O-notation analysis for the typical, best, and worst cases. For example, you can find many different algorithms for sorting data, but which one should you choose? Although it is probably the simplest sorting algorithm, the bubble sort is also one of the slowest. Its computational complexity is a horrible $O(n^2)$, meaning that if the number of elements to be sorted doubles, the elapsed time quadruples. The quicksort algorithm on the other hand has a significantly better computational time complexity of O(n *log n*). Table 6.1 compares the two sorting algorithms for a small, medium, and large numbers of elements to be sorted.

Table 6.1   Relative Typical Case Performance of Sorting Algorithms

	256 Elements	1000 Elements	10,000 Elements
Bubble Sort	65,000	1,000,000	100,000,000
Quicksort	2048	9965	133,000

The quicksort algorithm can be more than 1000 times faster than the bubble sort for the typical case involving a large number of elements. No matter how much effort you spend implementing and tuning the bubble sort algorithm, it can never be faster than the quicksort because of the nature of the algorithms and their computational complexities.

Computational complexity can be used to compare the expected performance of algorithms. But since computational complexity only takes into account loop iterations and not all of the factors affecting an algorithm's performance, you need to consider additional things to compare algorithms, especially when the computational complexities are similar.

Choice of Instructions

The instructions needed to implement an algorithm can have a big impact on performance and therefore on determining which algorithm to use. Some instructions, like integer addition, can be executed two per clock while other instructions, like integer division, can be only executed every 23 clocks. The speed of an instruction is specified by its latency and throughput.

Instruction latency is the number of clocks required to complete one instruction after the instruction's inputs are ready (that is, fetched from memory) and execution begins. For example, integer multiplication has a latency of about 15 to 18 clocks. So, the answer to a multiplication is available 15-18 clocks after it begins execution.

Instruction throughput is the number of clocks that the processor is required to wait before starting the execution of an identical instruction. Instruction throughput is always less than or equal to instruction latency. Throughput is 5 clocks for multiplication meaning that a new multiply can begin execution every 5 clocks even though it takes 15 to 18 clocks to get the answer to any specific multiplication. Instruction pipelining causes the number of clocks for throughput and latency to be different.

Table 6.2 lists the latency and throughput for most operations on the Pentium 4 processor.

Table 6.2   Approximate Instruction Performance on the Pentium 4 Processor

Instruction	Latency	Throughput
Addition, subtraction, increment, decrement, logic (AND, OR, XOR), compare, test, jump, memory move*, call, return	0.5	0.5
Push, pop, rotate, shift, SIMD memory moves, 64-bit technology operations except EMMS, floating-point absolute value, compare, add, subtract	1	1
128-bit SIMD integer operations, most SIMD single and double-precision floating-point operations except divide	2	2
Integer multiplication	15	4
Integer division, single-precision (32-bit) floating-point division and square root	23	23
SIMD single-precision floating-point divide and square root	32	32
Double-precision (64-bit) floating-point division and square root	38	38
Extended-precision (80-bit) floating-point division and square root	43	43
SIMD double-precision floating-point divide and square root	62	62
Transcendental functions (sine, cosine, tangent, arctangent)	130-170	130-170

* Memory operations may take much longer depending upon the state of the cache.

Taking latency and throughput into account can have a significant impact on algorithm selection. For example, if one algorithm uses ten additions while a second algorithm uses only one divide, the addition version will be faster because divides take forty times longer than additions to execute.

Finding the greatest common multiple of two numbers is a good example of using latency and throughput to select an algorithm. Elementary schools teach children to find the greatest common multiple of two numbers by going through the following steps.

1. Factor each number.
2. Find the factors that are common between both numbers.
3. Multiply the common factors together to get the greatest common multiple.

Example 6.1 Find the greatest common multiple of 40 and 48 the Elementary School way

1. Factor each number.
   40 = 2 * 2 * 2 * 5
   48 = 2 * 2 * 2 * 2 * 3
2. Find the common factors.
   2 * 2 * 2
3. Multiply the common factors to get the greatest common multiple.
   Greatest common multiple = 2 * 2 * 2 = 8

The elementary school algorithm is obviously very expensive for a computer; just the first step of factoring the two numbers would take a long time. Lucky for us, long ago Euclid found a much faster algorithm for finding the greatest common multiple. Euclid's Algorithm is:

1. Larger number = larger number - smaller number
2. If the numbers are the same, it is the greatest common multiple, otherwise go to step 1.

Example 6.2 Find the greatest common multiple of 40 and 48 using Euclid's Algorithm and repetitive subtraction

1. $48,40 \rightarrow 48\text{-}40, 40 \rightarrow 8, 40$
2. $8 \neq 40$ so repeat step 1
3. $8, 40 \rightarrow 40\text{-}8, 8 \rightarrow 32, 8$
4. $8 \neq 32$ so repeat step 1
5. $8, 32 \rightarrow 32\text{-}8, 8 \rightarrow 24, 8$
6. $8 \neq 24$ so repeat step 1
7. $8, 24 \rightarrow 24\text{-}8, 8 \rightarrow 16, 8$
8. $8 \neq 16$ so repeat step 1
9. $8, 16 \rightarrow 16\text{-}8, 8 \rightarrow 8, 8$
10. $8 = 8$ so 8 is the greatest common multiple

Euclid's Algorithm uses only five subtractions and ten compares for a total of fifteen instructions, which is much faster than just step 1 of the Elementary School version. It is written in C as follows:

```
while (a != b)
{
        if (a > b)
                a = a - b;
        else
                b = b - a;
}
gcm = a;
```

A variation on Euclid's Algorithm uses the modulo operation. In C it is written as follows:

```
while (1)
{
        a = a % b;
        if (a == 0)
        {
                gcm = b;
                break;
        }
        b = b % a;
        if (b == 0)
        {
                gcm = a;
                break;
        }
}
```

This implementation uses even fewer instructions. For a=40 and b=48, only three compares and three modulo operations are used for a total of six operations, nine fewer than the repetitive subtraction implementation. Since six instructions is less than fifteen, the modulo version seems like it should be faster, but it isn't because modulo uses integer division, which takes 23 clocks, while subtraction and compares only take 0.5 and 1 clock respectively. In this case, you would choose the repetitive subtraction algorithm, even though it executes more instructions, because the instructions used are much faster. Table 6.3 compares the two versions.

Table 6.3 A Rough Comparison of the Two Different Versions of Euclid's Algorithm

Repetitive Subtraction Version				Modulo Version			
Instruction	Quantity	Latency	Total clocks	Instruction	Quantity	Latency	Total clocks
Subtractions	5	0.5	2.5	Modulo (integer division)	3	23	69
Compares	10	1	10	Compares	3	1	3
Totals	15		12.5	Totals	6		72

Data Dependencies and Instruction Parallelism

In addition to instruction latency and throughput, data dependencies affect the processor's ability to execute instructions simultaneously, which improves algorithm performance. The Pentium 4 processor is capable of executing six instructions on every clock, but due to the instruction issues, the number of instructions that are executed simultaneously is usually lower.

Figure 6.1 is a Gantt chart showing how three multiplies might be executed together.

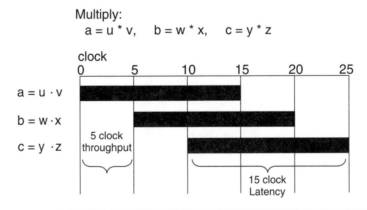

Multiply:
$$a = u * v, \quad b = w * x, \quad c = y * z$$

Figure 6.1 Sample Gantt Chart of Instruction Execution Without Data Dependencies

The Gantt chart in Figure 6.1 assumes no data dependencies exist among any of the instructions, allowing them to execute at the same time limited only by instruction latency and throughput. However, in the real world, data dependencies do exist, and they can make a huge difference. For example, if the three multiplies were data dependent, as in the statement a = w * x * y * z, the graph would look very different because the result of w * x would not be ready to be multiplied by y for fifteen clocks. The graph shown in Figure 6.2 is much longer because parallelism is not possible between the multiply operations.

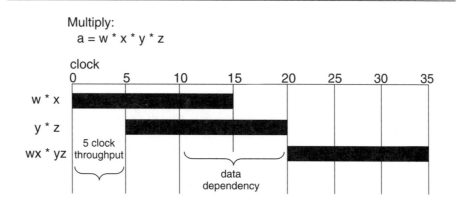

Figure 6.2 Gantt Chart of Instruction Execution With Data Dependencies

Instruction parallelism limited by data dependencies and latencies is a key limiting factor to algorithm performance. Additional instruction parallelism rules that are specific to each processor family do exist. However, using only the data dependencies and latencies makes for a good approximation of instruction execution, and you can disregard the additional unique parallelism rules.

Example 6.3 Improve the following loop.

Sometimes data dependencies are hard to spot because they are hiding in loop constructs or among multiple functions.

Problem

Reduce the hidden data dependencies in the following code to improve performance.

```
a = 0;
for (x=0; x<1000; x++)
        a += buffer[x];
```

Solution

Looking only at data dependencies, the increment of the variable x and the addition of a + buffer[x] can occur at the same time because the code appears to have no data dependencies. But that analysis overlooks the data dependencies that span across loop iterations. A better way to write the loop is to use four accumulators so that more arithmetic can occur on each clock due to fewer data dependencies.

```
a = b = c = d = 0;
for (x=0; x<250; x++)
{
        a += buffer[x];
        b += buffer[x+250];
        c += buffer[x+500];
        d += buffer[x+750];
}
a = a + b + c + d;
```

Even though this "unrolled" loop executes more instructions, the data dependencies are lower, so it has the potential to run faster. A good goal is to have low enough data dependencies so that the processor is able to execute at least four or more operations at the same time.

Memory Requirements

Fetching main memory is among the slowest operations for a processor and should be taken into account when selecting and implementing an algorithm. Algorithms have inherent memory requirements, and the ones that access less memory usually are faster. Some sorting algorithms sort data in place while others sort using additional memory. For example, selection sort is an in-place example while merge sort uses additional memory. Any benefit that an algorithm gains by using extra memory might be lost due to the speed of the memory accesses involved.

When evaluating the performance of an algorithm, treat memory accesses as high-latency instructions. A single value for memory latency cannot be defined because it depends upon many things, such as the cache state and data alignment. But as a general rule of thumb, the first time a memory location is accessed incurring a cache miss, it will be at least as expensive as a divide operation, and additional accesses to the same location are roughly free. Furthermore, the more data dependencies that an algorithm contains, the more limiting those memory latencies become, as the processor spends more time waiting for memory and less time executing non-data dependent instructions.

Detecting Algorithm Issues

Algorithm issues are primarily located by using the call graph feature in the VTune analyzer. Figure 6.3 shows the call graph results for the HUFF.EXE sample application.

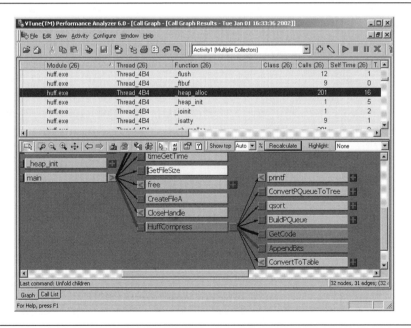

Figure 6.3 Call graph of the HUFF.EXE Application

On the surface, it might seem like you need to optimize the three functions `main`, `HuffCompress`, and `AppendBits` because they are on the critical path denoted by the thick red arrow. But in reality, those functions comprise the parts of the compression algorithm, and what you really need to optimize is the algorithm as a whole. Optimizing the complete algorithm instead of the individual functions will result in more optimization opportunities and higher performance.

Whenever time-based sampling shows that hotspots are spread across multiple functions, you should use call graph analysis to see the function hierarchy and determine whether the functions are somehow related to one another or are part of a larger algorithm that can be optimized as a whole entity.

Once the algorithm is identified, it is helpful to determine the degree of instruction parallelism in an algorithm, which indicates the amount of data dependencies and types of instructions involved. If the amount of instruction parallelism is low, it usually indicates that the algorithm should be improved or swapped out for a more efficient one.

You can determine the degree of parallelism by obtaining the event ratio of `Clockticks` versus `Instructions Retired` for a hotspot. As shown in Figure 6.4, the event ratio is approximately 0.8 for the `GetCode` function, which means that about 1.25 instructions are finishing per clock. But, since the Pentium 4 processor is capable of retiring three per clock, the processor is only operating at about ½ of its maximum speed, an indication that instruction parallelism issues such as data dependencies and long latency instructions are present and limiting performance.

Generally, when the Clockticks per Instructions Retired (CPI) ratio is above 1.0, the processor's capacity is not used completely, and optimizations should focus on removing data dependencies in the current algorithm or replacing it with a better one. On the other hand, a low ratio, roughly any below 0.75, means that the processor is efficiently executing instructions. Since a good CPI number depends largely on the specific code being executed, no general number can be used, in all situations and it doesn't make sense to use CPI guidance for anything but short regions of code.

When instruction parallelism is good but hotspots are still present, you usually find that executing fewer instructions by finding shortcuts or using a different algorithm leads to performance improvements.

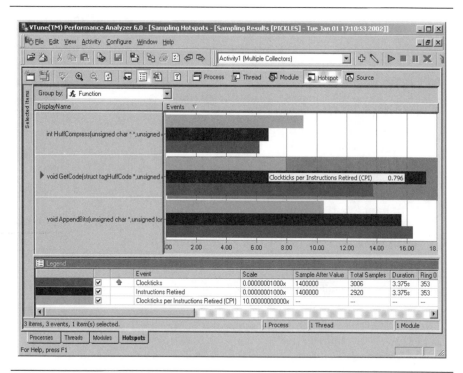

Figure 6.4 Clockticks, Instructions Retired, and ClockTicks per Instructions Retired (CPI) for HUFF.EXE

Key Points

In summary, remember these guidelines:

■ Selecting the right algorithm is absolutely critical to great performance. Computational complexity is the most critical performance attribute of an algorithm. Memory accesses, instruction selections, and avoiding processor issues are secondary.

■ Instruction latency, instruction throughput, and data dependencies greatly affect the performance of algorithms and they should be considered when selecting and implementing an algorithm.

■ Keep data dependencies low enough that the processor is able to execute at least four or more operations at the same time.

■ VTune analyzer's call graph can detect the algorithms that are the source of hotspots.

Chili Party Chili

Ingredients
- 1 pound sweet Italian sausage meat, no casings
- 3 pounds ground beef chuck
- 2 medium yellow onions, chopped
- ½ pound mushrooms, chopped
- 1 - 12 ounce can tomato paste
- 1 - 28 ounce can whole peeled tomatoes
- 1 - 15 ounce can crushed tomatoes
- 2 - 16 ounce cans dark red kidney beans, drained
- 1 - 16 ounce can black beans, drained
- ¼ cup olive oil
- 4 cloves minced fresh garlic
- 2 teaspoons ground cumin
- 3 tablespoons chili powder
- 1 tablespoon Dijon-style mustard
- 2 tablespoons dried basil
- 1 tablespoons dried oregano
- 1 cup Zinfandel wine + 1 glass for the chef
- 2 tablespoons lemon juice
- 1 tablespoon freshly ground pepper
- 3 large ancho chili peppers (mild heat) or chipotle pepper
  (medium heat), coarsely chopped
- Optional: 2 green Thai chili peppers, very finely diced, for high heat

Directions
1. Over low heat in a large 7-quart chili pot, cook the onions until tender in the olive oil, about 10 minutes.
2. Crumble the sausage meat and ground beef into the pot and cook over medium-high heat, stirring often, until meats are well browned. Pour off the excess fat.
3. Reduce heat to low and stir in ground pepper, tomato paste, garlic, cumin seed, chili powder, mustard, basil and oregano. Stir to blend.
4. Add all remaining ingredients and simmer uncovered, stirring often, for at least 30 minutes, but can be simmered for hours.
5. Serve with cheddar cheese, sour cream, corn bread, hot sauces, and more Zinfandel wine.

Chapter 7

Branching

O ne of the most basic operations of a computer language is the conditional branch. Unfortunately, conditional branches are also among the most difficult instructions for the processor to execute efficiently because they can break the in-order flow of instructions. Sometimes branches are executed in a single clock while other times they can take many dozens of clocks. For a detailed discussion of the reason that branching is a problem for processors, refer to Chapter 5 "Processor Architecture."

Branches come in two basic forms: conditional and unconditional. Conditional branches either jump to a designated group of instructions (taken branches) or go to the next instruction (fall through). Unconditional branches always jump to a new location, whose address may be known beforehand in the case of direct jumps or may not be known for indirect jumps. Table 7.1 shows examples of the two types of branches.

Table 7.1   Examples of the Two Types of Branches

Conditional	Unconditional
`if (a > 10)` `    a = 10;`	`Fn(a);`

`do {`
`    a++;`
`} while (a < 10);`
	`Goto end;`

`(a > 10) ? a=10 : a=0;`	`return a;`
`for (a=0; a<10; a++)` `    b++;`	`int 3;`
`while (!eof)` `    Read_another_byte();`	`fnPointer(a);`

To determine the next instruction, the Pentium 4 processor uses built-in rules and a branch history buffer to predict the outcome of a branch. The processor can correctly predict most branch outcomes, such as the odd/even pattern shown in the following code.

```
// simple branch pattern that will be correctly
// predicted by the Pentium 4 processor

for (a=0; a<100; a++)
{
    if (a % 2 == 0)
        do_even();
    else
        do_odd();
}
```

Generally, the Pentium 4 processor can predict all non-random branches. The odd/even branch above is very orderly and therefore very predictable. Just by looking at it, one can easily determine that 50 percent of the time the do_even function will be called and the other 50 percent of the time the do_odd function will be called. Most importantly, the branch pattern is exactly every other one. This pattern is very different from the code below that also branches each way about 50 percent of the time but is unpredictable.

```
// random branch pattern that is difficult to predict

for (a=0; a<100; a++)
{
    side = flip_coin();
    if (side == HEADS)
```

```
        NumHeads++;
else
        NumTails++;
}
```

The important difference between the two pieces of code is that one branch is predictable and the other is random and unpredictable. Just as the programmer could not predict the order of coin flip branches, neither can the processor. The best way to determine whether a branch will be correctly predicted is simply to think about the pattern of the branch. If a predictable pattern exists, the processor probably can detect it and correctly predict the outcome. Without a predictable pattern, the processor, with a strong possibility, will choose the wrong branch outcome, and performance will be lost.

Unfortunately, some random branches are unavoidable, such as the windows message loop. In these situations, you might think it would be advantageous to turn off branch prediction, but that is neither possible nor desirable. Branch prediction is more of a lost opportunity than a penalty. Without branch prediction, the processor would have to stop at every branch and wait many clocks for the compare to finish executing in the processor's pipeline. The performance lost by not performing branch prediction and by recovering from a mis-predicted branch is somewhat similar. Therefore, branch prediction is always a good thing, and it is important to allow branch prediction to help performance by avoiding unpredictable branches, especially in critical sections, so that the maximum performance benefit can be realized.

Unfortunately, it is impossible to avoid all mis-predicted branches and some are going to occur even in the critical areas and some performance opportunity will be lost. Even in the simplest loops, like the odd/even example above, one mis-predicted branch, the last comparison to exit the loop, is unavoidable. But one mis-predicted branch in a hundred is hardly worth spending any time to improve. The only mis-predicted branches worth improving are the ones that cause a significant amount of performance to be wasted.

Finding the Critical Mis-predicted Branches

You can find the branches to optimize using the VTune analyzer and going through the following steps.

Step 1: Find the Mis-predicted Branches

The first step is to locate those branches that the processor is mis-predicting. The event counter `Mispredicted Branches Retired` increments when a branch is mis-predicted and the VTune Performance Analyzer can be used to sample on this event. Figure 7.1 shows the sampling results for the `HUFF.EXE` application compressing a large text file.

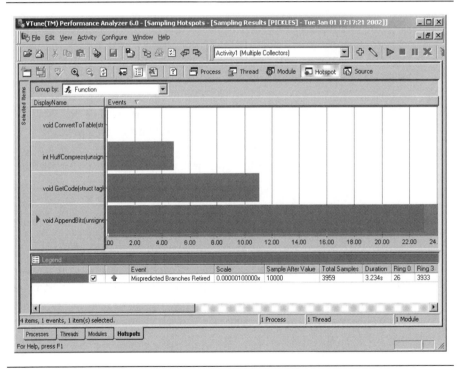

Figure 7.1 Mis-predicted Branches in the HUFF.EXE Application

The sampling results show that almost all the mis-predicted branches occur in the two functions `AppendBits` and `GetCode`. These two functions now become the focus of additional branch analysis.

Step 2: Find the Time-consuming Hotspots

It is always important to work on the areas of the application that consume a significant amount of time, but so far Step 1 has only identified the areas that have a significant amount of branch mis-predictions. A significant number of mis-predicted branches does not necessarily mean the area consumes enough time to make optimizations worth the effort. So, it is important to see if either of the two functions, `GetCode` or `AppendBits`, are also time-based hotspots.

The quickest way to determine how much time these functions consume is to use the VTune analyzer and sample on `Clockticks` that is shown in Figure 7.2.

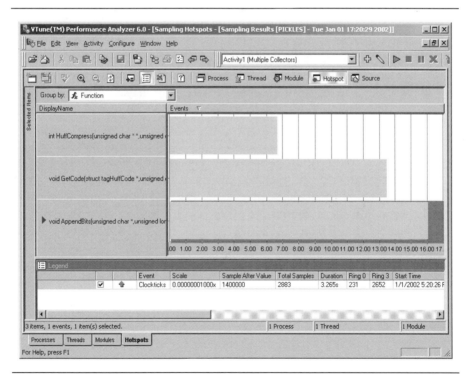

Figure 7.2 Time-based Hotspots in HUFF.EXE

The hotspots graph in Figure 7.2 shows that the functions GetCode and AppendBits are the two functions that consume the most time followed by HuffCompress. Since GetCode and AppendBits also contain a significant amount of mis-predicted branches, these two functions require additional analysis and probably branch prediction optimizations. Even though the hotspots graph in Figure 7.2 shows that HuffCompress consumes some time, a comparison shows that it consumes only half the time consumed by the other two functions. Since HuffCompress contains relatively few branch mis-predictions, it is not as important to optimize as GetCode and AppendBits.

Step 3: Determine the Percentage of Mis-predicted Branches

The final step is to determine the ratio of branches retired to branches mis-predicted. This ensures that optimization efforts are not wasted trying to optimize a good branch prediction ratio that only appears to be a hotspot because it is executed so many times. Only the branches that consume time and are frequently mis-predicted relative to the number of times executed are worth improving. If a branch were mis-predicted 1 out of 1000 times, it would not be worth optimizing. On the other hand, a mis-prediction rate of 1 out of 2 would be worth optimizing. The ratio of about 1 in 20 is roughly the crossover point.

The event counter Branches Retired counts every branch and by comparing that count to the Mispredicted Branches Retired event, the ratio can be determined and a decision made about whether or not to proceed with branch optimizations. Figure 7.3 shows that the mis-prediction rate in AppendBits is 0.124, meaning 1 out of every 8 branches is incorrectly predicted, but the rate in GetCode is 1 out of every 0.05 or 1 branch in 20 is mis-predicted. This discovery tells you that the branch predictability in AppendBits should be optimized first and GetCode second.

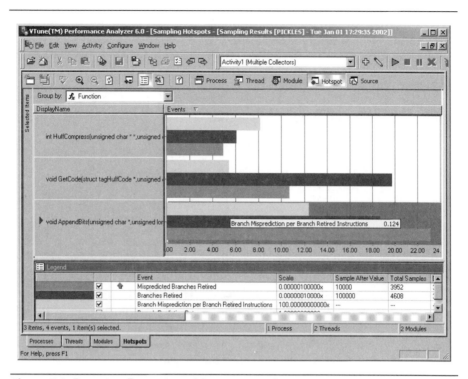

Figure 7.3 Branches Retired and Mis-predicted Branches

Final Sanity Check

These three steps make the assumption that analyzing the sampling data at the function level is equivalent to analyzing the data at the branch or instruction level, which is not 100 percent accurate. In almost all situations it is a great approximation, but in some cases, this assumption can be misleading. When working with long functions that could contain branchy regions that are independent from time-consuming regions, functions could be incorrectly included for performance optimizations. The easiest way to avoid this misstep is to look at the source code and confirm that assumption. Does the code that is expected to consume a significant amount of time contain unpredictable branches? As an alternative, you could drill down on each function in the VTune analyzer, and see the actual location of the samples, and compare the sample locations for the clock ticks and mis-predicted branches. If the sample locations do not match, be suspicious that optimizations might need something other than branch prediction improvements.

Now that the branches worth optimizing have been identified, it is time to start changing the code.

The Different Types of Branches

From an optimization point of view, branches can be grouped into five categories.

- *Conditional branches executed for the first time.* These branches are based upon the result of a compare operation that has not been executed previously or at least recently. In C, conditional statements such as if, do/while, and for generate conditional branches. In assembly, the jcc family of conditional jumps like jz and jne are conditional branches. The processor attempts to predict these branches based upon static branch prediction rules that "branches forward in memory are assumed to fall through" and "branches backward in memory are assumed to jump." These rules have been chosen to work best on TRUE if statements and on loops that repeat more than once. You only need to rewrite a branch to match the static branch prediction rules in those rare situations where the first pass through the code is time-critical. You get better results from improving the long-term branch predictability of a conditional statement than from optimizing its first execution. Generally speaking, do not worry about the static branch prediction algorithm unless one time through the branch is expected to consume a significant amount of time relative to the rest of the application.

- *Conditional branches that have been executed more than once.* These conditional branches have been executed before or at least recently, and the results of the previous branches are still in the processor's internal branch history buffer. These branches are predicted based upon the saved branch history and rules. When a branch is frequently mis-predicted, this dynamic branch prediction algorithm is having a difficult time. It is important to remove this type of branch or reduce its randomness to improve performance, but of course, only when it is consuming a significant amount of time.

■ *Call and Return.* For every call, the return address is pushed on the processor's internal return-stack buffer. When the processor executes the return statement, the top of the return-stack buffer is popped and used as the predicted address. Call/return prediction only fails when your application does not contain a matching return instruction for each call instruction. Optimizing for call/return branches is as simple as avoiding calls without matching returns.

■ *Indirect calls and jumps (function pointers and jump tables).* For indirect calls, the processor predicts that the branch target will be the same address as the last time the branch was encountered. These branches can be very difficult to predict because the code could have an infinite number of branch targets, unlike conditional branches that have only two targets: the next instruction and the jump target. To optimize indirect calls, focus on reducing the randomness of the target address. Testing the most likely case using a conditional branch then using a jump table usually helps. In C/C++, this test commonly is accomplished by placing an `if` statement before a `switch` statement that tests for the most common case.

■ *Unconditional direct branches/ jumps.* These branches always jump. They use the assembly instruction `jmp` or the C `goto` keyword and are always predicted correctly. No performance issues beyond instruction fetching and cache misses are associated with this kind of branch. Therefore, these branches need no optimizations.

Branches are improved in only two ways. You can remove them or you can make them less random. Whichever method is chosen, make sure to use the benchmark to verify performance improvement. Occasionally a mis-predicted branch will only cost a few clocks making it difficult to improve.

The following sections list the different kinds of branches and their optimization strategies.

Removing Branches with CMOV

The easiest branches to remove are the simple test and set variety. For example, consider the following sample code:

```
// In C
if (val > 255)
     val = 255;

// In assembly
     cmp val, 255
     jle skip_set_val_255
     mov val, 255
skip_set_val_255:
```

This branch is conditional on the value of a variable that could be random, so it might cause a branch mis-prediction and the loss of performance. But, these instructions are very efficient, using only two data dependent instructions when the value is less than 255 and three when the value is 256 or greater, with the possibility of a branch mis-prediction. Thus, the performance of this code is hard to beat when the branch is mostly predictable.

The easiest way to remove this type of branch is to use the CMOV instruction that was introduced on the Pentium Pro processor. The Pentium processor with MMX technology and older processors do not have the CMOV instruction, so using the instruction is not an option for the older processors.

The pseudo-code for using the CMOV instruction is shown in these two lines:

```
test (val > 255)
conditionally set val = 255 if true
```

In assembly language the code is written as follows:

```
mov eax, val
mov ebx, 255
cmp eax, ebx ; is val > 255
cmovg eax, ebx ; yes, val = 255
mov val, eax ; store val
```

Unfortunately, the CMOV instruction can have a register only as the destination and either a register or memory location as the source, so two extra instructions are used to load the immediate value and store the result. But, using the CMOV is instruction is fairly easy with inline assembly or the -Qxi option of the Intel C++ Compiler. The -Qxi option instructs the compiler that it is safe to use the CMOV instruction when compiling C/C++ code.

The CMOV version of the code contains five instructions, of which only four are data dependent because the first two instructions can occur at the same time. When using CMOV, it makes no difference if the value is greater than or less than 255 because all of the instructions are executed all the time. On the surface, it might look like these instructions would take longer than the branch version since it uses more data dependent instructions. And that would be the case if no performance were lost to mis-predicted branches. However, on truly random data, the processor would have a 50/50 chance of guessing correctly and that leaves plenty of room for the CMOV version to be much faster.

Doing a quick performance experiment using random data, the CMOV instruction is roughly two-and-a-half times faster than the branch version. The branch and the CMOV versions are roughly the same when the processor mis-predicts only about 1 in 100 branches. So, in this simple case, every branch mis-prediction is worth 50 data dependent instructions.

The decision to use branches or the CMOV instruction depends upon knowing something about the data. If the data is random, the CMOV version should be selected because it would avoid using branches and any possible branch mis-predictions that come along with using them. But if the data were uniform or mostly predictable, the branch version should be selected because it would be faster.

Further branch improvement requires using fewer data dependent instructions or doing more work per data dependent instruction.

Removing Branches with Masks

A mask can be generated by the SIMD instruction PCMP. It works by testing a condition then setting a register to all 1's (0xFFFFFFFF) or all 0's. The arithmetic OR and arithmetic AND instructions are used with the mask to obtain the desired results, as shown in the following sample pseudo-code, which clamps a variable to 255.

```
test (val > 255)
generate 2 masks with the following properties:
      mask 1 = 1's if val <= 255 or 0 if val >  255
      mask 2 = 1's if val >  255 or 0 if val <= 255
mask1 = mask1 AND val
mask2 = mask2 AND 255
val = mask1 + mask2
```

You can choose between two slightly different versions of creating a mask with the PCMP instruction: one uses the 8-byte MMX technology registers and the other uses the 16-byte Streaming SIMD Extensions (SSE) registers. You should decide which to use according to the quantity and alignment of the data that is being processed.

Support for the SIMD mask instruction exists in the Intel C++ compiler using inline assembly, intrinsics, and the C++ class libraries. The source code below clamps a variable at 255 using the MMX technology registers without branching.

```
Is16vec4 val4; // four 16 bit signed integers to clamp
Is16vec4 mask1, mask2;
mask1 = cmpgt (val4, 0x00ff00ff00ff00ff);
mask2 = cmple (val4, 0x00ff00ff00ff00ff);
val4 = (mask1 & 0x00ff00ff00ff00ff) + (mask2 & val4);
```

The same functionality written in assembly language is:

```
movq mm1, CONST_00ff00ff00ff00ff
movq mm0, val
pcmpgtw mm0, CONST_00fe00fe00fe00fe
pcmpgtw mm1, val
pand mm0, CONST_00ff00ff00ff00ff
pand mm1, val
paddw mm0, mm1
movq val, mm0
```

In this case, five data dependent instructions are used, one more than in the previous CMOV version. But since the CMOV version only works on one integer at a time and the SIMD version operates on four at a time, the SIMD version will be faster per variable. Doing four operations at a time taking only five clocks means that 1.25 instructions are required per result. Switch to using the 16-byte SSE registers and still only five data dependent instructions are required but for eight answers or 0.625 instructions per answer- over six times faster than CMOV and no need to use assembly language.

Removing Branches with Min/Max Instructions

In the special case of clamping values, you can use an even faster method than using the mask instructions. The SSE instruction set contains min and max instructions. Using these min and max instructions generates the fastest possible sequence to clamp a variable, as shown below using the C classes in the Intel C++ Compiler.

```
val = simd_min (val, 0x00ff00ff00ff00ff);
```

In assembly language, the same code is:

```
movq mm0, CONST_00ff00ff00ff00ff
pminsw mm0, val
movq val, mm0
```

This sequence uses only three data dependent instructions, so when using the 16-byte SSE registers, only 0.1875 instructions are required per answer.

Removing Branches By Doing Extra Work

Frequently, branches are used to avoid doing some work. For example, in the following code, the alpha value of 0 and 255 are checked first before calling the blend function.

```
for (i=0; i<BitmapSize; i++)
{
    SrcAlpha = GetAlpha(SrcPixel[i]);
    if (SrcAlpha == 255)
        DstPixel[i] = SrcPixel[i];
    else if (SrcAlpha != 0)
        DstPixel[i] = blend(SrcPixel[i],
                        DstPixel[i], SrcAlpha);
    // else, when SrcAlpha=0, do nothing
    // leave DstPixel alone
}
```

When the result of the blend operation is known ahead of time, like when SrcAlpha equals 0 or 255, the blend function need not be called, and if the blend function were rather slow, this would be a good optimization, because it avoids doing the extra work. But if SrcAlpha were random, the branches could be frequently mis-predicted and performance would be lost. The desire is that the net performance would be positive, since some time is lost due to a few mis-predicted branches but plenty of time is saved by not calling the blend function.

In some cases, especially when the data is random, you might find it is better to remove the branches and treat all the pixels (or data) in the same fashion. Once the decision is made to remove the branches, time can be spent improving the performance of the remaining work. Removing the branches also means that the program can use the SIMD instructions and that the performance of the code would no longer be sensitive to the data. The pseudo-code below executes the same loop without branches and can use the SIMD instructions.

```
for (i=0; i<BitmapSize; i+=4)
    Blend4Pixels (SrcPixel+i, DstPixel+i);
```

Of course, for maximum benefit, the function should be highly optimized and you should write the `Blend4Pixels()` function using the SIMD instructions.

Improving Branches

Sometimes random branches are unavoidable. In these situations, the best thing to do is to reorder them so that the most likely case is first. For example, `switch` statements usually have a most likely case that can be pulled out and moved before the `switch` statement, possibly reducing the number of mis-predicted branches. The following code is an example:

```
// Original version
switch (val)
{
       case 'A': // occurs 95% of the time
              a=val;
       break;
       case 'B': // occurs 4% of the time
              a=1;
       break;
       case 'C': // occurs 0.5% of the time
              a = 0;
       break;
       case 'D': // occurs 0.5% of the time
              a = val * 2;
       break;
}
// Improved version with leading if statements
if (val=='A')
       a=val;
else if (val=='B')
       a=1;
else switch (val) {
       case 'C':
              a = 0;
       break;
       case 'D':
              a = val * 2;
       break;
}
```

The `if` and `switch` combination has 25 times fewer branch mispredictions and runs about five times faster than the full switch statement.

Key Points

In summary, follow these guidelines when optimizing branches:

- Optimize the branches that are time-based hotspots, that are mis-predicted branch hotspots, and that have a high mis-prediction ratio (branches retired versus mis-predicted branches). Ignore all other branches. Only mis-predicted branches that cause a significant amount time to be lost are worth improving.

- Try to remove branches using masks and SIMD instructions to gain maximum benefit.

- Use the CMOV instruction to remove branches when SIMD instructions cannot be used.

- Use the benchmark to monitor changes in performance before and after branch optimizations to verify performance improvement.

Turkey Lasagna

Ingredients

8 oz lasagna noodles or enough for two layers in a 9x13-inch baking dish
1 pound ground turkey
16 ounces low-fat cottage cheese
4 cloves garlic, minced
14.5-oz can Italian-style diced tomatoes, with the thinnest,
    but not all, liquid drained
15-oz can tomato sauce
6-oz can tomato paste
2 tablespoons oregano
2 tablespoons thyme
1 egg, beaten
1 cup grated Parmesan cheese
10 ounces shredded mozzarella cheese

Directions

1. Preheat oven to 375°F.
2. Prepare lasagna noodles according to package. Rinse in cold water and let stand in cold water to prevent sticking while working on the rest of the recipe.
3. In a skillet, cook turkey and garlic until lightly browned. Pout off any excess fat.
4. In a large bowl, mix the egg, cottage cheese, diced tomatoes (including the thicker juice), tomato sauce, tomato paste, oregano, thyme, mozzarella cheese, and ½ cup of Parmesan. Add salt and freshly ground pepper to taste.
5. Assemble in a 9x13-inch baking dish. Layer half the noodles, half the turkey, and half the cottage cheese mixture. Repeat noodles, turkey, and cheese mixture for a second layer. Sprinkle the top with remaining ¼-cup Parmesan.
6. Cover with aluminum foil, being careful to leave a gap between the foil and the lasagna so the cheese does not stick, and bake for 45 minutes.
7. Remove the foil and bake for another 10 minutes.
8. Let cool for 10 minutes in baking dish before serving.

Chapter 8

Memory

No single issue effects software performance more globally than the speed of memory. From the Pentium 4 processor's point of view, memory is ridiculously slow. So slow, in fact, that nearly every application is limited by its performance. Slow memory hurts performance by forcing the processor to wait for instruction arguments to be fetched from memory before executing an instruction. Waiting instructions take up space in the instruction pool, which can fill up, leaving the processor with nothing to execute. Writing to memory also hurts performance because buffers used to execute the memory store become backed up waiting to write to slow memory. The programmer sees these waits as higher instruction latencies, meaning that instructions appear to take longer than expected to execute. For example, the following code sums an array.

```
total=0;
for (i=0; i<1000; i++)
   total += array[i];
```

The processor executes the loop using the following five steps:
1. Load array[i]
2. Execute total = total + array[i]
3. Increment loop counter i
4. Compare loop counter < 1000
5. Branch to step 1 if loop counter < 1000

Considering only the data dependencies, those five steps can be executed in three clocks because the load of the array in step one and the incrementing of the loop counter in step three can be executed at the same time as can steps two and four. But this loop is going to take much longer to execute than 3 * 1000 clocks because of the memory load latency. Before executing the addition on line two, the memory load on line one has to finish. While the processor waits for the load, it can skip ahead and do other non-dependent things, such as incrementing the loop counter, doing the compare, predicting the branch likely to be taken, and starting back at the top of the loop where it will encounter another memory load. Again, while waiting now for both the first and second loads, the processor can continue doing non-dependent things like the increment, the compare and so on. Eventually, the processor has executed as much code as it can and must just wait for memory. These memory latencies can add hundreds of clocks of execution time to an instruction.

Unfortunately, the memory issue is getting worse because processor speeds and memory demands are increasing at a faster rate than memory performance. As processors get faster but memory speeds stay the same, memory latency measured in processor clocks increases and even more processor clocks are wasted waiting for memory.

Buffers, caches, out-of-orders execution, cache hint instructions, automatic prefetch, and other processor features all work together to help improve memory performance and to minimize the time lost waiting for memory, but software design and implementation can play an even bigger role.

Memory Overview

Memory optimizations primarily deal with the L1 cache and the write buffers because all memory flows into and out of those points. Figure 8.1 is a block diagram of the memory system found in a computer containing a Pentium 4 processor.

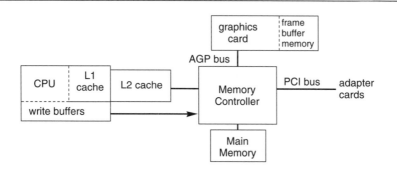

Figure 8.1 Block Diagram of a Pentium 4 Processor-based Computer

Main Memory and Virtual Memory

The amount of memory that a program can use is limited by the maximum address space of the processor. For the Pentium 4 processor the maximum address space is 64 gigabytes and it is comprised of physical memory, usually 128 megabytes or more, and of virtual memory, making up the remainder. An application uses *virtual memory* indirectly by requesting access to more memory than is physically available. When the operating system determines that it has run out of physical memory, a page fault is generated and, in response, a page of physical memory is saved to the hard disk freeing up memory to be used by the application, creating the illusion of an unlimited amount of physical memory. Unfortunately, this illusion comes at a huge performance penalty because swapping memory to and from the hard disk takes a very long time. For this reason, it is very important to carefully plan how much memory your application will use and to make sure that it can fit in a reasonable amount of physical memory to minimize page swapping.

Processor Caches

Small high-speed memories called *caches* are used to improve the latency of physical memory. The Pentium 4 processor always has two caches called the L1 cache and L2 cache, and it can have an optional L3 cache that is typically used on servers. The L1 cache is used for data only- the trace-buffer is used for instructions- and it is small but very fast. Called a unified cache, the L2 cache is used for both instructions and data. It is 32 times larger than the L1 cache and about three times slower. Main memory is much larger, typically more than 128 megabytes, but it is more than ten times slower than the L1 cache. Figure 8.2 shows the relative sizes and speeds of the caches and the 128-megabyte main memory.

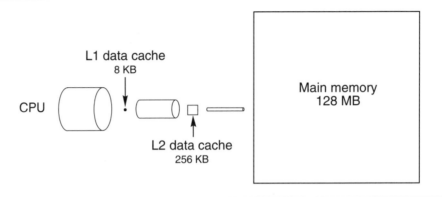

Figure 8.2 Relative Sizes and Speeds of the L1 and L2 Caches and Main Memory

When an application accesses a piece of memory, whether data is read or written, the processor first looks for the data in the cache. If the data is already in the cache, a *cache hit* occurs, and the data is accessed from the cache without touching main memory. When a *cache miss* occurs, the requested data is not in the cache and it needs to be fetched from main memory. Instead of retrieving just the requested byte or bytes, the processor fetches a 64-byte chunk into the cache expecting the extra memory to be used shortly. The 64-byte cache lines are aligned to 64 byte boundaries. So, a reference to byte 70 would load bytes 64-127.

Caches are based on the two principles of spatial and temporal locality.

Spatial locality. Memory locations near each other tend to be used together. Software does not randomly access a whole bunch of memory locations. Instead, memory accesses tend to clump together in local regions. So once an application accesses byte x, its next access is very likely going to be byte $x+1$ and so on. For this reason, when a cache miss occurs, the application retrieves more than a single byte from main memory. This extended retrieval improves performance because 1 transaction for 64 bytes is much faster than 64 transactions each for 1 byte.

Temporal locality. Memory just accessed is likely to be accessed again in the near future. Applications tend to access the same memory locations repeatedly, so recently used data is kept in the cache replacing older stale data. This principle is not the same as frequency of use; the number of times a memory location is accessed does not affect the cache.

L1 Cache Details

The L1 cache is the cornerstone of memory analysis and performance improvement because almost all memory used by an application flows through the L1 cache at some point. Improving the usage of the L1 cache will also improve L2 cache usage and will reduce operating system page swapping.

The L1 data cache on the Pentium 4 processor is organized in chunks of 64 bytes called *cache lines* and the cache can hold 128 lines for a total of 8192 bytes (128 lines * 64 bytes per line). Groups of four lines are called *sets* and columns of 32 lines are called *ways*. Figure 8.3 shows the lines, groups, sets, and ways of the L1 cache.

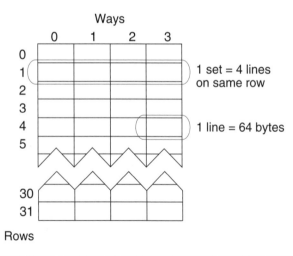

Figure 8.3 L1 Cache Showing Rows, Ways, Sets, and Lines

Each row has been designed to hold unique 2-kilobyte blocks of memory based upon the row number and the memory address, to speed up the time it takes to determine a cache hit. If all 128 lines could hold any memory location, the processor would have to test all 128 lines to determine a cache hit. But, by assigning each row a specific range of possible addresses, the processor tests only four lines to determine a cache hit. This arrangement makes the L1 data cache 2-kilobyte aligned.

The L2 cache, by comparison, is organized into 8 ways, 128 bytes per line, and 256 rows, equaling 256 kilobytes. The L2 cache is 8-kilobyte aligned.

Software Prefetch

The goal for memory optimizations is to transfer the minimum amount of memory required as quickly as possible, which requires the careful layout of data structures and memory buffers in a way that maximizes cache hits. But when the data is not in the cache, the processor's prefetch capability can be used to reduce the time spent waiting for memory.

The prefetch instruction tells the processor that an application is about to use a specific location of memory so the processor should get it ready by initiating a load. When bus bandwidth is available, the processor starts loading the memory into the cache before it is needed. By the time the memory is actually needed, the data should become available in the cache or at least have a head start getting there.

Four different types of prefetch instructions can be used to specify which cache(s) to preload, as shown in Table 8.1. Prefetching into the non-temporal buffer should be used when the application will be reading the data exactly one time. If the algorithm updates a memory location (read-modify-write) or otherwise accesses the data more than once, the T0 hint should be used.

Table 8.1 Four Different Types of Software Prefetch Instruction

Assembly Instruction	C++ Compiler Intrinsic Type Used as Second Parameter in _mm_prefetch(char *p, int Hint)	Description
PREFETCHNTA	_MM_HINT_NTA	Prefetch into non-temporal buffer useful for read once data
PREFETCHT0	_MM_HINT_T0	Prefetch data into all caches useful for read and/or write data
PREFETCHT1	_MM_HINT_T1	Prefetch data into L2 and L3 caches, but not the L1
PREFETCHT2	_MM_HINT_T2	Prefetch data into L3 cache only

The prefetch instruction works best when loading data far enough ahead of time so that the memory is already in the cache when needed. How far ahead depends upon many things, but about 100 clocks of execution time is a reasonable starting place. Frequently, prefetching the data used for a future loop iteration is easiest to program and it provides good results. Sometimes, circumstances require prefetching two, four, or even more loop iterations ahead to obtain maximum prefetch performance. A little trial- and- error should be used to determine where best to place the prefetch and which data to prefetch. But, be aware that as memory, memory controllers, and bus speeds change, the best placement of the prefetch instruction could vary also. The prefetch instruction loads a whole cache line, so prefetching 1 byte every 64 bytes is all that is required. Adding too many prefetch instructions actually can hurt performance. The following sample code issues a prefetch for data 16 loops iterations into the future.

```
for (i=0; i<1000; i++)
{
   x = fn(array[i]);
   // prefetch does not fault on invalid memory, so
   // it is safe to prefetch off the end of the array
   _mm_prefetch(array[i+16], MM_HINT_T0);
}
```

Writing Data Without the Cache:
Non-temporal Writes

With some exceptions, all reads and writes go through the L1 cache, which is desirable most of the time. However, in some cases, caching writes can harm performance and functionality for things like control registers on adapter cards and other hardware buffers. For that reason, the operating system and device drivers can define regions of memory as *uncacheable*. Uncacheable data is written immediately and in the exact order specified, bypassing the cache. Unfortunately, uncacheable memory has horrible performance because every piece of data has to be written with its own memory bus transaction.

A similar, but much higher performance memory type, is called uncacheable write-combining memory or just *Write Combining* (WC). WC memory is used when the sequence and urgency of the writes is not important but performance is. WC memory uses internal memory buffers to save a contiguous series of memory writes before issuing one large transaction to store the whole chunk to main memory. The operating system and device drivers can define areas of memory as WC. This type of memory commonly is used for things like the frame buffer on graphics cards and buffers on hard disk controllers, since the order and urgency of writing the data is not important in these cases and the processor does not need to use the data again. A special instruction called SFENCE can be issued to immediately flush the write buffers just before the data is needed, just before repainting the display, for instance.

In addition to writing to hardware, applications can use Write Combining memory buffers to bypass the cache for data that only needs to be written which can result in a performance improvement. An application can use the write combining buffers by writing data using one of the streaming store instructions. When the processor executes a streaming store instruction and the data is not already in the cache, the write buffers are used and the cache is bypassed. The streaming store instructions can write 32-, 64-, or 128-bit variables, and these instructions are available in assembly language, intrinsics, and the C++ class library packaged with the Intel C++ compiler. Table 8.2 lists the available streaming store instructions.

Table 8.2   Streaming/Non-temporal Store Instructions on the Pentium 4 Processor

Data Type	Intrinsic	Assembly Instruction
Integer Doubleword—32 bit	_mm_stream_si32	MOVNTI
Integer Quadword—64 bit	_mm_stream_pi	MOVNTQ
Integer Double Quadword—128 bits	_mm_stream_si128	MOVNTDQ
Two double-precision floating-point values—128 bits	_mm_stream_pd	MOVNTPD
Four single-precision floating-point values—128 bits	_mm_stream_ps	MOVNTPS
Selected bytes of a Quad-word—64 bits	_mm_maskmove_si64	MASKMOVQ
Selected bytes of a Double Quadword—128 bits	_mm_maskmoveu_si128	MASKMOVDQU

The following code writes 64 bytes using the streaming store instructions.

```
// assembly
movntdq mem, xmm0

// intrinsics
_mm_stream_si128(mem, a);

// C++ class library
store_nta(mem, a);
```

The only requirement for maximum performance is that the memory be written without skipping any bytes and follow the data alignment rules. The processor event counters Write WC Full and Write WC Partial can be used to identify the locations where this requirement is not being met.

Issues Affecting Memory Performance

Ideally, memory would be as fast as the processor, and you would not have to deal with caches or any of the issues that come along with using them. Unfortunately, the downside of building a system like that would be increased cost of memory components. So, it remains the programmer's responsibility to write applications in a way that avoids the side effects of the cache while maintaining maximum performance.

Cache Compulsory Loads

Three things cause cache loads: compulsory, conflicts, and capacity misses. *Cache compulsory loads* occur when data is loaded for the first time. Since the data was never in the cache, the processor must load it for the first time causing a compulsory cache load. The number of compulsory loads can be reduced but not avoided totally.

The number of compulsory loads is determined by how much memory the application uses. The total amount of unique memory bytes used by the application divided by the number of bytes in a cache line determines the minimum number of compulsory cache loads. Since it is very difficult to account for all the memory that a program uses due to function calls, stack usage, the operating system tasks, and so on, calculating the number usually only makes sense for a small portion of the application, such as a loop or a short function.

Changing the application to access less memory is the only way to reduce the number of compulsory cache misses. More important than the number of compulsory cache misses is the time lost due to them. Since the processor executes instructions out-of-order, cache misses do not necessarily cause a loss in performance. Performance is lost only when the processor cannot execute any other instructions and must wait for memory. Locations where data dependencies are high and lots of memory is being used are the areas where performance is most likely to be limited by compulsory cache misses.

Using tools like the VTune analyzer, you can find where the cache misses are occurring and where performance experiments can help you to determine how much time is being lost due to them.

Cache Capacity Loads

Cache capacity is the second reason that cache misses occur. *Cache capacity loads* occur when data that was already in the cache is being reloaded. If the processor had a larger cache, if it had more lines, or if each line were larger, the capacity load would have been avoided because the data could have stayed in the cache.

Algorithmic changes to use a smaller working set of data can reduce the number of cache capacity loads. Instead of operating on a large data set that is too big to fit in the cache, it is usually better to operate on smaller chunks that do fit in the cache. This optimization is called *strip mining* or blocking.

Just like all cache loads, the number of loads is not as important as the time lost.

Cache Conflict Loads

Conflicting addresses, which occur due to the way the cache is organized, cause cache loads. *Cache conflicts loads* occur because every cache row can only hold specific memory addresses. If five or more pieces of data are being accessed that all use the same row (which happens when bits 6-10 of the address are identical) but those pieces of data are located in different cache lines (separated by more than 64 bytes), they will not all fit in the cache since a cache row can only hold four lines, maximum. For example, consider an image-processing algorithm that adds two planar images together into one packed image, as shown in Figure 8.4. It requires eight separate read pointers, one for each color channel, and one write pointer for the destination. Cache conflicts occur if the bitmaps are 2-kilobyte aligned because eight pointers always contend for the same cache row and for a ninth when the destination bitmap happens to be similarly aligned.

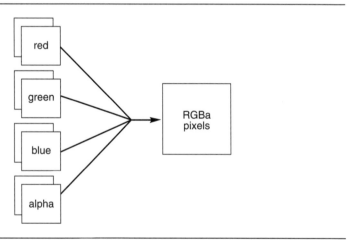

Figure 8.4 Example of Converting Planar Image Data to Packed Data

Avoiding cache conflicts is as easy as changing the memory alignment, keeping data in registers, or using an algorithm that accesses fewer regions of memory. In Figure 8.4, if the buffers were aligned to different 128-byte alignments (use 128-byte alignment to avoid L2 cache conflict misses, too.), no cache conflicts would occur and the performance would be more than twice as fast.

Due to the design of the cache controller, 64-kilobyte alignment also causes conflicts. Avoid using two or more 64-kilobyte aligned buffers to avoid these conflicts. The event counter, 64K Aliasing Conflicts, is used to detect this issue.

Cache Efficiency

Cache efficiency is the measure of how much memory is loaded into the cache versus how much memory is used. Two things affect cache efficiency: how many bytes per cache line are used and how many times the same cache line is loaded. For example, if an algorithm accesses every other element in an array of numbers, time is wasted loading the unused values because the cache always loads whole cache lines, even if only one byte is used. Cache conflicts and capacity loads also lower cache efficiency. If the same cache line must be reloaded due to a conflict or capacity issue, twice as much data has been transferred and cache efficiency is halved.

Poorly organized data structures can result in low cache efficiencies. It is important to organize data structures so that elements that are used together are located next to each other, placing them on the same cache line.

Data Alignment

Unaligned data can be a major headache for the processor in two ways. If a variable is split across two cache lines, then two cache lines must be accessed, halving memory performance. Additionally, the processor eventually has to combine the two halves of the variable, wasting even more time. For example, trying to read a double-word variable (four bytes) at address 126 incurs this penalty. Two bytes are in one cache line and two bytes are in a second cache line.

Data alignment also affects which instructions can be used. Some SIMD instructions always require aligned data and will fault on unaligned data.

Making sure data is aligned is one of the easiest ways to gain a performance improvement. Table 8.3 shows the proper alignment for the various data types.

Table 8.3 Data Alignment Rules

Data Type	Alignment
1 byte, 8-bits, BYTE	Any alignment
2 bytes, 16-bits, WORD	2 byte alignment
4 bytes, 32-bits, DWORD	4 byte alignment
8 bytes, 64-bits, QWORD	8 byte alignment
10 bytes, 80-bits, double extended floating point	16 byte alignment
16 bytes, 128-bits	16 byte alignment

Misaligned data accesses that do not cross L1 cache lines do not incur a performance penalty, with the exception of the SSE2 instructions that require aligned memory and will fault. Only MOVUPS, MOVUPD, and MOVDQU can access unaligned SIMD data. All other SSE and SSE2 instructions will fault upon accessing unaligned data even if the access does not cross a cache line boundary.

Misaligned data can be detected in the following two ways:

- The misaligned data accesses that cross L1 cache line boundaries (64 bytes) but do not use the SIMD instructions are called a split load or split store. The VTune Performance Analyzer has two event counters that detect split accesses: Split Loads Retired and Split Stores Retired.

- The misaligned data that is accessed using the SSE2 instructions but does not use MOVUPS, MOVUPD, or MOVDQU are detected by waiting for an unhandled exception fault, as shown in Figure 8.5. Be careful, the error message does not specifically indicate that unaligned data is the cause.

Figure 8.5 An Attempt To Use The SSE2 Instructions To Access Unaligned Data

Compilers and Data Alignment

Compilers are required to align variables on their natural alignment meaning a 4-byte variable is guaranteed to be four byte aligned. Data alignment issues can only occur when casting variables, as shown in the following sample code.

```
// the return value from malloc is cast to a double
// this may have an alignment issue
double* pDblArray = (double*)malloc (48*sizeof(double));

// pointer is cast from float pointer to
// F32vec4 pointer (4 floats)
// this may have an alignment issue
float ArrayOfFloats[128];
F32vec4 * pSIMDFloats = (F32vec4 *)ArrayOfFloats;
```

Detecting Memory Issues

Memory optimizations rely upon accurate detection of the location of and the reason for a memory problem. Memory can be a problem anytime the processor has to wait for its data, a situation often caused by things like page swapping and cache misses. Tracking down these locations then knowing what optimizations you can perform to make the biggest difference is the focus of this section.

Some insight into the application is very helpful for setting expectations. Does the application use a small or large amount of memory relative to the amount of physical memory? Do you expect to see continuous page swapping or maybe just a little during initialization? Are data structures carefully planned to minimize cache misses or are they haphazardly thrown together?

Finding Page Misses

Page swapping is always a sign that the processor is waiting for memory and these situations should be eliminated where possible. The quickest way to detect page swapping is to sample on the Pages/sec operating system counter in the Memory performance object, using either the VTune Performance Analyzer or the Microsoft Performance Monitor (PERFMON.EXE). Figure 8.6 shows the Performance Monitor sampling on the event.

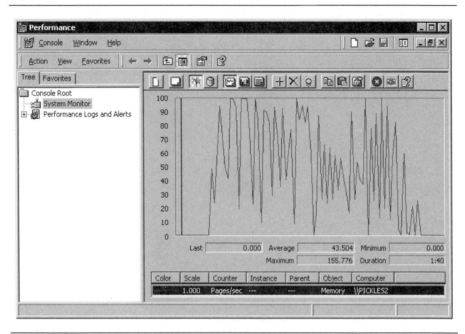

Figure 8.6 The Performance Monitor Tracking Pages/sec

The graph in Figure 8.6 shows that the system is generating a large amount of page misses. Since every page miss costs a huge amount of time, it is important to focus optimizations on removing or at least minimizing the page misses. Aside from adding more memory to the computer, the only way to avoid page misses is by changing the application to use less memory or to use it differently to increase page locality, and therefore processor cache locality. It should be fairly easy to determine what part of the application is generating page misses by examining where large buffers and memory allocations are occurring. Make sure to consider calls made by the application to operating system functions or other applications that may be causing page misses on the application's behalf.

Page misses can be transient, meaning that the second time the application is run, different pages will be in memory and the profile may look different.

The Counter Monitor feature in the VTune analyzer can help pinpoint what code was running when page misses occurred. Figure 8.7 shows that the HUFF.EXE sample program causes a bunch of page misses, but only right at the start, which is the initialization code.

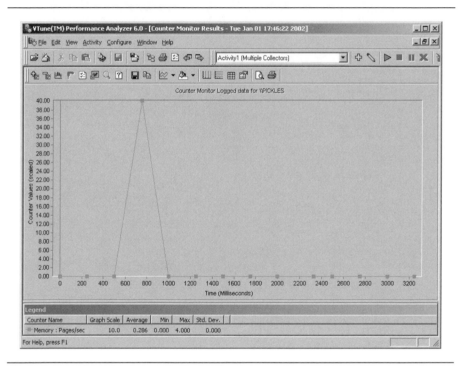

Figure 8.7 VTune analyzer, Counter Monitor sampling Memory Object, Pages/sec

Concentrating on the spike in the graph reveals that HUFF.EXE was the only active process, as shown in Figure 8.8.

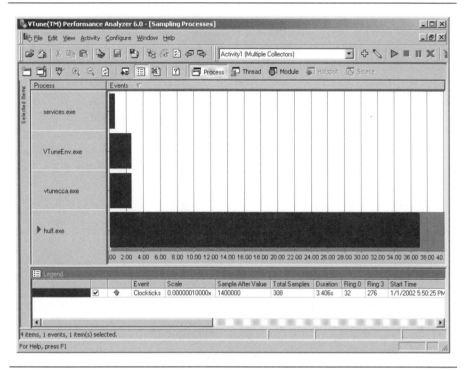

Figure 8.8 Clocktick Samples from Drilling Down on the First Part of the Counter Monitor Graph in Figure 8.7

With this information and specific knowledge about how the program works, the load of the uncompressed data file is very likely the cause of the page misses. Since no page misses occur after the beginning and loading the data file is unavoidable, this program does not have a page miss issue worth optimizing.

Finding L1 Cache Misses

Once page swapping is under control, it is time to focus on the L1 cache. Except for write combining (WC) memory stores and uncacheable memory, all memory accesses go through the L1 cache. Sampling on L1 cache misses identifies the portions of the application that are accessing memory or at least missing the L1 cache. Comparing those locations to the application's time-based hotspots will show where the processor is waiting for memory. You should examine only the locations that consume a significant amount of time and have L1 cache misses.

Sampling on the 1st Level Cache Load Misses Retired counter in the VTune Performance Analyzer will show where all the L1 cache load misses are occurring, as shown in Figure 8.9 for the HUFF.EXE application.

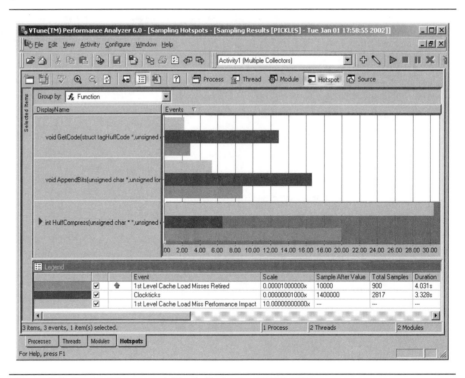

Figure 8.9 Cache Misses and Clock Ticks for HUFF.EXE

The graph in Figure 8.9 shows that the time-based hotspots and the location of the L1 cache misses are not correlated. The function `HuffCompress` contains the most L1 cache misses but does not consume the most time. And the function `AppendBits` consumes the most time but does not contain the most cache misses. In this case, optimization efforts would focus on the functions that consume the most time first. So the order of optimizations would be `AppendBits,GetCode`, then `HuffCompress`.

Since only three functions have L1 cache misses and they are relatively short, it would be worth the effort to examine the source code and list by hand all memory accesses. The goal would be to find cache misses occurring on the same buffers, low cache efficiency, or cache conflicts caused by multiple aligned pointers accessing memory.

Understanding Potential Improvement

Before fixing memory problems, it is important to make sure that memory really is the bottleneck. Just because sampling identifies a location of the application that contains many cache misses, it does not automatically mean that a significant amount of performance is being lost.

Due to out-of-order execution, it is hard to tell exactly how much time is lost waiting for memory accesses by only looking at the sampling data from the VTune analyzer. Performance experiments should be used to supplement the sampling analysis to determine how much performance is being lost. For example, let's say that time-based sampling has identified a hotspot on a function that is also an L1 cache misses hotspot. This discovery is a very strong sign that memory accesses are causing the bottleneck, but it is still not a sure thing. Verification and quantification of the size of the bottleneck can be determined with performance experiments. The following sample piece of code adds a constant value to every element in an array.

```
for (x=0; x<len; x++)
    DestArray[x] = SourceArray[x] + K;
```

This loop breaks down into the following steps:

1. Load SourceArray[x].

2. Add K.

3. Store DestArray[x].

4. Increment x.

5. Compare x and len.

6. Jump to step 1 when x is less than len.

By inspection alone, it should be obvious that memory is the bottleneck because this loop does nothing else that is time consuming. But, how bad is the bottleneck? Considering only the data dependencies, one time through the six steps of this loop can be executed in three clocks. But, timing this loop using 256,000 elements shows that it takes about nine clocks per element.

A performance experiment would be to remove the possibility of read cache misses to see what happens. The performance experiment code would look like:

```
for (x=0; x<len; x++)
    DestArray[x] = SourceArray[0] + K;
```

Timing this new loop shows that the execution time drops to about five clocks per element. A second experiment would be to remove the possibility of write cache misses, as shown in the following sample.

```
for (x=0; x<len; x++)
    DestArray[0] = SourceArray[x] + K;
```

The performance is now roughly four clocks per element. The final experiment with no cache misses is shown below.

```
for (x=0; x<len; x++)
    DestArray[0] = SourceArray[0] + K;
```

This code executes in about two clocks per element. Compared with the original timing of nine clocks per element, accessing memory is causing the loop to be more than four times slower than the performance experiment with no memory accesses. This information leads to two conclusions. First, seven clocks per element are wasted waiting for cache misses. And secondly, write cache misses are a little more costly than read cache misses in this case. With this detailed analysis complete, it is time to start fixing the memory problems.

Fixing Memory Problems

Once the details of where and why a memory access is a bottleneck, optimizations can be made. The following list describes the techniques used to improve memory performance.

- *Use less memory to reduce compulsory cache misses.* Selecting a different algorithm that uses less memory can help. For example, some sorting algorithms like insertion sort operate on the array in-place while other sorting algorithms like merge sort require additional temporary memory. Make sure to select a computationally and memory efficient algorithm. Remember, computationally efficient algorithms can make a much bigger difference than a few extra cache misses so don't automatically select an algorithm based solely on its use of memory.

  Changing data types can also reduce the amount of memory. If 32-bit integers are not needed, try words or bytes or even bits.

  Sampling on 1st Level Cache Misses Retired will show the locations where the application is using memory. Use this as a guide to steer you towards the areas of your application that when using less memory will have the biggest impact.

- *Increase cache efficiency.* Examine what cache lines are being loaded to make sure that all the memory is being used. Adjust data structures and memory buffers to place items used at the same time next to each other in memory.

No tools exist today that show cache efficiency. But, you can get an idea of the cache efficiency by seeing how many cache lines have been loaded versus the amount of memory you expected your application to use.

■ *Read memory sooner with prefetch.* The prefetch instruction provides a hint to the processor that a memory location is about to be used. By issuing the prefetch instruction far enough before the data is needed, a cache miss still occurs, but now the data waits in the cache for the processor instead of the processor waiting for the data. Remember that the processor is also doing its own hardware prefetch by watching memory access patterns so don't go nuts adding prefetch instructions ahead of every memory access. Be sure to always use the benchmark to test that the use of the prefetch instruction improves performance by a significant amount.

■ *Write memory faster with non-temporal instructions.* The streaming, non-temporal instructions write data without using the cache, saving one cache read, caused by the read-for-ownership cache policy, and one cache write. When using the non-temporal instructions, make sure that the data will not be loaded in the near future by another function. Writing memory with the non-temporal instructions just to read it back into the cache will not improve overall performance. The non-temporal instructions work best when writing data that will never be used again by the processor, such as frame buffer data that will only be used by the graphics card.

■ *Avoid conflicts.* The address of the data being accessed determines where in the cache it can be placed. Avoid reading or writing five or more buffers at the same time with the same 2-kilobyte alignment or the L1 cache will have to evict a cache line even if the cache is not full.

Detecting the 2-kilobyte L1 cache alignment conflicts is rather difficult because the processor does not have an event counter that tracks this situation. A combination of looking at the suspected source code, inspecting the accessed data addresses in a debugger, and running performance experiments can be used to identify L1 cache conflicts. When developing a performance experiment to detect L1 cache conflicts, force the addresses to be aligned differently or stop accessing a memory buffer or two. If L1 cache conflicts were occurring, you will be able to detect a change in the number of L1 cache misses using the VTune analyzer.

The 64-kilobyte cache controller conflicts can be detected by sampling on the `64K Aliasing Conflicts` processor event counter with the VTune analyzer.

- *Avoid capacity issues.* Capacity issues are caused by the eviction of data before all references to it are finished. This problem usually occurs in two-pass algorithms where a large buffer is processed by one function, followed by a second-pass over the same buffer by a second function. Both functions cause cache misses even though the same data is used. Instead, try operating on smaller cache sized buffers. So, run the first function on a cache-sized subset of data, then run the second function on the same cache-sized subset of data. If everything goes as planned, the second function will have no cache misses because the data is still in the cache from when the first function loaded it. Then, repeat both the first and second functions on the next cache-sized subset of data, and so on.

  Be careful when determining a cache-sized subset of data to operate on because all memory accesses, including stack variables, global variables, and the buffers, all contribute to capacity issues. It is very rare that the full L1 cache size (8 KB) can be used because of all the other variables. Try to pick a size that is easy to program and avoids capacity issues, such as 4 kilobytes of memory.

  Use the `1st Level Cache Misses Retired` event counter to find the locations of the cache misses events. Then, by just looking at the source code, determine whether the memory was just in the cache.

- *Add more work.* The processor can execute non-dependent instructions while waiting for memory to be fetched. Where possible, take advantage of these "free" clocks by moving non-data dependent work to the locations of cache misses. The cache misses still take the same amount of time, but now the processor can execute other instructions during the wait instead of just wasting time.

Example 8.1 Optimize a Function

An important optimization skill is being able to look at a piece of code and predict the performance issues and solutions without using a performance analyzer. Look at the following loop and determine what issues exist.

Problem

Improve the following function assuming that the Dest array will not be used in the near future, that the arrays are aligned, and that len is a multiple of four.

```
void AddKtoArray (int Dest [], int Src[], int len, int K)
{
    int i;
    for (i=0; i<len; i++)
        Dest [i] = Src [i] + K;
}
```

Solution

The first thing to notice is that this loop will be memory bound when the arrays are not already in the cache because it does nothing else that is time-consuming. Since the problem statement says that the destination array will not be used in the near future, the streaming store instructions should be used.

The best way to improve this loop is to use the streaming store instructions and the SIMD instructions to add four integers at a time. These changes improve performance by about 33 percent, but the loop is still very memory bound. Further improvements can be made by adding more work to this loop using the time that would be wasted waiting for memory, by reducing the amount of memory used which also reduces the number of cache misses, or by making sure that the memory was in the cache using a strip-mining technique with another function that accessed the same memory. The following code uses the intrinsics and the Intel C++ Compiler's class libraries.

```
// assumes: arrays are 16 byte aligned
//          len is a multiple of 4
void AddKtoArray4s (int Dest [], int Src[], int len, int K)
{
    int i;
    __m128i *Dest4 = (__m128i *)Dest;
    Is32vec4 *Src4  = (Is32vec4 *)Src;
    Is32vec4 K4(K, K, K, K);
```

```
Is32vec4 K4(K, K, K, K);

for (i=0; i<len/4; i++)
        _mm_stream_si128(Dest4+i, Src4[i] + K4);
}
```

Example 8.2 Optimize a Data Structure

Looking at data structures and immediately identifying cache issues is an important part of software optimization. Look at the following data structure and identify possible performance issues and improvements.

Problem

Optimize a phone book data structure to improve searching. The data structure is:

```
#define MAX_LAST_NAME_SIZE 16
typedef struct _TAGPHONE_BOOK_ENTRY {
      char LastName[MAX_LAST_NAME_SIZE];
      char FirstName[16];
      char email[16];
      char phone[10];
      char cell[10];
      char addr1[16];
      char addr2[16];
      char city[16];
      char state[2];
      char zip[5];
      _TAGPHONE_BOOK_ENTRY *pNext;
} PhoneBook;
```

The search function is:

```
PhoneBook * FindName(char Last[], PhoneBook * pHead)
{
      while (pHead != NULL)
      {
            if (stricmp(Last, pHead->LastName) == 0)
                  return pHead;
            pHead = pHead->pNext;
      }
      return NULL;
}
```

Solution

First, recognize that the problem is that the function makes horrible use of the cache. Each structure takes up 127 bytes, but only 16 bytes are used for each pass through the search loop. This arrangement wastes 48 bytes of the 64-byte L1 cache line and 111 bytes of the 128-byte L2 cache line meaning the L1 cache efficiency is at best 25 percent. To improve performance, rearrange the structure so that all the last name variables are in one continuous array and place the other less frequently used data somewhere else. The two arrays would be declared as shown in the following sample.

```
char LastNames[MAX_ENTRIES * MAX_LAST_NAME_SIZE];
PhoneBook PhoneBookHead[MAX_ENTRIES];
```

Since last names can be any length, up to `MAX_LAST_NAME_SIZE-1` bytes still might be wasted in the array, but you have made a big improvement over the previous version. Taking into consideration variable length strings, the find function can now be written:

```
PhoneBook * FindName(char Last[], char *pNamesHead,
PhoneBook *pDataHead, int NumEntries)
{
      int i = 0;
      while (i < NumEntries)
      {
            if (stricmp(Last, pNamesHead) == 0)
                  return (pDataHead+i);
            i++;
            pNamesHead += strlen(pNamesHead) + 1;
      }
      return NULL;
}
```

The bottleneck in this code shifts to the string compare and string length functions, which should now be optimized with application specific versions. See Chapter 10, "Slow Operations," for additional information.

A further improvement would be to replace the sequential search algorithm with a binary search or other higher-performance algorithm.

Key Points

In summary, remember these guidelines:

- Avoid operating system paging and virtual memory.

- Focus analysis on determining where and why L1 cache misses are occurring.

- Optimize applications by reading memory sooner using software prefetch and avoiding cache issues.

- The processor events 1st Level Cache Misses Retired, Write WC Full, Write WC Partial, and 64K Aliasing Conflicts can be used to locate memory hotspots.

- Use performance experiments to determine the severity of memory issues and possible solutions.

Ahi Tuna Burger

Ingredients

1 pound Ahi tuna, sushi grade, diced
4 large hamburger buns
2 teaspoons fresh ginger root, minced
2 tablespoons low-sodium soy sauce
2 tablespoons sesame oil
1 clove garlic, minced
pinch of wasabi powder or more to taste

Directions

1. In a bowl, whisk ginger, sesame oil, soy sauce, garlic, and wasabi together. Adjust taste with fresh ground pepper and more wasabi. Stir in diced Ahi tuna.
2. Make mixture into 4 patties.
3. Over medium-high heat, in a non-stick skillet, lightly cook tuna burgers for about 1-2 minutes per side, keeping the center raw.
4. Serve in a toasted bun.

Chapter 9

Loops

Loops are the most common sources of hotspots due solely to their repetitive nature; do anything enough times and it will be a hotspot. A loop in and of itself is not a performance issue, and loops can actually help performance in a few ways. First, loops reduce the number of instructions. Programs with fewer instructions require less memory to store program instructions, so less time is spent waiting for instructions to be fetched from main memory. Secondly, the Pentium 4 processor caches decoded instructions, so when the same instruction is executed at the same memory location for the second time, the decode time is saved.

On the downside, loops add some overhead. For example, the following code adds four integers together.

```
sum = 0;
for (i=0; i<4; i++)
    sum = sum + array[i];
```

These same four integers can be added together with one statement without using a loop.

```
sum = array[0] + array[1] + array[2] + array[3];
```

The loop version executes the same three addition instructions, but also includes one assignment, four increments, four compares, three branches, and one branch misprediction. Not only does the loop version run slower, it contains and executes more instructions. Clearly, the loop was not the most efficient method in this case. But, if the array had 10,000 elements, the loop would be fastest. Knowing why a particular loop is slow, or fast, is half the battle and Table 9.1 summarizes the key reasons.

Table 9.1 Loop Advantages and Disadvantages

Things that can make loops fast	Things that can make loops slow
Less instruction memory used	Extra instructions/overhead required for loop construct
Decode time saved when same instruction is executed more than once	Loops add at least one branch misprediction
Processor is able to internally unroll loop to increase chances of instruction parallelism	Loop constructs add extra data dependencies
Compilers look at loops for opportunities to use SIMD instructions and threading	Loops may hide data dependencies.

Most modern compilers generate loop-optimized code and can perform some of the optimizations listed in this chapter automatically. Be sure to read all compiler documentation to understand what loop optimizations are possible and what switches you must use to enable them. Before attempting to change your code to perform an optimization, make sure that the compiler has not already automatically performed the optimization or that it cannot be told to do so.

Common Loop Problems

Loop issues fall into three categories.

Loop overhead. At very least, a loop requires an extra addition, compare, one jump per iteration, and one branch misprediction at the end exiting the loop. Usually, the body of the loop consumes so much time that these extra instructions take comparatively little or no time. But, when performing a simple operation, like summing an array, loop overhead can add up.

Data dependencies. It is nearly impossible to write a useful function that is not in some way limited by data dependencies and by an amount of instruction parallelism that is less than optimal. But finding the dependencies and reducing them is not impossible if you know where to look. For example, in the previous code sample for summing an array, data dependencies are hiding between loop iterations. The processor cannot add the third element of the array to the total until the first two elements have been added together creating the dependency across loop iterations. Furthermore, the loop variable is used as an index into the array, making the load of `array[i]` dependent upon the increment of variable `i`. These dependencies tend to be harder to find and harder to fix.

Lack of parallelism. You should always be looking for ways to do more things at the same time. Reducing data dependencies, using the SIMD instructions, and using multithreading all introduce parallelism into an application. Loops are code sequences in the application that can benefit greatly from making sure instructions are being executed in parallel.

Loop Unrolling

One of the most common loop optimizations is *loop unrolling*. Loop unrolling is the combination of two or more loop iterations and reduction of the loop count as shown in the following code sample.

```
// Original
sum = 0;
for (i=0; i<16; i++)
      sum += array[i];

// Unrolled 4 times
sum = 0;
for (i=0; i<16; i+=4)
{
      sum += array[i];
      sum += array[i+1];
      sum += array[i+2];
      sum += array[i+3];
}
```

The unrolled version of the loop contains three additional add instructions, increasing the size of the code size, but in turn, executing fewer instructions. The same sixteen additions occur in both versions, but the loop variable is incremented sixteen times in the original version and only four times in the unrolled version. The performance of this loop depends upon both the trace cache and L1 cache state, but in general, the unrolled version runs faster because fewer instructions are executed. However, at some point the performance benefit from fewer instructions is lost due to the added expense of fetching and decoding more instructions. For example, little benefit comes from replacing the loop with sixteen add instructions (a completely unrolled loop).

To improve this code further, you might reduce the data dependencies as shown in the following sample.

```
t1 = t2 = t3 = t4 = 0;
for (i=0; i<16; i+=4)
{
        t1 += array[i];
        t2 += array[i+1];
        t3 += array[i+2];
        t4 += array[i+3];
}
sum = t1+t2+t3+t4;
```

This version is faster because the performance gained by reducing the data dependencies exceeds the performance lost executing the three additions at the end. Reduction of data dependencies is always desirable.

No universal rule-of-thumb dictates when to unroll a loop and by how much. Further complicating the unroll decision, optimizing compilers can unroll loops automatically. But, some guidelines do exist, and it is easy to examine the compiler output to see what optimizations, if any, have been made automatically. In the simple loop examples discussed so far, unrolling hardly makes a difference, but in other applications, it could make a significant difference. Most importantly, think about why the loop is slow and address that problem. Unrolling a loop full of expensive data-dependent operations is silly. But unrolling a loop that results in fewer data dependencies and a better blend of instructions is beneficial. As with all optimizations, make sure to use the benchmark to verify performance improvement.

Use the following guidelines to help you decide when unrolling can be helpful and how to maximize its potential.

Low loop counts, short bodies. Replace loops with low loop counts and short bodies with a non-loop version of the code. This optimization is similar to the example of summing an array of four elements by using four adds instead of a loop. Removing the loop entirely and leaving four add instructions would likely be faster, but be careful, you don't want to change something that is not broken. These loops probably are not hotspots unless the loop body is doing a very expensive operation like trigonometry operations or random memory access. Avoid fixing the loop construct when something else is really the problem.

Low loop counts, long bodies. Unroll loops with low loop counts and long bodies to reduce data dependencies. If the loop body is long, the processor might not be able to detect the maximum amount of parallelism. You should unroll the loop and interleave the iterations so that multiple instructions can be executed together by giving the processor a good blend of instructions and fewer data dependencies.

High loop counts, short bodies. Consider unrolling loops that have high loop counts and short bodies. The processor and compiler can usually do a good job optimizing these kinds of loops and the Intel C++ Compiler automatically can unroll them, but unrolling by hand can sometimes provide additional performance benefit. When unrolling these loops, try to remove data dependencies and use a good blend of instructions. An unrolled loop full of floating-point divides or memory accesses does not qualify as a good blend of instructions. These loops are perfect for SIMD instructions. Try using the Intel C++ Compiler to vectorize these loops automatically, or you might use the C++ classes, intrinsics, or inline assembly. Small loops are also easier to convert to using the SIMD instructions.

High loop counts, long bodies. Unroll only to reduce data dependencies and to provide a better blend of instructions. The additional amount of source code, trace-cache space requirements, and decode time all work against you when unrolling loops with many instructions, plus the loop overhead will be lost in a long loop body anyway.

Loops with branches. Be careful when loops contain branches. Mispredicted branches can destroy a loop's performance and unrolling a loop just creates more unpredictable branches. Before unrolling, attempt to remove all branches from within loops.

Example 9.1 Optimize by Unrolling the Loop

Sometimes, unrolling a loop makes the code simpler and faster. Try to optimize the following loop.

Problem

Improve the performance of the following code by unrolling the loop to remove the branch and reduce the number of instructions.

```
for (i=0; i<1000; i++)
{
        if (i & 0x01)
                do_odd(i);
        else
                do_even(i);
}
```

Solution

Don't overlook the obvious reason for unrolling a loop; it makes sense. The solution is to unroll the loop once to remove the branch from within the loop.

```
for (i=0; i<1000; i+=2)
{
        do_even(i);
        do_odd(i+1);
}
```

Loop Invariant Work

Calculations that do not change between loop iterations are called *invariant work*. When optimizing compilers find invariant work, they move it outside the loop to increase performance. But, unfortunately compilers cannot detect and remove all invariant operations, so the programmer needs to help. For example, the calculation of val/3 in the following loop example does not change inside the loop so it can be moved before the loop. Or can it?

```
// all variables are integers
for (x=0; x<end; x++)
    array[x] = x * val / 3;
```

Due to the order of operations of integer arithmetic, moving val/3 outside the loop and multiplying by a temporary value inside the loop might change the result. Only when the variable val is a multiple of three and the multiplication does not overflow an integer is this optimization safe. In this case, the compiler would not move the division outside the loop, but it still might be safe for the programmer to do so.

Function calls can also be invariant. In the following loop, the compiler does not know whether the call to foo(end) is invariant, so it calls that function every time through the loop. If the programmer knows that the function call is invariant and it is safe to call it only once, that invariant work should be placed outside the loop.

```
for (x=0; x<100; x++)
    array[x] = x * val / 3 * foo(y);
```

The best way to detect loop invariant code is by looking at the source code and using the VTune analyzer's Tuning Assistant, as shown in Figure 9.1.

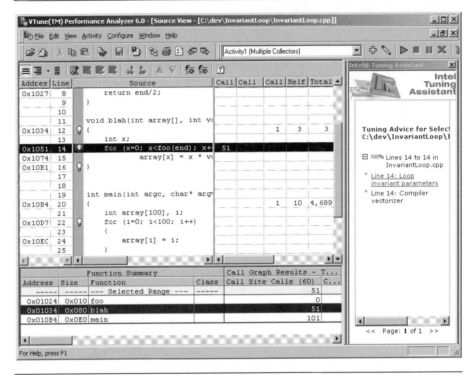

Figure 9.1 VTune Analyzer Tuning Assistant Detects Loop Invariant Code

Loop Invariant Branches

Removing branches inside loops is especially important because they make it harder for compilers to perform loop optimizations and harder for programmers, and compilers, to use the SIMD instructions. Invariant branches can sometimes be moved before a loop, as shown in the following sample code.

```
void BlendBitmap(BYTE Dest[],
                 BYTE Src1[], BYTE Src2[],
                 int size, BYTE blend)
{
   int i;
   for (i=0; i<size; i++) // one loop
   {
      if (blend == 255) // invariant branch
         Dest[i] = Src1[i];
      else if (blend == 0) // invariant branch
         Dest[i] = Src2[i];
      else
         Dest[i] = (Src1[i] * blend +
                   Src2[i] * (255-blend)) / 256;
   }
}

// improved version
// no branches inside loops
void BlendArray(BYTE Dest[],
                BYTE Src1[], BYTE Src2[],
                int size, BYTE blend)
{
   int i;
   if (blend == 255) // invariant branch before loop
      for (i=0; i<size; i++) // loop without branches
         Dest[i] = Src1[i];
   else if (blend == 0) // invariant branch before loop
      for (i=0; i<size; i++) // loop without branches
         Dest[i] = Src2[i];
   else
      for (i=0; i<size; i++)
         Dest[i] = (Src1[i] * blend +
                   Src2[i] * (255-blend)) / 256;
}
```

Iteration Dependencies

Data dependencies and lack of ready instructions are two basic issues that slow down performance. Loops are especially susceptible to data dependencies issues because to write a loop with them is easy but to spot them is difficult. The following code computes the factorial for zero to eleven and stores the result in an array.

```
int i, FactorialArray[12];
FactorialArray [0] = 1;
for (i=1; i<12; i++)
      FactorialArray [i] = FactorialArray [i-1] * i;
```

This loop is jammed full of data dependencies- so much so that every iteration is dependent upon all previous iterations. In pseudo assembly language, the sequence is:

1. store 1 at FatorialArray[0]

2. i = 1

3. load reg with FactorialArray[i-1]

4. multiply reg = i * reg

5. store reg at FatorialArray[i]

6. increment I

7. compare i and 12

8. jump less than to step 3

You can see that lines 1 to 5 are dependent upon each other, plus they include two memory accesses and an integer multiply, which are all long latency operations. This loop is limited to running no faster than one instruction per clock. Plus dependencies exist between iterations. On the second time through the loop, the load on line 3 must wait until the previous iteration's line 6 finishes. Basically nothing is performance-oriented about this loop, and it should be completely rewritten if it were the cause of a hotspot. The simplest way to rewrite this loop is by pre-calculating the factorials at compile time or program initialization and just storing the values with the following code.

```
int FactorialArray[12] = {1, 1, 2, 6,
     24, 120, 720, 5040,
     40320, 362880, 3628800, 39916800};
```

Memory Address Dependencies

As with all data dependencies, starting the dependent operation as early as possible reduces the time spent waiting for the result. Long latency operations such as reading memory are especially hard on data dependencies.

Most loops take the form:

1. load memory from LoadPtr

2. do computations

3. store memory to StorePtr

4. calculate new load and store pointers

5. increment loop counter

6. branch to line 1 if not done yet

Just as with all loops, plenty of data dependencies are present, but two especially nasty ones are limiting performance in this example. First, the memory load on line 1 is dependent on line 4 from the previous loop iteration. Therefore, the processor cannot start the memory fetch for the next loop iteration until the previous loop iteration, specifically line 4, finishes. In the ideal case, the processor would be fetching the data for the next iteration during the computations for the current iteration. By moving the calculation of the new memory pointers up in the loop, along with a possible load or prefetch, memory can be accessed earlier. At the very least, make sure to calculate load and store addresses as early as possible.

The second issue is called *unknown store address blocking*. When the address of a memory store is not known, the processor cannot speculatively load other memory locations because it cannot be certain that the memory will not be changed by the store. Lines 1 and 3 above are going to have this problem if the calculation of the store address is not quickly executed. As a result, the processor waits to load memory for the next iteration until the store pointer for the current iteration is known.

Key Points

Keep these three general rules in mind:

■ Because of repetitive execution, loops are usually the source of performance issues.

■ Write loops so that data dependencies are low, loop overhead is small compared to the total execution time, and memory addresses are known well in advance of their use.

■ Loops are usually a great place to add parallelism to an application. Instruction parallelism can be added by lowering data dependencies through the use of unrolling, using the SIMD instructions, or adding multiple threads.

Creamy Baked Mac and Cheese

Ingredients

2 tablespoons butter
6 ounces evaporated milk
2 cups macaroni, corkscrew, or spiral shaped pasta
10 ounces sharp cheddar cheese, grated

Directions

1. Preheat oven to 400°F.
2. Boil macaroni in salt water in a large pot until almost tender. Drain.
3. Reduce heat to low. Add butter, evaporated milk, and cheese and stir constantly until creamy, about 5 minutes.
4. Place into a baking dish and bake until lightly brown on top, about 20 minutes.

Chapter 10

Slow Operations

O ccasionally, a hotspot is located in a piece of code that is just plain slow. It might be a system call, an expensive sequence of calculations, or maybe just an expensive instruction like cosine-whatever it is, it's slow. It is common to think that slow operations are just that, slow, and nothing can be done to improve performance. But, don't give up too soon. Usually, you still can improve performance significantly by finding a way to avoid the slow operation altogether or by modifying it saving just the good parts.

Operations are slow, for the most part, because they are written to solve a general problem. For example, string functions like `scanf` work for all types of input. If only a subset of the functionality were required, like the conversion of hexadecimal values, `scanf` would not take advantage of that fact and would still execute the full general version. In this case, and many others, a special purpose function could easily beat the performance of the generalized function. Especially when building into the code assumptions about the data, such as the length, alignments, and cache state, a specialized function usually is easier to write and its performance is higher.

Slow Instructions

Instructions are slow due to one or more of the following reasons:

■ Long latency. Latency is the time in processor clocks from the time that the instruction first starts executing until the time that it is completed. For instructions like addition and subtraction, the latency is a quick 0.5 clocks. But for instructions like floating-point division, latency can be 23 or more clocks depending upon the precision. Long latency instructions hurt performance only when other operations are dependent upon the result. Executing a long latency instruction when other non-dependent instructions are ready for execution does not usually present a performance issue. Some common long latency operations are: memory accesses that miss the cache, division, multiplication, square root, logarithms, rounding, exponentials, and trigonometry functions.

■ Low throughput. Throughput measures how many of the same kind of instruction can be executed at the same time. This measurement is expressed as the minimum number of clocks required between starts of two of the same type of instruction. For example, floating-point multiplies have a throughput of two clocks, so every two clocks another floating-point multiply can be started even though it takes longer than two clocks to get any one answer. Single-precision division, on the other hand, has a throughput and latency of 23 clocks, so only one divide can be executed at a time.

■ Arguments are not ready. Data dependencies are probably the most common reason that instructions appear to execute slowly. When instruction arguments are not available due to dependencies on previous calculations or memory fetches, the instructions wait around inside the processor and have the appearance of taking a long time to execute.

■ No available execution ports. The Pentium 4 processor can execute many instructions at the same time, but limits do apply. For example, a floating-point square root and a divide cannot occur at the same time because they require the use of the same execution port. However, multiple ALU instructions like addition, subtraction, and compares can be executed at a time because the processor provides multiple execution ports that are capable of processing ALU instructions. The processor has been designed to handle a blend of instructions for maximum performance.

■ Serializing. Serializing instructions are in a class of performance killers all their own because these instructions stop the out-of-order flow of execution. Two common examples are changing the floating-point control register and executing CPUID that is typically used to determine the type of processor.

Improving slow instruction issues involves finding other work to do during the latency or finding a way to avoid using the slow instruction in the first place. For example, if an algorithm requires division, it would be a good idea to find 23 clocks of non-data-dependent instructions to execute in the meantime or to find a way to avoid the division by using subtraction, shifts, or lookup tables. Sometimes merging two functions or unrolling a loop can help find the additional work and discover more optimization opportunities.

Lookup Tables

A common approach used to avoid executing slow instructions is to use a lookup table to store pre-calculated results. When lookup tables work, they do so because memory speeds are faster than calculation speeds. But as processors get more powerful and memory speeds stay the same, lookup tables can be less effective. You should remember three things when using lookup tables:

■ Organize the table to maximize cache hits. Memory fetched from the cache is very fast but accesses that miss the cache are very slow. When designing the table, be sure to consider which entries are likely to be used together and how to best organize the table to maximize cache hits. Sometimes, a less than obvious index function or a little table compression can be used to improve performance.

■ Keep the table small. The smaller the table, the more room there will be in the cache for other things. Even if the cache is large enough to store the whole table, still try to use the smallest possible size because you are trying to improve the performance of the whole application and not just the lookup table. Save the cache for other more critical operations.

■ Store as many calculations as possible. Always try to create the table with the largest amount of precalculated values including as many slow instructions as possible. But be careful, more calculations sometimes lead to more memory requirements which can reduce performance. A balance between using extra memory and doing more calculations has to be met.

Example 10.1 Optimizations Using Lookup Tables

Multiple lookup tables can be used at the same time to dramatically improve performance while keeping additional memory requirements to a minimum. This example demonstrates the technique.

Problem

The following function converts a 32-bit per pixel RGBA (red, green, blue, alpha) bitmap to black and white. Improve the performance of this function using one or more lookup tables.

```
void RGBtoBW(DWORD *pBitmap, DWORD width, DWORD height,
          long stride)
{
  DWORD row, col;
  DWORD pixel, red, green, blue, alpha, bw;
  for (row=0; row<height; row++)
  {
    for (col=0; col<width; col++)
    {
      pixel = pBitmap[col + row*stride/4];
      alpha = (pixel >> 24) & 0xff;
      red   = (pixel >> 16) & 0xff;
      green = (pixel >> 8) & 0xff;
      blue  = pixel & 0xff;
      bw = (DWORD)(red   * 0.299 +
                   green * 0.587 +
                   blue  * 0.114);
      pBitmap[col + row*stride/4] =
            (alpha<<24) + (bw<<16) + (bw<<8) + (bw);
    }
  }
}
```

Solution

The first thing to notice is that the black and white pixel is a scaling of the three individual color components of the RGB pixel and a copy of the alpha channel. The table with the most number of calculations would be:

```
BlackWhitePixel = BigTable[RGBpixel];
```

Unfortunately, this table is huge. Since there are 2^{32} possible pixel values and each value is 32 bits, the table is $2^{32}*4$ bytes or 16 GB, clearly way too large.

The math that takes the most time is the three floating-point multiplies followed by the floating-point to integer conversion. A table that contained these calculations would be used with the following code:

```
BlackWhitePixel = BigTable[RGBpixel & 0x00ffffff] +
                  RGBpixel & 0xff00000000;
```

This table would be 2^{24} bytes or 16 MB, still huge. A good compromise is to use three 256-byte tables one for each multiply. The line would then change to:

```
bw = (DWORD)mul299[red] +
     (DWORD)mul587[green] +
     (DWORD)mul144[blue];
pBitmap[col + row*stride/4] =
     (alpha<<24) + (bw<<16) + (bw<<8) + bw;
```

Using the three look-up tables speeds up performance by about 400 percent, but you can still make more optimizations. Using a fourth table can avoid the shifts and additions on the last assignment. The line would then change to:

```
pBitmap[col + row*stride/4] = (alpha<<24) + BWMerge[bw];
```

Using the fourth table for the merge improves performance by another 50 percent, using only 256*4 or 1 KB of additional memory. Also, with a simple mask, you can avoid the two shifts for the alpha channel.

So using three 256-byte tables, one 1024-byte table for a total of 1772 bytes, and removing the two shifts improves performance by about 700 percent. The new function using tables is:

```
void tblRGBtoBW(DWORD*pBitmap,DWORD width,
                DWORD height,long stride)
{
    DWORD row, col;
    DWORD pixel, red, green, blue, alpha, bw;
    for (row=0; row<height; row++)
    {
        for (col=0; col<width; col++)
        {
```

```
                         pixel = pBitmap[col + row*stride/4];
                         alpha = pixel & 0xff000000;
                         red   = (pixel>>16) & 0xff;
                         green = (pixel>>8) & 0xff;
                         blue  = pixel & 0xff;
                         bw = (DWORD)mul299[red] +
                              (DWORD)mul587[green] +
                              (DWORD)mul144[blue];
                         pBitmap[col + row*stride/4] =
                              alpha + BWMerge[bw];
                    }
              }
      }
```

And the code to make the tables is:

```
BYTE mul299[256];
BYTE mul587[256];
BYTE mul144[256];
DWORD BWMerge[256];
for (i=0; i<256; i++)
{
      mul299[i] = (BYTE)((float)i * 0.299f);
      mul587[i] = (BYTE)((float)i * 0.587f);
      mul144[i] = (BYTE)((float)i * 0.144f);
      BWMerge[i] = (i<<16) + (i<<8) + i;
}
```

A further refinement would reduce the size of the tables. The red table changes values about every three entries and the blue table only about every seven values. Using convenient powers of two, the red table could be half as large and the blue table a quarter as large. The memory requirements would drop by 192 bytes, which is hardly worth saving unless cache space is at a premium.

System Calls

Sometimes, you will find hotspots in places other than the application itself, such as the operating system, external libraries, or device drivers. When you do, you are not necessarily finished optimizing. You just need to use a different strategy to improve performance. Four things help in these situations:

■ Make fewer calls. Many functions operate most efficiently on large data sets, because of the amortized overhead. For example, 3D graphics libraries perform best when operating on large buffers of vertices which helps to minimize call overhead and calculation data dependencies. Using intuition and performance experiments, it should be possible to discover the most efficient way to combine multiple function calls into one call that operates on more data at the same time. Memory allocation is another very common function call that has high overhead when used for small requests. It would be much better to allocate a large block of memory and divide it yourself than to make many calls for small blocks of memory. Don't forget to review documentation and search the Internet for information that might help to direct you. Once you have an idea why a function call is slow, you can rewrite your application to call it more efficiently.

■ Call the same function differently. Some functions have dramatically different performance depending upon their arguments. Things like memory alignment and buffer lengths can greatly change performance. For example, the copy memory function works significantly better on aligned buffers.

■ Call a different function. Some functions are just slow and the best thing to do is to spend time searching for an alternative. Sometimes a similar function that has higher performance or an optimized version of the same library can be found and substituted. A great place to look for optimized functions are the Intel® Performance Libraries which are a collection of highly optimized libraries good for matrix math, digital signal processing, speech, and image processing. They can be found at The Intel Performance Libraries Web site on the Intel® Software Development Products Home page. The Intel Performance Libraries contain the BLAS (Basic Linear Algebra Subprograms) routines which are routines for performing basic vector and matrix operations. More information on BLAS can be found on the Internet and in many books.

The Intel C++ Compiler also contains a few C run-time function intrinsics such as memcpy, memset, and strcpy that provide very high performance and can be called in place of the standard C run-time library.

■ Write the functionality yourself. When all else fails, it is time to write your own version of the function. Most functions, especially ones written by external companies, are intended for general-purpose use. Since you have the advantage of specific knowledge about your application and its algorithms, data structures, and cache state, chances are good that you can beat the best general-purpose functions. Keep this point in mind: when writing the algorithm, you should be looking for things that are specific to your implementation and exploit them for maximum performance.

Example 10.2 Improve the Following Function

Find a way to exploit specific knowledge about the algorithm to improve performance.

Problem

The following function takes as input an array of two-digit hexadecimal characters and generates a second array of the equivalent integers. For example, if the text buffer had four characters "AE92" the hex buffer would have two unsigned bytes 0xAE (174d) and 0x92 (146d).

```c
void TxtToHex (BYTE * pHex, char Txt[], int length)
{
        int i, x;
        for (i=0; i<length; i++)
        {
                sscanf (Txt+2*i, "%02x", &x);
                pHex[i] = (BYTE)x;
        }
}
```

Solution

The problem is that the C run-time function sscanf is a general-purpose routine that is extremely inefficient for this usage. The best solution is to write a 2-character, text-to-hexadecimal function that takes advantage of knowing that exactly two characters must be converted with no spaces. The new and improved function is:

```c
void TxtToHexFast (BYTE * pHex, char Txt[], int length)
{
        int i, a, b;
        for (i=0; i<length; i++)
        {
                a = (int)Txt[i*2];
                b = (int)Txt[i*2+1];
                if (a >= 'A')
                        a = a - 'A';
                else
                        a = a - '0';
                if (b >= 'A')
```

```
                        b = b - 'A';
            else
                        b = b - '0';
            pHex[i] = (BYTE)((a<<4) + b);
      }
}
```

This new version is about 1000 times faster than using `sscanf`. Unfortunately, branch mis-predictions are occurring because the multiple `if` statements are based on somewhat random data. An even faster method would be to use a lookup table, as shown in the following code.

```
BYTE LookupA[23] = {
        0x00, 0x10, 0x20, 0x30, 0x40,
        0x50, 0x60, 0x70, 0x80, 0x90,
        0xff, 0xff, 0xff, 0xff, 0xff,
        0xff, 0xff, // skip : ; < = > ? @
        0xa0, 0xb0, 0xc0, 0xd0, 0xe0, 0xf0};
BYTE LookupB[23] = {
        0x00, 0x01, 0x02, 0x03, 0x04,
        0x05, 0x06, 0x07, 0x08, 0x09,
        0xff, 0xff, 0xff, 0xff, 0xff,
        0xff, 0xff, // skip : ; < = > ? @
        0x0a, 0x0b, 0x0c, 0x0d, 0x0e, 0x0f};
void TxtToHexTable (BYTE * pHex, char Txt[], int length)
{
      int i, a, b;
      for (i=0; i<length; i++)
      {
            a = (int)Txt[i*2-'0'];
            b = (int)Txt[i*2+1-'0'];
            pHex[i] = LookupA[a] + LookupB[b];
      }
}
```

This new function uses two tables with a total of 46 bytes and executes another seven times faster, for a total result that is almost 8000 times faster than the `sscanf` version.

System Idle Process

The king of all slow operations is the system idle loop. The operating system automatically runs this process when no processes are ready to be executed. When the System Idle process runs, it is always a sign that the processor is wasting time waiting for something to occur.

Slow input/output devices such as hard disks and synchronization events usually cause your application to sleep, allowing the System Idle process to run. A goal for performance optimizations is to have no system idle time.

System idle time can be detected using the Performance Monitor with the Process object counter/ % Processor Time/ Instance Idle as shown in Figure 10.1. When the System Idle process is at 100 percent, the system is completely idle. In Figure 10.1, the system is idle from anywhere between 0 and 90 percent.

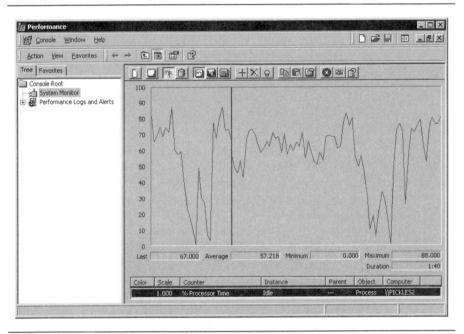

Figure 10.1 The Performance Monitor Displaying System Idle Time

The VTune analyzer can also be used to detect system idle time. Figure 10.2 is a screen shot of the VTune analyzer displaying the System Idle process labeled pid_0x0. If you were to drill down on pid_0x0, hall.dll would be the module and `HalProcessorIdle` would be the function.

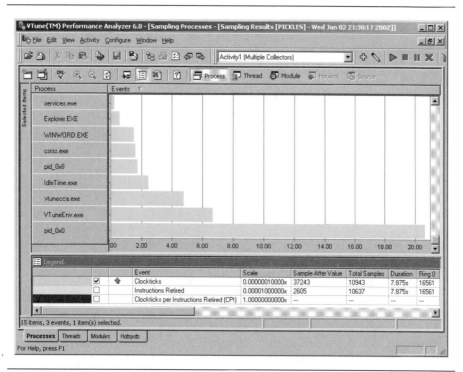

Figure 10.2 The System Idle Process in the VTune Analyzer

When the CPU is not at 100-percent utilization, optimization efforts should focus on detecting why the system waiting. Sometimes the reason will be obvious- a word processor waiting for user input, for example- but other times some detective work is needed. Unfortunately, drilling down on the system idle bar in the VTune analyzer only displays the assembly code for the system idle task, which is not helpful because you need to know why the system is running the idle process, not to see the assembly language instructions for the System Idle process. However, switching to the Counter Monitor feature can offer some hints. The Counter Monitor feature displays the collected samples versus time and allows you to zoom in on a specific period of time, as shown in Figure 10.3.

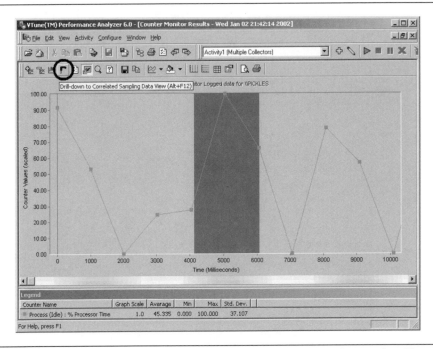

Figure 10.3 Counter Monitor Isolating the Highest Peak of the System Idle Time

Once a region is selected, like the one shown in Figure 10.3, you can drill-down to obtain a histogram that contains only the samples that were collected during the isolated slice of time. Usually, you can determine what the application was doing by examining the samples. Look for loops in the application that called operating system functions such as disk reads, network access, and synchronization calls- any function that might wait.

The Call Graph feature can be used to help narrow down the possible functions that are waiting. By using the VTune analyzer to highlight Top 10 Self Wait Time, shown in Figure 10.4, the functions that are outlined and on the critical path are most likely the source of the idle time.

Sometimes a performance experiment is required to increase your confidence that you know exactly why the system idle loop is running. By intentionally breaking the code to avoid calling the suspected function, you should be able to determine which operations are causing idle time and how much.

Fixing idle-time issues is just like fixing system call issues. First determine why the function is waiting and then determine how to best improve the situation by calling the same function with different parameters, calling a different function, or writing your own function.

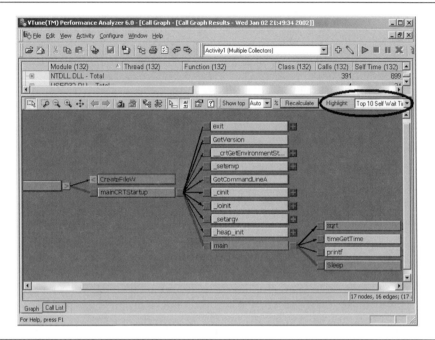

Figure 10.4 Call Graph Highlighting the Top 10 Self Wait Functions

Key Points

When optimizing slow instructions, keep the following in mind:

- Instructions and operations can be slow because they are general purpose. Writing your own function that specifically exploits knowledge about your application's requirements can result in huge performance increases.

- Determine how to call functions for maximum efficiency. Buffer sizes and data alignment usually cause dramatic changes in function performance.

- Use lookup tables to avoid slow calculations, especially when table sizes are small and the number of precalculated values is high.

- When you see the System Idle process running, relentlessly investigate the cause and improve the situation.

Not-Your-Kid's
Grilled Cheese Sandwich

Ingredients for 2 sandwiches
4 thickly sliced sourdough bread slices
6 ounces shaved sharp cheddar cheese
Handful of spinach leaves
4 tomato slices
6 turkey bacon slices
2 tablespoons butter

Directions
1. Cook bacon in microwave on paper towels until crisp.
2. Heat a cast-iron skillet on medium heat.
3. Lightly butter one side of two slices of bread. Place butter side down on skillet.
4. Assemble sandwich with cheese, spinach, bacon, tomato, more cheese, and piece of unbuttered bread.
5. Push sandwich down with hand or plate until the bottom bread starts browning and cheese starts melting, about 2-3 minutes.
6. If you accidentally buttered the top bread, wipe butter off your hand.
7. Lightly butter the top slice of bread, then turn the whole sandwich over, compress, and wait for melting and browning, about 2-3 more minutes.

Chapter **11**

Floating Point

Before the Pentium processor, floating-point math was executed either by a separate co-processor or a floating-point emulation software package. Either way, using floating-point numbers just about guaranteed a slow application. But those days are long gone and floating-point performance is now on par with the rest of the processor and even faster in some cases. However, the same issues that affect all instructions, such as data dependencies, available instructions ports, and memory latencies, also affect floating-point math operations. In addition to the common problems, you should be aware of a few additional issues that are specific to floating-point operations, which include numeric exceptions, precision control, and floating-point to integer conversions.

Floating-point operations can occur using the x87 floating-point unit (FPU), the 64-bit or 128-bit SIMD units, or by direct manipulation of the stored floating-point value using integer instructions. Each method has different performance advantages, capabilities, and issues that are discussed in this chapter.

Numeric Exceptions

The x87 floating-point unit and the SIMD floating-point unit can generate exceptions in response to certain input and calculation conditions. The processor handles exceptions by calling software handlers or, if masked, ignoring them and doing something reasonable like creating a denormal number. It is important to detect and eliminate floating-point exceptions because they usually indicate error conditions and almost always hurt performance. Table 11.1 is a list of all the possible floating-point exceptions.

Table 11.1 List of Floating-point Exceptions

Exception	Description
Stack Overflow or Underflow	Attempt to load a non-empty register location. Always indicates a critical error condition. **NOTE:** Valid only for x87 FPU, which is stack based. The SIMD units are register based.
Invalid Operation	Attempt to use data bytes that do not represent a floating-point number called NaNs or Not-A-Number. Also caused by improper use of infinity or negative operands. Always indicates a critical error condition.
Divide-by-zero	Attempt to divide-by-zero. Always indicates a critical error condition.
Denormal Operand	Occurs when using extremely small numbers that cannot be encoded in the standard normalized floating-point format. The use of denormal operands always indicates a loss of precision and usually indicates a calculation condition that is worth fixing.
Numeric Overflow/ Numeric Underflow	Occurs whenever a rounded result of an operation exceeds the largest or smaller possible finite value that will fit in the destination format. This condition can usually be fixed by scaling values, using greater precision, or by flushing the result to zero.
Inexact-result /Precision	Occurs when the result of an operation is not exactly representable in the destination format. This is the only exception that can be safely ignored.

Detecting floating-point exceptions is accomplished by unmasking the exceptions in the floating-point control word. Figure 11.1 is a diagram of the bit assignments of the x87 control word and Figure 11.2 is a diagram for the SIMD control word.

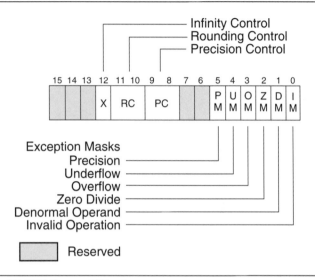

Figure 11.1 x87 FPU Control Word

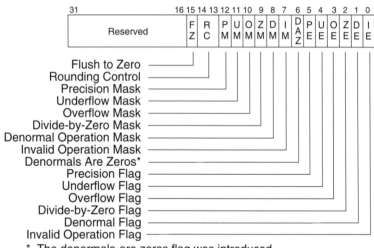

Figure 11.2 SSE and SSE2 Control Register

If a bit is set (one) then the exception is masked and will not occur. When the bit is cleared (zero) the exception will occur. A good way to detect whether any exceptions exist is to enable all exceptions at the start of an application then run the benchmark and quality assurance tests. The simplest method to unmask exceptions is to call one of the following functions:

```
WORD UnmaskAllx87FPExceptions (void)
{
        WORD OldCtrl;
        WORD NewCtrl;
        _asm {
                FSTCW OldCtrl
                mov ax, OldCtrl
                and ax, 0ffc0h
                mov NewCtrl, ax
                FLDCW NewCtrl
        }
        return OldCtrl;
}
DWORD UnmaskAllSSEFPExceptions (void)
{
        DWORD OldCtrl;
        DWORD NewCtrl;
        _asm {
                STMXCSR OldCtrl
                mov eax,OldCtrl
                and eax, 0ffffe07fh
                mov NewCtrl, eax
                LDMXCSR NewCtrl
        }
        return OldCtrl;
}
```

Both of these functions return the original value of the floating-point control register for use when restoring the values.

Floating-point exceptions are reported with an Application Error dialog box as shown in Figure 11.3.

The debugger will place you on the instruction that caused the floating-point exception so that you can immediately debug and correct the situation.

Figure 11.3 Sample Application Error Dialog Box

Flush-to-Zero and Denormals are Zero

When floating-point numbers become very tiny and the standard normalized-number format can no longer be used, the processor generates an approximate denormalized number. Denormal numbers always indicate a loss of precision, an underflow condition, and usually an error or at least a less than desirable condition. Denormal numbers can be used as inputs to future arithmetic, but at the expense of lost performance.

Starting with the Pentium 4 processor, SIMD floating-point computations that generate denormal results can be set to zero, improving performance using the flush-to-zero and denormals are zero modes. These modes are not compatible with the IEEE Standard 754, and they have been included to provide improved performance when working with values so close to zero that treating them as zero does not appreciably affect the quality of the result. The following function sets flush-to-zero mode:

```
void SIMDFlushToZero (void)
{
    DWORD SIMDCtrl;
    _asm
    {
        STMXCSR SIMDCtrl
        mov eax, SIMDCtrl
        // flush-to-zero = bit 15
        // mask underflow = bit 11
        // denormals are zero = bit 6
        or eax, 08840h
        mov SIMDCtrl, eax
        LDMXCSR SIMDCtrl
    }
}
```

Precision

Floating-point numbers are stored in memory in one of three formats: single (4 bytes), double (8 bytes), and double-extended (10 bytes) precision. Regardless of the format used, the processor always performs calculations based upon global calculation precision that is also called single, double, and double-extended.

The quickest way to improve performance is to lower the floating-point calculation precision, which effects the performance of addition, subtraction, multiplication, division, and square root. Table 11.2 shows the difference in performance among the different precisions for division.

Table 11.2 Performance in Clocks of the Floating-point Divide Instructions

Instruction	Single	Double	Double Extended
FDIV x87 divide	23	38	43
DIVSS/ DIVSD scalar SIMD divide	22	35	—
DIVPS/ DIVPD packed SIMD divide	32	62	—

The first step is to determine how much precision is required. Precision specifies the maximum magnitude of a number as well as how many digits can be represented. Figure 11.4 is a diagram of how floating-point numbers are mapped into the real number system.

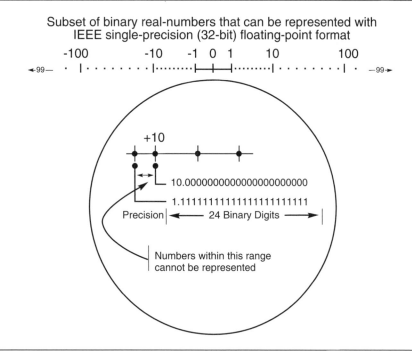

Figure 11.4 Single-precision Floating-point Number Representation

The Pentium 4 processor can operate on and store floating-point numbers with 32, 64, or 80 bits of precision. You should choose the lowest precision that satisfies your application's computational requirements. The smallest possible and largest possible numbers that can be represented by each of the data types are shown in Table 11.3.

Table 11.3 Length and Range of Floating-Point Data Types

Data Type	Length	Approximate Normalized Decimal Range
Single Precision	32	1.18×10^{-38} to 3.4×10^{38}
Double Precision	64	2.23×10^{-308} to 1.79×10^{308}
Double Extended Precision	80	3.37×10^{-4932} to 1.18×10^{4932}

Once you have determined the minimum precision required, you can adjust the floating-point control register to match the desired precision. By default, double extended precision is used. The data type in memory is independent of the processor's internal precision setting. So, declaring a variable as a float instead of a double does not alter the calculation precision. Table 11.4 shows the bit value for the PC field in the control register.

Table 11.4 Precision Control Field (bits 8 and 9) of the x87 Floating-point Control Register

Precision	PC Field
Single Precision	00B
Reserved	01B
Double Precision	10B
Double Extended Precision	11B

The following code can be used to set the precision of the x87 floating-point control register.

```
#define PRECISION_SINGLE       0x0000
#define PRECISION_DOUBLE       0x0200
#define PRECISION_EXTENDED     0x0300
WORD Setx87Precision(WORD precision)
{
      WORD OldCtrl;
      WORD NewCtrl;
      _asm {
            FSTCW OldCtrl
            mov ax, OldCtrl
            and ax, 0fcffh
            or ax, precision
            mov NewCtrl, ax
            FLDCW NewCtrl

      }
      return OldCtrl;
}
```

This function returns the value of the control register before changing the precision. It is important to restore the value before calling any functions that rely upon the default floating-point precision behavior or any external functions that use or could use floating-point math in the future. When adjusting the x87 floating-point unit precision, be sure to do so infrequently because changing the control word is an expensive operation. The following function can be used to restore the control word.

```
WORD Setx87ControlWord(WORD NewCtrlWord)
{
        WORD OldCtrlWord;
        _asm {
                fnstcw OldCtrlWord
                fldcw NewCtrlWord
        }
        return OldCtrlWord;
}
```

For floating-point SIMD, different instructions are used for single or double precision so there is no need to change the Streaming SIMD Extensions (SSE) control word (MXCSR) to control the precision. In assembly language, SIMD floating-point division is written as follows:

```
; four divides (32-bits each) single precision
DIVPS xmm1, xmm0

; two divides (64-bits each) double precision
DIVPD xmm1, xmm0
```

The Intel C++ Compiler with the C++ data types can be also used to divide single and double precision SIMD data.

```
F32vec4 a, b;       // single precision
a = a/b;            // four divides (32-bit each)

F64vec2 c, d;       // double precision
c = c/d;            // two divides (64-bits each)
```

Scalar-SIMD Floating Point

SIMD floating-point operations operate on one, two, or four pieces of data at the same time. Operating on one piece of data at a time is called scalar-SIMD while operating on two or four pieces is called packed-SIMD. Scalar-SIMD can be very beneficial when mixing single- and double-precision floating-point calculations in the same function since the control word need not be changed like it does with X87 floating-point. The scalar SIMD instructions easily can be used with the Intel C++ Compiler. The following lines of code are examples of single-precision scalar-SIMD using the SSE instructions.

```
// using the Intel C++ Compiler C++ Class Data Types
F32vec1 a, b;  // scalar only 1 single precision value
a = b / 6.0f;  // division using scalar SIMD
// using the Intel C++ Compiler Intrinsics
RetVal = _mm_sqrt_ss(single_fp); // square root
RetVal = _mm_rsqrt_ss(single_fp); // reciprocal square root
```

Float-to-Integer Conversions, Rounding

Very frequently, the results of a floating-point operation are converted to an integer. This conversion is especially common for computer graphics applications because pixels and coordinates are integers, but computations are sometimes done with floating-point arithmetic. Unfortunately, the conversion from floating-point to integer values can be costly. The C language specifies that floating-point to integer conversions, as shown in the following code, must perform truncation (rounding towards zero).

```
float a = 3.5f;
int b;
b = (int)a;  // float to integer conversion
// b will equal 3
```

Unfortunately, the processor, by default, rounds floating-point values to the nearest integer. So, when the compiler is asked to cast a floating-point value to an integer, the x87 floating-point control register is changed twice, once before the conversion and once after the conversion, to restore the original value. The following four distinct steps detail the compiler's process for converting floating-point numbers to integer numbers.

1. Save floating-point control word.
2. Switch control word to truncate mode.
3. Execute a floating-point to integer store (FISTP).
4. Restore the floating-point control word to round mode.

The compiler executes all four steps each time a conversion takes place, potentially adding a huge amount of unnecessary overhead. The VTune Performance Analyzer can be used to identify where floating-point to integer truncations are occurring by detecting calls to _ftol. Figure 11.5 shows the sampling results of an application that has many calls to ftol.

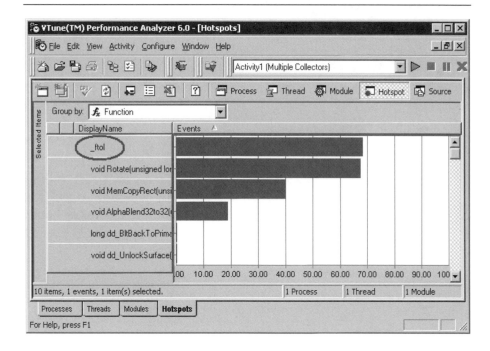

Figure 11.5 Floating-point to Integer Conversions Detected via Sampling

Performance can be improved by avoiding the use of the default compiler behavior using one of the following four methods:

- Use the Intel C++ Compiler specific command-line switch that performs rounding instead of truncation when converting floating-point numbers to integers.

- Use assembly language to change the rounding mode once, do all the conversions without the compiler (FLID, FISTP), and then restore the rounding mode.

- Use the SIMD packed or scalar convert with truncation instructions.

- Do direct bit manipulation using integer instructions.

Choosing one of the four methods is a matter of preference, convenience, and performance. The use of the SIMD instructions is likely to provide the highest performance because four values can be converted at once.

Using the Intel C++ Compiler's Round Instead of Truncate Switch

The Intel C++ Compiler's - Qrcd command-line switch disables the truncation behavior and uses rounding for all floating-point to integer conversions. While this choice does produce faster code, it does not conform to the C specification and could cause compatibility issues. This switch should be used on a file- by- file basis to limit the possibility of compatibility issues.

Assembly Language

The second way to convert floating-point numbers to integers with truncation is to change the rounding mode to truncation once, perform all the conversions in assembly language, and then restore the control word. The following assembly code converts a floating-point number to an integer based upon the current rounding mode.

```
float x;
int y;
_asm {
        fld x  // load a floating-point value
        fistp y  // store as an integer
}
```

To truncate the number, the rounding mode must be changed to truncation before executing the two instructions. The rounding mode is controlled by bits 10 and 11 of the x87 floating-point control register and by bits 13 and 14 of the SIMD floating-point control register. Table 11.5 shows the encoding for the rounding mode bits in the control register, which is shown in Figure 11.1.

Table 11.5 Rounding Modes and Encoding of the Rounding Control (RC) Field

Rounding Mode	RC Field	Description
Round to nearest	00B	Rounded result is the closest to the infinitely precise result. If two values are equally close, the result is the even value. Default.
Round down	01B	Rounded result is closest to but no greater than the infinitely precise result.
Round up	10B	Rounded result is closest to but no less than the infinitely precise result.
Round toward zero (truncate)	11B	Rounded result is closest to but no greater in absolute value than the infinitely precise result.

The following function changes the rounding mode to truncation for the x87 floating-point unit:

```
WORD Changex87FPToTrunc(void)
{
        WORD NewCtrlWord, OldCtrlWord;
        _asm {
                fnstcw OldCtrlWord
                mov ax, OldCtrlWord
                or ax, 0c00h
                mov NewCtrlWord, ax
                fldcw NewCtrlWord
        }
        return OldCtrlWord;
}
```

The following function changes the rounding mode to truncation for the SIMD floating-point unit:

```
DWORD ChangeSEEToTrunc(void)
{
        DWORD NewCtrlWord, OldCtrlWord;
        _asm {
                stmxcsr OldCtrlWord
                mov eax, OldCtrlWord
                or eax, 06000h
                mov NewCtrlWord, eax
                ldmxcsr NewCtrlWord
        }
        return OldCtrlWord;
}
```

Both functions return the value of the old control word so that you can restore it before calling a function that needs the original rounding mode. The following functions can be used to restore the value of the floating-point control words:

```
WORD Setx87ControlWord(WORD NewCtrlWord)
{
        WORD OldCtrlWord;
        _asm {
                fnstcw OldCtrlWord
                fldcw NewCtrlWord
        }
        return OldCtrlWord;
}



DWORD SetSSEControlWord(DWORD NewCtrlWord)
{
        DWORD OldCtrlWord;
        _asm {
                stmxcsr OldCtrlWord
                ldmxcsr NewCtrlWord
        }
        return OldCtrlWord;
}
```

SIMD Convert with Truncation Instructions

The third method for converting floats to integers with truncation is to use the scalar or packed SIMD convert with truncation instructions. These instructions can be used with inline assembly or with the Intel C++ Compiler intrinsics. The instructions all start with CVTT as the first four letters of the mnemonic, which means ConVerT with Truncation. These instructions are relatively fast, with throughputs of two clocks. Furthermore, these instructions can operate on one, two, or four values at the same time. The following code converts four single-precision floating-point values to four integer values with truncation:

```
float fa[4];   // 16 byte alignment required
int ia[4];     // 16 byte alignment required
_asm {
      cvttps2dq xmm0, fa
      movdqa ia, xmm0
}
```

This code assumes that both arrays are 16-byte aligned. If they are not, the conversion requires an unaligned load and store that reduces performance, as follows:

```
_asm {
      movdqu xmm0, fa    // no alignment required
      cvttps2dq xmm0, xmm0
      movdqu ia, xmm0    // no alignment required
}
```

Direct Bit Manipulation

Once the floating-point value is in memory, the bits can be manipulated directly with integer instructions. The following code can be used to approximate the conversion of a positive single-precision floating-point value to a truncated (rounded towards negative infinity) integer:

```
#define FLOAT_FTOI_MAGIC_NUM (float)(3<<21)
#define IT_FTOI_MAGIC_NUM 0x4ac00000
int FastFloatToInt(float f)
{
      f += FLOAT_FTOI_MAGIC_NUM;
      return (*((int *)&f) - IT_FTOI_MAGIC_NUM) >>1;
}
```

Floating-Point Manipulation Tricks

You can use a few floating-point manipulation tricks, like the floating-point to integer conversion shown in the preceding code sample, to approximate some floating-point calculations. These tricks should only be used when reduced accuracy is acceptable and when floating-point operations are the bottleneck. Do not use these floating-point tricks in all cases, only those specific cases where the performance boost has significant impact.

Square Root

This function approximates the square root for positive numbers with roughly a 5 percent error, for example, the `FastSqrt(144.0) = 12.5`.

```
float FastSqrt (float f)
{
      float RetVal;
      _asm {
            mov eax, f
            sub eax, 0x3f800000
            sar eax, 1
            add eax, 0x3f800000
            mov RetVal, eax
      }
      return RetVal;
}
```

Reciprocal Square Root

This function approximates 1/square root (x) for values > 0.25 with less than 0.6% error:

```
#define ONE_AS_INT 0x3f800000
float FastInvSqrt (float x)
{
      long tmp = ((ONE_AS_INT << 1) +
                  ONE_AS_INT - *(long*)&x) >> 1;
      float y = *(float *)&tmp;
      return y * (1.47f - 0.47f * x * y * y);
}
```

Key Points

When working with floating-point numbers, keep in mind the following points:

- Keep data dependencies and memory latencies low.
- Avoid penalties due to exceptions and denormal numbers.
- Use the lowest precision possible for calculations.
- Avoid floating-point to integer conversions using the compiler.
- Use scalar and packed SIMD floating-point calculations where possible.

Ingredients for dough

2¼ cups unbleached flour
½ cup wheat or rye flour
2 teaspoons kosher salt
¼ teaspoon fresh ground pepper
1 teaspoon active-dry yeast
2 tablespoons olive oil
¾-to-1 cup warm (~100°F) water

Directions

1. Using the paddle attachment of a mixer, mix all the ingredients together, in the order listed, with only ¾ cup water.
2. While mixing, add as little water as possible until the dough forms a ball.
3. Switch to the dough hook and knead on low speed for 10 minutes. Dough will be a ball, rather dry, and not too sticky.
4. Form into ball and place in an oiled bowl. Cover with plastic wrap, place in refrigerator, and let rise for about 10 hours.

Ingredients for sauce and toppings

8 ounces (½ can) tomato sauce
2 tablespoons olive oil
½ teaspoon ground fennel
1 teaspoon oregano
1 teaspoon basil
¼ teaspoon ground pepper
¼ teaspoon garlic powder
¼ teaspoon crushed red pepper
1½ cups mozzarella, grated
Toppings of your choice, pepperoni, sausage, spinach, etc.

Directions

1. Place pizza stone on lowest rack in oven and preheat oven on maximum temperature for 20 minutes.
2. Mix the ingredients for the sauce together.
3. Remove dough from refrigerator and shape into a 16 inch diameter pie.
4. Spread sauce on pie, then any toppings, then cheese.
5. Place on pizza stone and bake for 7-10 minutes until cheese bubbles and starts to brown.
6. Remove from oven and cool for a few minutes before cutting.

Chapter **12**

SIMD

Single-instruction multiple-data or SIMD is a very significant performance feature that was added to Intel Architecture processors, starting with the Pentium processor with MMX technology. Since then, all 32-bit Intel Architecture processors have been built with more SIMD instructions. SIMD works by operating on multiple pieces of data at the same time using only one instruction, as shown in Figure 12.1.

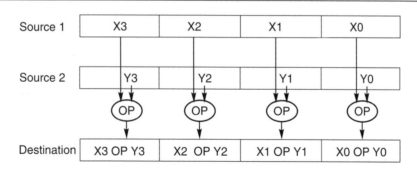

Figure 12.1 Block Diagram of SIMD Execution Model

As new processors were introduced, SIMD technology has expanded to include floating-point in addition to integer operations, as shown in Table 12.1.

Table 12.1   Brief History of SIMD Technology

Technology	First Appeared	Description
MMX technology	Pentium processor with MMX technology	Introduced an 8-byte data type for packed integers.
Streaming SIMD Extensions (SSE)	Pentium III processor	Added a 16-byte data type for packed single-precision floating point.
Streaming SIMD Extensions 2 (SSE2)	Pentium 4 processor	Added a 16-byte data type for packed double-precision floating-point and packed integers.

This chapter discusses the simple things that can be done to make using the SIMD instructions easier and tells you how to achieve higher performance. Details of the specific instructions are located in the *IA-32 Intel Architecture Software Developer's Manual*, Volumes 1 and 2.

Using the SIMD Instructions

The standard C/C++ language does not contain any built-in support for the SIMD instructions, so non-standard methods must be used. The four methods used to program the SIMD instructions are shown in Table 12.2.

Table 12.2   Four Different Ways to Use the SIMD Instructions

Method	Description	Advantages (+) / Disadvantages (-)
Assembly language	Whether inline assembly in C/C++ source code or by using an assembler, both methods use the actual assembly language instructions, specifying everything including registers.	+ Direct control and access to all instructions and registers. – Harder to read, debug, code, learn, and maintain. – Does not guarantee highest performance. – Code is specific to a class of processors.
Intrinsics	Similar to the actual assembly instructions, the intrinsics specify instructions but not registers.	+ Access to all instructions without the need to deal with registers and scheduling. + Integrates well with C/C++. – Hard to read, debug, code, learn, and maintain. – Does not guarantee highest performance. – Code is specific to a class of processors.

continued

Table 12.2 Four Different Ways to Use the SIMD Instructions (continued)

Method	Description	Advantages (+)/Disadvantages (-)
C++ class data types	Uses data types very similar to standard C/C++.	+ Easy to read, debug, code, learn, and maintain.
		+ Code is not specific to one class of processor.
		+ Guarantees the performance boost from using the SIMD instructions.
		– Cannot access all possible instructions and data type combinations.
Auto-vectorize	Let the compiler do all the work.	+ No source code changes.
		– Only loops are vectorized.
		– Due to C compiler issues, some loops are hard for the compiler to use the SIMD instructions.

The following code is an example of a simple function that sums an array of numbers using all four different methods.

```
// Auto-vectorize, Compile with /QxW
int SumArray(int *pBuf, int NumInts)
{
        int i, accum=0;
        for (i=0; i<NumInts; i++)
            accum += pBuf[i];
        return accum;
}

// Using the C++ class data types
int SumArrayClass(int *pBuf, int NumInts)
{
        int i;
        Is32vec4 *pBufVec4 = (Is32vec4 *)pBuf;
        Is32vec4 accum(0,0,0,0);
        for (i=0; i<NumInts/4; i++)
            accum += pBufVec4[i];
        return accum[0] + accum[1] + accum[2] + accum[3];
}

// Using Intrinsics
int SumArrayIntrin(int *pBuf, int NumInts)
{
        int i;
        __m128i accum;
        __m128i *pBuf128 = (__m128i *)pBuf;
        accum = _mm_sub_epi32 (accum, accum); // set to zero
        for (i=0; i<NumInts/4; i++)
            accum = _mm_add_epi32(accum, pBuf128[i]);
```

```
      accum = _mm_add_epi32(accum, _mm_srli_si128(accum, 8));
      accum = _mm_add_epi32(accum, _mm_srli_si128(accum, 4));
      return _mm_cvtsi128_si32 (accum);
}

// Using inline assembly language
int SumArrayAsm(int *pBuf, int NumInts)
{
      _asm {
            mov ecx, 0  ; used for loop counter
            mov esi, pBuf
            pxor xmm0, xmm0  ; init accumulator
      loop:
            paddd xmm0, [esi+ecx*4]  ; accum += pBuf[...]
            add ecx, 4 ; move by four integers
            cmp ecx, NumInts ; done yet?
            jnz loop
            ; add across the register
            movdqa xmm1, xmm0
            psrldq xmm1, 8
            paddd xmm0, xmm1
            movdqa xmm1, xmm0
            psrldq xmm1, 4
            paddd xmm0, xmm1
            movd eax, xmm0 ; return value in eax
      }
}
```

SIMD Instruction Issues

To convert a function to use the SIMD instructions, start by using one of the SIMD data types and adjusting a loop count or otherwise changing the application to execute fewer instructions. Once you have taken care of those things, it is important to handle data alignment, calculation compatibility, and data simplifying buffer lengths.

Data Alignment

The arguments of SIMD instructions must be aligned for maximum performance. Alignment should be at least 8 bytes when using MMX technology or 16 bytes when using the Streaming SIMD Extensions (SSE) or the Streaming SIMD Extensions 2 (SSE2). An exception will occur in any program that operates on unaligned memory with the SSE or SSE2 instructions without using the special-purpose, slower, unaligned memory move instructions.

Proper alignment is needed for all accesses, such as stack-based variables, data structures, and memory buffers, as shown in Table 12.3.

Table 12.3 Different Memory Alignment Methods

Object Being Aligned	How to Align
Stack-based variables	Use the command-line option -Qsfalign16 with the Intel C++ Compiler or declspec(align()) before each variable.
Elements within a data structure	Use the command-line option /Zp or the pragma pack.
Statically allocated variables	Use the align() attribute with declspec and the Intel C++ Compiler as shown in the following example. __declspec(align(16)) float array[1000];
Dynamically allocated variables	Use _mm_malloc() with the Intel C++ Compiler or align the pointer returned by malloc().

The following code allocates 512 bytes of memory on a 16-byte boundary using the C run-time library and the Intel C++ Compiler intrinsics.

```
// Version 1: Using the C runtime library
DWORD *pBuf, *pBufOrig;
pBufOrig = (DWORD *)malloc(128*sizeof(DWORD)+15);
pBuf = (DWORD *)(((DWORD)pBufOrig + 15) & ~0x0f);
...
free(pBufOrig);

// Version 2:Using the Intel C++ Compiler
// intrinsics
DWORD *pBuf;
pBuf = (DWORD )_mm_malloc (128*sizeof(DWORD), 16);
...
_mm_free(pBuf);
```

With all memory allocations, it is very important to observe the memory alias issues that are discussed in Chapter 8.

Compatibility of SIMD and x87 FPU Floating-Point Calculations

The floating-point SIMD instructions and the x87 FPU both operate on the same single-precision and double-precision floating-point data types. However, when operating on these data types, the SIMD instructions operate on them in their native format (single-precision or double-precision), in contrast to the x87 FPU, which extends them to double extended-precision floating-point format to perform computations, and then rounds the result back to a single-precision or double-precision format before writing results to memory. Because it operates on a higher precision format then rounds the result to a lower precision format, the x87 FPU may return a slightly different result when performing the same operation on the same single-precision or double-precision floating-point values than the one that is returned by the floating-point SIMD instructions. The difference occurs only in the least-significant bits.

Data Simplifying Buffer Lengths/Padding

To keep algorithms as simple as possible, it is a great benefit to operate on buffers that are multiples of the SIMD data size being used. For example, when using the four integers SIMD data type, make sure that the buffer is a multiple of four integers. Padding or adding extra, unused bytes at the end of buffers is usually a very easy way to satisfy this requirement. Using multiples of the SIMD data size avoids the special case of dealing with an odd amount of remaining variables.

You can avoid extra programming, testing, and overhead by spending a little time making sure that the memory was allocated with the proper alignment and padding.

In the previous example of summing an array, an assumption about alignment and padding was made. For the function to work correctly in all cases, the buffer must be aligned to at least a 16-byte boundary, and the length must be a multiple of four integers. If these conditions could not be met, the function would need to accommodate buffers with less than four elements, unaligned buffers, and unpadded buffers, adding lots of code.

Integer SIMD

The Pentium 4 processor's integer SIMD is a combination of MMX technology, Streaming SIMD Extensions, and Streaming SIMD Extensions 2. Together, these three technologies offer 8- and 16-byte integer SIMD technology that operates on 1-, 2-, 4-, 8-, and 16-byte integers.

MMX technology (8-byte data types) shares its registers with the x87 floating-point register stack, and therefore, they cannot both be used at the same time. Furthermore, the Empty MMX State (EMMS) instruction must be executed after an MMX technology instruction and before an x87 floating-point instruction or a call to a function that uses or could use x87 floating-point instructions in the future. The EMMS instruction is needed to initialize the floating-point stack, avoiding a possible exception due to misinterpreting SIMD data as floating-point data. The EMMS instruction should be treated as overhead that should be minimized because too many EMMS instructions will hurt performance.

Most of the time, you can avoid the use of the 8-byte MMX technology registers by using the 16-byte SSE/SSE2 registers. Not only are the 16-byte registers not shared with the x87 floating-point unit, but they also operate on twice as much data at a time.

Integer SIMD can be used to do many operations: transfer data, initialize data, convert among different types of integer data, add, subtract, bitwise logical instructions, comparisons, shifts, rotates, averages, min, max, and moves with masks.

Single-Precision Floating-Point SIMD

Streaming SIMD Extensions (SSE), first introduced on the Pentium III processor, added support for single-precision, floating-point SIMD arithmetic using the 16-byte XMM registers.

The SSE instructions support a limited set of the total floating-point operations supported in the x87 floating-point unit. They are: aligned data movement, unaligned data movement, addition, subtraction, division, square root, max, min, compares, shuffles, conversions and approximations of reciprocals, and reciprocal square root.

As a convenience, most SSE instructions can operate on one or four floats at a time, called scalar and packed operations respectively. Unlike MMX technology, these registers are not shared with the x87 floating-point stack, therefore executing the EMMS instruction is not required.

An example of summing an array of floats is shown below using the C++ class data types, again with the assumptions of alignment and padding. You can see how similar it is to the integer version.

```
// Using the C++ class data types
// Assumption: pBuf is 16-byte aligned
// Assumption: NumFPs is a multiple of 4
float SumArrayClass(float *pBuf, int NumFPs)
{
    int i;
    F32vec4 *pBufVec4 = (F32vec4 *)pBuf;
    F32vec4 accum(0,0,0,0);
    for (i=0; i<NumFPs/4; i++)
        accum += pBufVec4[i];
    return accum[0] + accum[1] + accum[2] + accum[3];
}
```

Reciprocal Approximations Accuracy

Using the Newton-Raphson Method can increase the accuracy of the results from the SSE reciprocal and reciprocal square root. Application Note 803 *Increasing the Accuracy of the Results from the Reciprocal and Reciprocal Square Root Instructions using the Newton-Raphson Method* (listed in "References") has a complete explanation of the technique and sample code.

Double-Precision Floating-Point SIMD

The Streaming SIMD Extensions 2 (SSE2) instructions include a collection of double-precision floating-point SIMD operations. Except for the reciprocal approximations instructions, the same SIMD single-precision floating-point operations are available for SIMD double-precision floating-point numbers except they operate on two values instead of four values at once. The operations use the same 16-byte XMM registers as the single-precision SSE, but unlike the x87 floating-point unit, the instruction itself, not a control register, determines the calculation precision.

The following code sample sums an array of doubles using the C++ class data types:

```
// Assumption: pBuf is 16-byte aligned
// Assumption: NumFPs is a multiple of 2
double SumArrayClass(double *pBuf, int NumFPs)
{
    int i;
    F64vec2 *pBufVec2 = (F64vec2 *)pBuf;
    F64vec2 accum(0,0);
    for (i=0; i<NumFPs/2; i++)
        accum += pBufVec2[i];
    return accum[0] + accum[1];
}
```

The differences between using double- and single-precision floating-point arithmetic are: declarations are doubles instead of floats and F64vec2 instead of F32vec4, loops are halved instead of quartered, and only two elements are operated on at a time instead of four.

SIMD Data Organization

The data organization and layout presents a very common problem when using the SIMD instructions. Nothing illustrates this problem better than the matrix multiplication of a 1x4 matrix times a 4x1, as shown in Equation 12.1.

$$\begin{bmatrix} x1 \\ x2 \\ x3 \\ x4 \end{bmatrix} \bullet \begin{bmatrix} y1 \\ y2 \\ y3 \\ y4 \end{bmatrix} = x1\,y1 + x2\,y2 + x3\,y3 + x4\,y4$$

Equation 12.1 Dot Product of Two Matrices

In standard C, this multiplication is trivial, as shown in the following code sample:

```
float dot (float x[], float y[])
{
   return x[0]*y[0]  +  x[1]*y[1]  +
          x[2]*y[2]  +  x[3]*y[3];
}
```

Obviously, executing four multiplies should be a perfect application for the SIMD instructions, and it is, but a little complication arises because the addition requires that the individual elements of one register be added together. This is called summing across a register, which unfortunately does not exist as a single instruction. However, you can accomplish summing across a register with shifts and additions, as shown in Figure 12.2, or by storing the data to memory and adding it with the x87 floating-point unit.

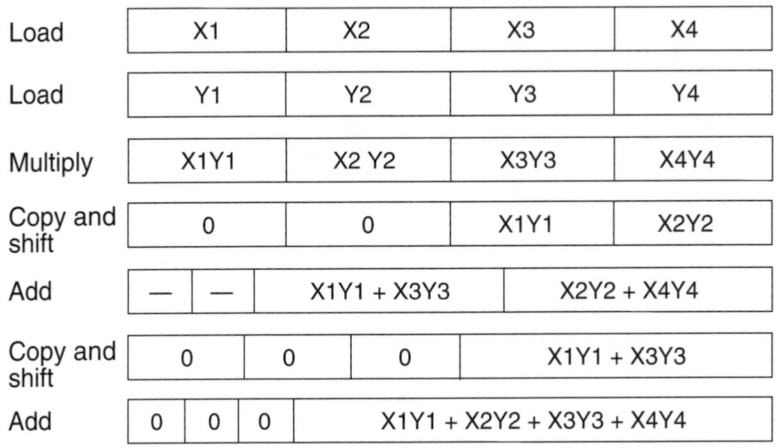

Load	X1	X2	X3	X4

Load	Y1	Y2	Y3	Y4

Multiply	X1Y1	X2 Y2	X3Y3	X4Y4

Copy and shift	0	0	X1Y1	X2Y2

Add	—	—	X1Y1 + X3Y3	X2Y2 + X4Y4

Copy and shift	0	0	0	X1Y1 + X3Y3

Add	0	0	0	X1Y1 + X2Y2 + X3Y3 + X4Y4

Figure 12.2 Diagram of Dot Product Using Single-Precision Floats

The code for the dot product using SIMD follows:

```
float DotSimd(float x[], float y[])
{
        F32vec4 *pX = (F32vec4 *)x;
        F32vec4 *pY = (F32vec4 *)y;
        F32vec4 val;

        val = pX[0] * pY[0];
        return val[0] + val[1] + val[2] + val[3];
}
```

Summing across a register (the calculation in the return statement) is a slow operation, and using it all but removes any performance advantage from using SIMD for this operation. The trick is to find a different way of storing the data, so that summing across a register is not required nor is any operation that requires access to the individual pieces of the SIMD register. The solution is to do four dot products at the same time.

Let's suppose that we have eight vectors called A, B, C, D, W, X, Y, and Z, and that we want the dot product of AW, BX, CY, and DZ. Instead of storing the data in eight separate arrays, the data could be interleaved in an array-of-structures format, as shown in Figure 12.3.

Structure-of-arrays layout

a1	a2	a3	a4	b1	b2	b3	b4	c1	c2	c3	c4	d1	d2	d3	d4

w1	w2	w3	w4	x1	x2	x3	x4	y1	y2	y3	y4	z1	z2	z3	z4

Array-of-structures layout

a1	b1	c1	d1	a2	b2	c2	d2	a3	b3	c3	d3	a4	b4	c4	d4

w1	x1	y1	z1	w2	x2	y2	z2	w3	x3	y3	z3	w4	x4	y4	z4

Figure 12.3 Array-of-Structures Versus Structure-of-Arrays Data Layout

The dot product function can now be written using only four multiplies and three additions to generate four results using the intrinsics, as shown in the following code sample:

```
__m128 Dot4Simd( __m128 abcd[], __m128 wxyz[])
{
    __m128 temp1, temp2, temp3, temp4;

    temp1 = _mm_mul_ps(abcd[0], wxyz[0]);
    temp2 = _mm_mul_ps(abcd[1], wxyz[1]),
    temp3 = _mm_mul_ps(abcd[2], wxyz[2]),
    temp4 = _mm_mul_ps(abcd[3], wxyz[3]),
    temp1 = _mm_add_ps(temp1, temp2);
    temp1 = _mm_add_ps(temp1, temp3);
    return  _mm_add_ps(temp1, temp4);
}
```

The same number of instructions are executed in both of the functions, Dot4Simd and dot, but in Dot4Simd, four products are calculated instead of one, increasing performance by about two times.

Data layout is a major performance factor when using the SIMD instructions. With the right data layout, alignment, and padding, you can realize the full performance advantages of SIMD. But, with a poor data layout, much of the performance boost from using SIMD will be lost.

Example 12.1 Optimize a Function Using the SIMD Instructions

Make sure that the data is in a SIMD instruction friendly format and use the SIMD instructions to improve performance.

Problem

The following function performs bilinear interpolation on a bitmap and returns a calculated pixel. Since bitmaps have integer coordinates, something must be done when the code requests a fractional pixel, such as the pixel at (1.5, 2.25). Bilinear interpolation performs linear interpolation in both x and y axes, effectively interpolating fractional pixels.

The function assumes 32-bit RGBA (red, green, blue, alpha) pixels and that the coordinates passed to the function have already been verified to be within the bitmap.

```
DWORD GetBilinearFilteredPixel(float x, float y,
            DWORD *pBitmap, long stride)
{
        stride = stride / 4;      // using DWORD ptr access
        long loc = (long)x+(long)y*stride;
        DWORD TopLeftPixel     = pBitmap[loc];
        DWORD TopRightPixel    = pBitmap[loc+1];
        DWORD BottomLeftPixel  = pBitmap[loc+stride];
        DWORD BottomRightPixel = pBitmap[loc+stride+1];

        float fx, fy;   // get the fractional part
        fx = x - (int)x;
        fy = y - (int)y;

        // 32-bit RGBA pixels
        float alphaFP =
            (TopLeftPixel     >> 24) * (1.0f-fx) * (1.0f-fy)+
            (TopRightPixel    >> 24) *       fx * (1.0f-fy)+
            (BottomLeftPixel  >> 24) * (1.0f-fx) *       fy +
            (BottomRightPixel >> 24) *       fx *       fy;

        float redFP =
            (TopLeftPixel     >> 16 & 0xff) * (1.0f-fx) * (1.0f-fy) +
            (TopRightPixel    >> 16 & 0xff) *       fx * (1.0f-fy) +
            (BottomLeftPixel>>16 & 0xff) * (1.0f-fx) *       fy +
            (BottomRightPixel>>16& 0xff) *       fx *       fy;

        float blueFP =
            (TopLeftPixel     >> 8 & 0xff) * (1.0f-fx) * (1.0f-fy) +
            (TopRightPixel    >> 8 & 0xff) *       fx * (1.0f-fy) +
            (BottomLeftPixel>> 8 & 0xff) * (1.0f-fx) *       fy +
            (BottomRightPixel>>8 & 0xff) *       fx *       fy;
```

```
float greenFP =
    (TopLeftPixel      & 0xff) * (1.0f-fx) * (1.0f-fy) +
    (TopRightPixel     & 0xff) *        fx * (1.0f-fy) +
    (BottomLeftPixel   & 0xff) * (1.0f-fx) *        fy +
    (BottomRightPixel  & 0xff) *        fx *        fy;

return ((DWORD)(alphaFP+0.5f) << 24) +
       ((DWORD)(redFP   +0.5f) << 16) +
       ((DWORD)(greenFP +0.5f) << 8)  +
       ((DWORD)(blueFP  +0.5f));
}
```

Solution

The first thing to notice is that the four color components are multiplied by the same four things which is perfect for the use of SIMD instructions. Converting a function to use the SIMD instructions is a little easier when working from the desired end format of the data backwards towards the start of the function. In this case, the optimal end format is one 4-byte value that contains the three color components and the alpha channel. To achieve the desired data format, the previous step has to be three additions, as shown in Figure 12.4.

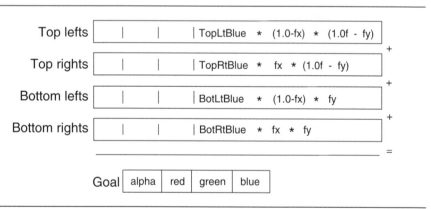

Figure 12.4 Three SIMD Additions After Multiplications

Working backwards one more step, you arrive at the multiply operations for the top left calculation, shown in Figure 12.5.

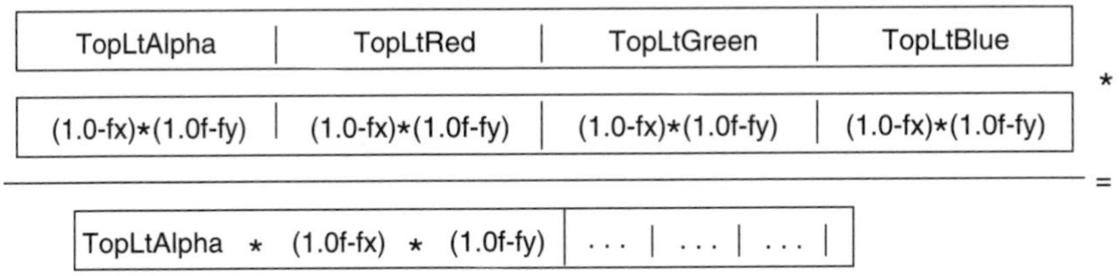

TopLtAlpha	TopLtRed	TopLtGreen	TopLtBlue
(1.0-fx)∗(1.0f-fy)	(1.0-fx)∗(1.0f-fy)	(1.0-fx)∗(1.0f-fy)	(1.0-fx)∗(1.0f-fy)

∗

=

TopLtAlpha ∗ (1.0f-fx) ∗ (1.0f-fy)	...	...	...

Figure 12.5 Organization for Easy Multiplies

Continually working backwards to the original data format fills in the rest of the function, shown in the following code using the SIMD intrinsics.

```
DWORD GetBilinearFilteredPixelSIMD(float x, float y,
                DWORD *pBitmap, int stride)
{
    stride = stride / 4;      // using DWORD ptr access
    long loc = (long)x+(long)y*stride;

    float fx, fy;   // get the fractional part
    fx = x - (int)x;
    fy = y - (int)y;
    float TopLeft = (1.0f-fx)*(1.0f-fy);
    float TopRight = fx * (1.0f-fy);
    float BottomLeft = (1.0f-fx) * fy;
    float BottomRight = fx * fy;

    __m128i zeros = _mm_setzero_si128();

    // load both top pixels
    __m64 TopPixels = *(__m64 *)(pBitmap+loc);

    // load both bottom pixels
    __m64 BottomPixels = *(__m64 *)(pBitmap+loc+stride);

    // Begin the conversion of bytes to floating-point values
    // expand each byte to a word
    __m128i iTopLeftPixels     =
        _mm_movpi64_epi64(_mm_unpacklo_pi8(TopPixels, 0));
    __m128i iTopRightPixels     =
        _mm_movpi64_epi64(_mm_unpackhi_pi8(TopPixels, 0));
    __m128i iBottomLeftPixels   =
        _mm_movpi64_epi64(_mm_unpacklo_pi8(BottomPixels, 0));
    __m128i iBottomRightPixels =
        _mm_movpi64_epi64(_mm_unpackhi_pi8(BottomPixels, 0));

    // expand each word to a double-word and then to FP
```

```
    __m128 FpTopLeftPixels  =
        _mm_cvtepi32_ps(
            _mm_unpacklo_epi16(iTopLeftPixels, zeros));
    __m128 FpTopRightPixels =
        _mm_cvtepi32_ps(
            _mm_unpacklo_epi16(iTopRightPixels, zeros));
    __m128 FpBottomLeftPixels  =
        _mm_cvtepi32_ps(
            _mm_unpacklo_epi16(iBottomLeftPixels, zeros));
    __m128 FpBottomRightPixels =
        mm_cvtepi32_ps(
            _mm_unpacklo_epi16(iBottomRightPixels, zeros));

    // load the multipliers
    __m128 TopLeftMultiplier     = _mm_load_ps1(&TopLeft);
    __m128 TopRightMultiplier    = _mm_load_ps1(&TopRight);
    __m128 BottomLeftMultiplier  = _mm_load_ps1(&BottomLeft);
    __m128 BottomRightMultiplier = _mm_load_ps1(&BottomRight);

    // do the multiplies
    FpTopLeftPixels      =
        _mm_mul_ps(FpTopLeftPixels, TopLeftMultiplier);
    FpTopRightPixels     =
        _mm_mul_ps(FpTopRightPixels,TopRightMultiplier);
    FpBottomLeftPixels   =
        _mm_mul_ps(FpBottomLeftPixels, BottomLeftMultiplier);
    FpBottomRightPixels =
        _mm_mul_ps(FpBottomRightPixels,BottomRightMultiplier);

    // do the additions
    __m128 pixel = _mm_add_ps(FpTopLeftPixels,FpTopRightPixels);
    pixel = _mm_add_ps(FpBottomLeftPixels, pixel);
    pixel = _mm_add_ps(FpBottomRightPixels, pixel);

    // convert 4 single-precision values back to a double word
    __m128i iPixel = _mm_cvtps_epi32(pixel);
    iPixel = _mm_packs_epi32(iPixel, zeros);
    iPixel = _mm_packs_epi16(iPixel, zeros);

    DWORD NewPixel = _mm_cvtsi128_si32(iPixel);

    _mm_empty();
    return NewPixel;
}
```

The source data format is four pixels, each containing four bytes packed into a 32-bit integer. While this format takes a few extra instructions to convert to four floating-point values, the memory savings is significant over having the source values as four floating-point values and not having to convert. (You can conduct a performance experiment to verify the savings.) Since the individual portions of a SIMD register are not accessed independently, like they were when summing across the register, this data format is sufficient and does not need to be altered.

Determining Where to Use SIMD

You can use the SIMD instructions everywhere and anywhere in an application. But, as with all optimizations, it is important to focus optimization efforts on the pieces of the application that will make the biggest impact. Using SIMD instructions all over the application does not guarantee a performance improvement.

The main difficultly you could encounter when using the SIMD instructions is having a SIMD friendly data layout. When designing and writing the application and its individual algorithms, take care always to organize the data in a way that maximizes cache efficiency and SIMD friendliness. SIMD friendly data is data that is properly aligned, properly padded, and easy to operate on with the SIMD instructions, avoiding the need to operate on the individual pieces of a register.

The application's time-based hotspots are the best places to use the SIMD instructions. Once the hotspots are identified using a tool like the VTune analyzer, each location should be analyzed to determine the data that is accessed. From the amount, layout, alignment, and padding of the data plus the calculations that are performed on the data, you can determine whether it makes sense to use the SIMD instructions. Look for places where the data can be altered to make more efficient use of the SIMD instructions. Don't overlook the simple cases like an aligned memory copy or one floating-point reciprocal square root calculation.

Key Points

When considering the use of the SIMD instructions, keep in mind the following:

- Data alignment is critical for maximum SIMD performance.

- Data padding can help reduce extra work when arrays are not multiples of the SIMD data size.

- Make sure to organize your data to maximize use of the cache and the SIMD instruction set by determining if a structure-of-arrays layout is better than an array-of-structures.

- Every hotspot in an application that operates on array-based data is a possible place to use the SIMD instructions.

Shrimp Stir-Fry

Ingredients

1 pound medium shrimp, peeled and deveined
1 pound asparagus, ends snapped off, cut diagonally into bite-sized pieces
1 pound snow or snap-peas, trimmed, strings removed
1 medium yellow bell pepper, seeded, cut into bite-sized pieces
1 tablespoon minced scallions
1 tablespoon minced fresh garlic
1 tablespoon minced fresh gingerroot
6 tablespoons soy sauce
2 tablespoons sesame oil
1 tablespoon rice vinegar
3 tablespoons vegetable oil

Directions

Since the four ingredients take different amounts of time to stir-fry, cook each separately and then combine at the end. Use four bowls (1 large) and have everything ready to go before turning on the heat.

1. Marinade shrimp in a large bowl with 2 tablespoons soy sauce, 1 tablespoon rice vinegar, and 1 tablespoon sesame oil.
2. In three separate bowls, marinade asparagus, peas, and yellow pepper in 1 tablespoon soy sauce and 1 tablespoon vegetable oil each.
3. Preheat a large non-stick pan on medium-high.
4. Pick shrimp out of bowl shaking off excess liquid and stir-fry for about 2 minutes until completely cooked. Place back in bowl.
5. Pick out asparagus, stir-fry for about 1-2 minutes, until lightly browned, dump into shrimp bowl. Repeat for the peas and the yellow pepper.
6. Reduce heat to medium-low. Using 1 tablespoon sesame oil and 1 tablespoon soy sauce sauté scallions, garlic, and ginger for about 1 minute until lightly browned.
7. Dump everything including liquids back in pan and heat together for about 1 minute to combine flavors. Add salt and fresh ground pepper.

Chapter 13

Processor-Specific Optimizations

All of the optimization concepts discussed in this book are useful on all Intel processors. But a few optimizations require specific knowledge of the features and cache architecture of a particular 32-bit Intel Architecture processor. Some issues require the use of assembly language while others need just a small adjustment in a high-level language. This chapter compares the major 32-bit Intel Architectures and discusses optimizations specific to the most recent ones.

32-bit Intel Architectures

The 32-bit Intel architecture started with the Intel386™ microprocessor back in 1985. Optimizing specifically for the Intel386 primarily relied upon carefully selecting which assembly language instructions to use and how to order them. Tedious and time consuming, only the most demanding applications got hand-coded assembly language attention. A few years later, the Intel486™ processor was introduced, and it also relied on assembly language. But in 1993, optimizations for the Pentium processor really got things cooking. By writing an algorithm following a set of pairing rules, performance could be, in some cases, doubled. Compilers and optimization tools were provided to help with optimizations and with analyzing the sequence of instructions to make sure that the maximum performance was obtained. The new processors and tools have shifted the focus away from the specific order of instructions to high-level concepts, such as organizing data for efficient memory access, use of SIMD instructions, and reduction of data dependencies.

Optimizations specific to processor architecture fall into the following categories:

■ Using new processor instructions like MMX technology and Streaming SIMD Extensions.

■ Using new processor features like L1 and L2 caches and automatic hardware prefetch.

■ Using the fastest possible sequence of code while avoiding slow ones. For example, adding one to the register contents using the add instruction is faster than using the increment-by-one instruction on the Pentium 4 processor.

■ Using tools and compilers that help to identify architecture issues and can generate code optimized for a specific group, or groups, of processors.

Table 13.1 below illustrates the major Intel Architectures and high-level optimization strategies.

Table 13.1   Overview of IA-32 Intel Architecture

Architectures	Processors	Major Differences	Optimization Strategies
Early 32-bit	Intel386, Intel486	First processors to use 32-bit registers and greater memory addressability	Assembly tricks
Pentium family of processors	Pentium processor, Pentium processor with MMX technology	Level 1 and Level 2 caches, dual-pipeline (two instructions at the same time)	Assembly U-V pairing to guarantee that two instructions could be executed on every clock. Use new MMX technology instructions.

continued

Table 13.1 Overview of IA-32 Intel Architecture (continued)

Architectures	Processors	Major Differences	Optimization Strategies
P6 micro-architecture	Pentium Pro processor, Pentium II processor, Pentium III processor	Super-scalar architecture–instructions are decoded to µOps. Three µOps per clock can be executed. Introduction of out-of-order execution, multi-stage deep pipeline, branch prediction algorithm, speculative execution, cache hint instructions, more SIMD instructions.	Use additional processor features. Organize data for the L1 and L2 caches; organize code to follow 4:1:1 decode pattern. Use new SIMD single-precision floating-point instructions, and avoid slow operations like floating-point to integer conversions and partial register stalls. Reduce data dependencies and branch mis-predictions. Use optimizing compilers.
Intel® NetBurst™ microarchitecture	Pentium 4 processor	Double-speed execution units can execute instructions in ½ a clock. Trace-cache replaces instruction cache; more SIMD instructions are introduced.	Take advantage of larger L1 cache line size, of new double-precision floating-point SIMD and additional integer SIMD instructions, and of automatic hardware prefetch. Reduce data dependencies and branch-mispredictions. Use optimizing compilers.
Hyper-Threading Technology	Forthcoming	One processor can execute tasks on behalf of multiple threads simultaneously.	Use multithreaded applications.

When developing an application, focus your optimization efforts on the latest processors for a few reasons. First, people who are running performance sensitive applications are almost certain to have a newer computer. And secondly, people who buy new computers tend to buy the majority of the new software. With this in mind, this chapter will focus on the details of the Pentium III processor and the Pentium 4 processor.

The Pentium III Processor

Figure 13.1 is a block diagram of the major functional blocks of the Pentium III processor.

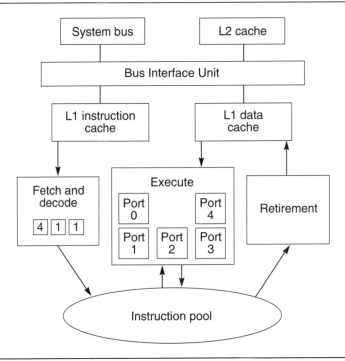

Figure 13.1 Block Diagram of the Pentium III Processor's Functional Units

Instructions get executed through similar processes on both the Pentium III processor and the Pentium 4 processor, with the few differences discussed in the remainder of this chapter.

L1 Instruction Cache

On the Pentium III processor, the L1 cache is split into two 16-kilobyte regions, one for instructions and the other for data, for a total of 32 kilobytes. The L1 instruction cache retrieves instructions from memory and delivers them to the decoders for conversion into μOps. Since instructions can be a few bytes or more in length, it is possible for an instruction to begin in one cache line and end in a second. When this happens, the processor must wait until both cache lines have been fetched from memory before instruction decoding can begin. The potential time loss is roughly equal to one cache line fetch, which can be as high as hundred or so clocks. Usually, split instructions do not present a problem because the processor is in a steady state of fetching, decoding, executing, and retiring instructions, and the delay to fetch a second cache line is rarely the bottleneck. However, in some cases, when executing a short function that is a branch target and demands high performance, it may be beneficial to avoid this wait by aligning jump targets to cache line boundaries.

This issue mostly affects interrupt service routines, device drivers, and other short functions that are not in the L1 cache.

Instruction Decoding

The Pentium III processor uses three decode units to break down IA-32 instructions into µOps. One of the decode units can handle all types of instructions while the other two decode units can only handle simple instructions that convert to exactly one µOp as shown in Figure 13.2.

Decoder 0 Can decode all instructions	Decoder 1 1 µOp only	Decoder 2 1 µOp only

Figure 13.2 Three Decoders on the Pentium III Processor

On every clock, the processor attempts to decode three instructions. But this can only happen if the instructions are in an order that matches the capabilities of the decoder units. So, when an instruction sequence contains instructions that decode to two, one, and one µOps, all instructions are decoded in the same clock, whereas instructions that decode to one, one, and two µOps take two clocks to decode.

It is possible to improve the efficiency of instruction decoding by rearranging the instructions to match the 4:1:1 sequence. The 4 is chosen for the first decoder because decoding an instruction to 5 or more µOps can only be done one at a time. But, unlike the Pentium processor where U-V pairing improved execution performance, 4:1:1 instruction ordering does not guarantee an overall performance boost, only a more efficient instruction decoding.

Using an optimizing compiler that can schedule code for both the Pentium III and Pentium 4 processors is the best and easiest way to handle efficient instruction decoding.

The VTune analyzer can detect instruction decoding issues on the Pentium III processor by sampling on `Instructions Decoded` versus `Clockticks`. But don't spend too much time analyzing instruction decoding because the reduction of data dependencies is far more important. Lowering data dependencies by moving data dependent instructions as far apart as possible helps all processors by giving them the opportunity to execute more instructions per clock, which has a bigger positive impact on performance than instruction decoding.

Instruction Latencies

The Pentium III processor executes instructions in different amounts of time than the Pentium 4 processor. Table 13.2 is a list of the more common instructions.

Table 13.2 Instruction Latency and Throughput (Latency / Throughput)

Instruction	Performance for the Pentium III Processor	Pentium 4 Processor
Integer ALU instructions (add, subtract, bitwise OR, AND...)	1 / 1	0.5 / 0.5
Integer multiplication	4 / 1	14-18 / 3 - 5
Floating-point multiply	5 / 2	7 / 2
Division	Single-precision 18 / 18 Double-precision 32 / 32 Extended-precision 38 / 38	Single 23 / 23 Double 38 / 38 Extended 43 / 43
MMX Technology ALU	1 / 1	2 / 2
MMX Technology Multiply	3 / 1	8 / 2
Most SSE Instructions	3-5 / 1-3	4-6 / 2
SSE divide	Scalar 18 / 18 Packed 36 / 36	Scalar 22 / 22 Packed 32 / 32
Most SSE2 Instructions	Only on the Pentium 4 processor	2-8 / 2-4

The biggest difference is that the Pentium 4 processor can execute twice as many integer ALU instructions per clock as the Pentium III processor. But, overall the processors are fairly similar, and again, greater focus on reducing data dependencies is easier and benefits all processors.

Instruction Set

New instructions usually come along with every new processor. For example, MMX Technology, Streaming SIMD Extensions (SSE), Streaming SIMD Extensions 2 (SSE2), and the cache control instructions have all been added since the Pentium processor. Using the new instructions, where appropriate, usually opens up new optimization opportunities and big performance increases. It is important to review the processor and compiler documentation to see what new features are available and where in your application they could be used. You can find details of the additional instructions that have been designed into each processor in *Volume 1: Basic Architecture* of the *IA-32 Intel Architecture Software Developer's Manual*.

You must use the new instructions judiciously to make sure that they do not get executed on older processors. If a new instruction is executed on an older processor, an invalid instruction fault will occur and the application will crash. The current processor can be detected using the CPUID instruction or the processor dispatch feature in the Intel C++ Compiler. See Chapter 3, "Tools," for the details of the processor dispatch feature.

Floating-Point Control Register

A common cause of performance loss is floating-point to integer conversions. See Chapter 11, "Floating-point Optimizations," for details. The instruction that loads the floating-point control register (assembly instruction FLDCW) causes serialization on the Pentium III processor, which can be a huge performance issue. On the Pentium 4 processor, however, toggling the control register between any two rounding modes has been greatly improved, but is still not free. Plus on all processors, additional overhead results from calling the C run-time library function (_ftol) that performs the actual conversion or the equivalent instructions that have been placed inline by the compiler.

Optimizations for all processors should attempt to reduce the amount of floating-point to integer conversions using the C run-time libraries, which in turn switches the floating-point control register. See Chapter 11 for the details of the floating-point control register.

L1 Data Cache

The Pentium 4 processor has bus bandwidth that is roughly three times greater than Pentium III processor, greatly improving performance for most applications. However on both processors, cache misses are still expensive and need to be minimized.

The organization of the Pentium III processor's L1 data cache is shown in Figure 13.3.

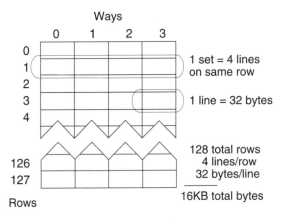

Figure 13.3 L1 Data Cache Architecture on the Pentium III Processor

The main difference is the 32-byte line size, which is half as large as the Pentium 4 processor. This feature is important to consider when designing data structures and allocating memory. Luckily, optimizations for the Pentium 4 processor work perfectly well on the Pentium III processor. Remember, the goal is to increase cache efficiency by decreasing the amount of compulsory cache misses, cache conflicts, and cache capacity issues. See Chapter 8, "Memory," for details.

Memory Prefetch

Both processors have software prefetch, but only the Pentium 4 processor has automatic hardware prefetch. When the Pentium 4 processor can prefetch data via hardware, it is better not to use the software prefetch instruction because the processor can do the prefetch more efficiently. When all of the following conditions are met, the Pentium 4 processor's automatic prefetch detects the loads and software prefetch is unnecessary:

- Only one stream, either reading or writing, per 4-kilobyte page is accessed.

- No more than eight streams from eight different 4-kilobyte pages.

- Accessing cacheable memory, not write-combining or uncacheable memory.

You can determine where the Pentium 4 processor automatically prefetches data by comparing the `Bus Accesses` event counter to the `Reads Non-Prefetch` event counter in the VTune analyzer.

Processor Events

Over 100 processor events can be sampled using tools like the VTune Performance Analyzer. Each processor has the same basic set of events, such as branch mis-predictions and cache misses and a few counters specific to the processor. The details of the event counters for the Pentium 4 processor are documented in the *Intel Pentium 4 Processor Optimization Reference Manual*, "Appendix B: Intel Pentium 4 Processor Performance Metrics." The event counters for the Pentium III processor are documented in the *Intel Architecture Optimization Reference Manual* "Appendix B: Performance-Monitoring Events and Counters." Both books are located on the CD-ROM included with this book.

Partial Register Stalls

A partial register stall plagues the Pentium III processor. The stall occurs when a write operation on a partial register is followed by use of the full register. Figure 13.4 shows how the general-purpose registers are divided into pieces.

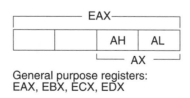

General purpose registers:
EAX, EBX, ECX, EDX

Figure 13.4 Pieces of the General-Purpose Registers

The following code causes a partial register stall on the Pentium III processor:

```
mov ax, 20 ; loads only the lower 16 bits
mov variable, eax ; stalls trying to write 32 bits
```

The first line loads the lower 16 bits of the EAX register and then the second line uses the full 32-bit register. The problem arises because the processor does not know what data is contained in the upper 16 bits, so it waits for the complete retirement of the first instruction. By loading the full register- that is, by setting the upper 16-bits to zero or sign extending- the processor does not wait for the load to retire, as shown in the following code:

```
movzx ax, 20 ; loads the full register
mov variable, eax ; does not stall
```

Another way to avoid the problem is by zeroing the register before use with the SUB or XOR instructions as shown in this code segment:

```
sub eax, eax ; zeros the register
mov ax, 20    ; loads the lower 16-bits with the
              ; upper 16-bits guaranteed to be zero
              ; zero from the previous subtraction
mov variable, eax ; no stall
```

On the Pentium III processor, it is very important to avoid these partial register stalls, which can be detected by sampling on the `Partial Register Stalls` event counter using the VTune analyzer. The Pentium 4 processor does not have this particular partial register stall. However, for a good blended code sequence, avoid the partial register code sequence entirely.

The Pentium 4 processor has a different partial register performance issue when using the ah, bh, ch, or dh registers- that is, bit positions 8 through 16 of the general purpose registers. The only way to avoid this stall is to avoid using those partial registers.

Modern compilers do not generate code with this type of partial register stall. However, if you find partial register stalls, look for assembly language or compiler optimization settings that target processors older than the Pentium Pro processor.

Partial Flag Stall

On the Pentium 4 processor, a dependency stall occurs when using instructions that do not update all the flags, such as the INC and DEC instructions, which do not update the carry flag (CF). In these cases, using ADD and SUB is faster. The use of INC and DEC is especially common for loop counters, so be sure to examine loops during the optimization process.

Pause Instruction

The PAUSE instruction was introduced on the Pentium 4 processor, but it can be executed on all processors, because they all treat the instruction as a no-operation instruction (NOP). The PAUSE instruction should be added to spin-wait loops to avoid a possible memory-order issue and to reduce power. The PAUSE instruction is basically a NOP that introduces a slight delay, effectively limiting memory requests to the maximum speed of the memory system bus, which is the highest speed at which the memory can be changed by another processor. Trying to issue requests any faster than this is pointless. The following code includes the PAUSE instruction executed using the Intel C++ Compiler intrinsics:

```
while (sync_var != READY)
        _mm_pause();  // issues the PAUSE instruction
```

Key Points

When developing code specific to a processor, keep in mind the following:

- Optimizations targeted at the Pentium 4 processor will work perfectly well on the Pentium III processor.
- Make sure to optimize cache and memory usage on both processors by observing the slight difference in L1 cache line sizes and write buffers.
- Avoid partial register and flag stalls.
- Use a compiler like the Intel C++ Compiler that can generate code that favors execution on the Pentium 4 processor and can automatically generate multiple code paths one per processor.
- Avoid the use of SSE2 instructions on the Pentium III processor, because they generate an invalid instruction fault.

Chicken Monterey

From The Silver Palate Cookbook

Ingredients

5 tablespoons best-quality olive oil
1 chicken, 2½ to 3 pounds, quartered
salt and freshly ground black pepper, to taste
1 cup finely chopped yellow onions
2 carrots, peeled and chopped
4 garlic cloves, peeled and minced
1 cup canned chicken broth
½ cup fresh orange juice
½ cup canned crushed tomatoes
1 tablespoon dried rosemary
1 medium sized sweet red pepper, stemmed and cored, cut into julienne
½ large zucchini and ½ large yellow summer squash, cleaned
    and sliced diagonally
1/3 cup chopped Italian parsley (garnish)
grated zest of one orange (garnish)

Directions

1. Heat 3 tablespoons of the oil in a large skillet. Pat the chicken pieces dry, season them with salt and pepper, and cook gently in the oil for 5 minutes. Turn the chicken, season again, then cook for another 5 minutes. Do not attempt to brown chicken or you will overcook it; it should be pale gold. Remove chicken from skillet and reserve.
2. Add the onions, carrots and garlic to the oil remaining in the skillet and cook, covered, over low heat until vegetables are tender, about 25 minutes.
3. Uncover skillet and add the stock, orange juice, tomatoes and rosemary. Season to taste with salt and pepper and simmer the mixture, uncovered, for 15 minutes.
4. Return chicken pieces to the pan and simmer further, 20 to 25 minutes, or until the chicken is nearly done. Baste the pieces with the sauce and turn them once at the 15-minute mark. (If you wish, you may complete the recipe to this point the day before serving. Refrigerate chicken in the sauce and reheat gently before proceeding.)
5. Heat remaining 2 tablespoons of olive oil in another skillet and sauté the pepper julienne for 5 minutes. Add sliced zucchini and yellow squash and season with salt and pepper. Raise the heat and toss the vegetables in the oil until they are tender but still firm, another 5 minutes or so.
6. With a slotted spoon, transfer vegetables to the skillet with the chicken and simmer together for 5 minutes. Sprinkle with the chopped parsley orange zest and serve immediately.

Chapter 14

Introduction to Multiprocessing

Multiprocessing is the area of computer science that deals with the execution of more than one instruction at the same time. Parallel execution can be accomplished in five different ways, as shown in Figure 14.1.

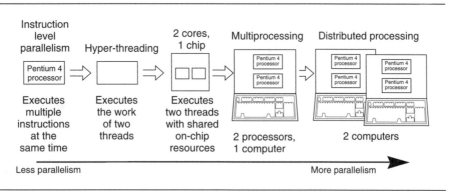

Figure 14.1 Five Different Methods for Executing Instructions in Parallel

Desktop computers rely on instruction-level parallelism for parallel execution, but that is about to change. Hyper-Threading technology, which will begin appearing in Intel® Xeon® processor based systems, will allow one processor to execute the instructions of two threads at the same time-driving down cost and increasing the availability of multi-processing. As multiprocessor computers and processors with Hyper-Threading Technology become more common, it makes sense to use parallel processing techniques more often to increase performance. This chapter introduces the performance and software design issues of parallel processing so that you can get ready for the future.

For detailed information on OpenMP and parallel programming, obtain one of the books dedicated entirely to the subject, such as *Parallel Programming in OpenMP* by Chandra, Menon, Dagum, Kohr, Maydan, and McDonald.

Parallel Programming

Concurrency is one of the key techniques for getting more performance from a system by performing more than one action at a time. The most common application of concurrency is in the design of modern operating systems where it is used to hide the latency associated with access to system resources.

For software optimization, concurrency is used to do more work in less time. At the level of a single processor, instruction-level parallelism gives the processor the ability to execute more than one instruction at the same time, as is the case with the Pentium 4 processor, which has the ability to execute six microinstructions at one time. Instruction-level parallelism is primarily possible due to the specific instructions used, their order, their data dependencies, and the micro-architecture of the processor. Higher levels of parallelism can be achieved by using multiple processors or Hyper-Threading Technology.

For multiple processor systems, concurrency is achieved by using multiple threads in a single application. In some cases, a sophisticated compiler automatically can create multithreaded code. But, in most cases the programmer must explicitly create a parallel algorithm by hand and code it in a parallel program.

To write a multithreaded program, you must identify the tasks that can be executed concurrently. Once these tasks have been found, you must manage the data to make the tasks relatively independent. In other words, the problem must be decomposed in terms of tasks and data.

Usually, either the data decomposition or the task decomposition becomes more obvious and takes a primary role in the design of the parallel program, which in turn leads to two different strategies in writing a multithreaded program: task parallelism and data parallelism.

■ *Task Parallelism.* Coarse-grained task parallelism is very common in desktop applications. For example, a word processor contains tasks that periodically save a backup copy of the document, verify spelling and grammar, and process user input, which are all different tasks. Other programs might run the same task but on different data, such as a server that uses one thread per user.

In other cases, fine-grained task parallelism breaks down a single problem into many independent sub-tasks. In each case, an application whose threads are organized by the tasks they execute is said to have task parallelism.

■ *Data Parallelism.* Applications that operate on large data sets can divide the calculations among multiple threads based upon the different sections of data. For example, if an algorithm uses a large matrix in a calculation, multiple threads can work on independent sections of the matrix, creating parallelism based upon data. In this case, the data drives the parallelism and is called data parallelism.

Both types of parallelism can be used in the same program and no one method is globally better than the other. You should make the choice based upon the specific application.

In both cases, it is essential that all processors are kept busy by load balancing the tasks and minimizing overhead. Load balancing is accomplished by designing the algorithm so all processors are equally occupied. If one processor spends more time working than the others, the unbalanced load becomes a limiting factor for performance. Minimizing the overhead incurred when creating, managing, and synchronizing the threads helps to keep the processor executing useful code. The more work each thread independently performs, the lower the overhead and the higher the performance will be.

Thread Management

In some cases, an intelligent compiler can analyze a program and automatically create a multithreaded program. Unfortunately, this technique rarely works as well in real applications as it does in sample problems and benchmarks. Therefore, if you want a multithreaded application, you most likely have to code it yourself.

The two categories of multithreading API's are: low-level thread libraries such as POSIX threads or Win32[†] and high-level such as OpenMP. Thread libraries give the programmer complete control over how the threads are managed and synchronized. Unfortunately, complete control requires the programmer to deal with all the details of thread management, making threads cumbersome to use. With high-level schemes such as OpenMP, the programmer tells the compiler what to do with the threads at an abstract level and leaves the low-level details to the compiler. This approach makes OpenMP much easier to use, but at the expense of some control and maybe some performance. Low-level thread libraries versus high-level threaded API's is similar to assembly language versus C programming; you gain a little more control, and maybe some performance, at the expense of additional programming and maintenance effort.

Low-level Thread Libraries

Threads can be created and terminated using the Win32 API functions `CreateThread` and `ExitThread` or the C runtime library functions `_beginthread` and `_endthread`. The Microsoft Foundation Class Library (MFC) also provides thread functions such as `AfxBeginThread` and `AfxEndThread` which both use the `CWinThread` object. All of these methods explicitly create additional threads of execution. You can use threads for task parallelism like user interface processing or saving backup data or for data parallelism for lengthy calculations on independent data.

High-Level Thread Management with OpenMP

OpenMP is a set of pragmas, environment variables, and run-time libraries that tell the compilers (C/C++ and Fortran) when, where, and how to create multithreaded code. OpenMP uses a fork-join model where one master thread creates a team of threads then joins the results at the end as shown in Figure 14.2.

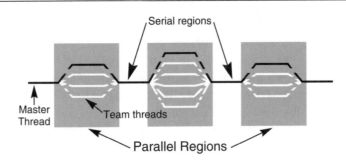

Figure 14.2 Fork-Join Model of OpenMP

Once the threads are created, they can execute the same code on each thread, allowing the programmer to write general task-level programs. OpenMP really shines, however, when it is used to split up work between groups of threads. This is called *worksharing*. The most common form of worksharing is when the iterations of a loop are split up between a team of threads, which also is the easiest and most common way to use OpenMP. If done correctly, worksharing has the further advantage of allowing the programmer to add parallelism incrementally to an application and to write code that is semantically equivalent to the original sequential code.

To learn more about OpenMP, look at the OpenMP documentation at OpenMP Architecture Review Board's Web site. The following code computes a numerical approximation to an integral using trapezoid integration. The integrand and ranges of integration are selected, so the resulting integral should approximate the value of π. The code sample shows three different ways to write this program: without threads, using explicit Win32 threads, and using OpenMP. (For the Intel C++ Compiler, be sure to compile with the /Qopenmp command line option.)

```
static long num_steps = 100000;

double pi_nothreads (void)
{
      double step, x, pi, sum;
      int i;

      sum = 0.0;

      step = 1.0/num_steps;

      for (i=0; i<=num_steps; i++)
      {
            x = (i-0.5)*step;
            sum = sum + 4.0 / (1.0+x*x);
      }
      pi=step*sum;

      return pi;
}

#define NUM_THREADS 2
HANDLE hThread[NUM_THREADS];
CRITICAL_SECTION hUpdateMutex;

double step;
double global_sum = 0.0;
DWORD WINAPI Pi(void *arg)
{
```

```
        int i, start;
        double x, sum=0.0;
        start = *(int *)arg;
        step = 1.0/num_steps;
        for (i=start; i<num_steps; i+=NUM_THREADS)
        {
              x = (i-0.5)*step;
              sum = sum + 4.0 / (1.0+x*x);
        }
        EnterCriticalSection(&hUpdateMutex);
        global_sum += sum;
        LeaveCriticalSection(&hUpdateMutex);

        return 0; // unused
}

double pi_Win32(void)
{
        double pi;
        int i;
        DWORD threadID;
        int threadArg[NUM_THREADS];
        InitializeCriticalSection(&hUpdateMutex);
        for (i=0; i<NUM_THREADS; i++)
        {
              threadArg[i] = i+1;
              hThread[i] = CreateThread(NULL, 0,
                   (LPTHREAD_START_ROUTINE )Pi,
                   &threadArg[i], 0, &threadID);
        }
        WaitForMultipleObjects (NUM_THREADS, hThread, TRUE,
                                 INFINITE);
        pi = global_sum * step;

        return pi;
}

#include <omp.h>
double pi_OpenMP (void)
{
        int i;
        double x, pi, sum = 0.0;
        step = 1.0/(double) num_steps;
        omp_set_num_threads(NUM_THREADS);
        #pragma omp parallel for reduction(+:sum)
                  private(x)
        for (i=1; i<=num_steps; i++)
        {
              x = (i-0.5)*step;
              sum = sum + 4.0/(1.0+x*x);
        }
        pi = step * sum;
        return pi;
```

```
}

int main(int argc, char* argv[])
{
        printf ("nothreads pi = %f\n", pi_nothreads());
        printf ("Win32 pi = %f\n", pi_Win32());
        printf ("OpenMP pi = %f\n", pi_OpenMP());
        return 0;
}
```

Threading Goals

Converting a program to use multiple processors or Hyper-Threading Technology with high performance is a matter of keeping the following things in mind.

■ *Focus on hotspots.* If you are converting an already running application, make sure to use a performance analyzer to determine what areas of the application should be threaded. Don't bother threading or using any optimization techniques on a piece of the application that consumes an insignificant amount of time, i.e. cold spots.

  If the application is in the design stage, research the expensive tasks, algorithms, and calculations to see how they might be implemented efficiently, using the fastest possible single and multi-threaded solutions. Run performance experiments to verify performance expectations.

■ *Load Balancing threads.* In parallel computing, you want to keep all the resources as busy as possible. If one processor is more heavily loaded than the others, that processor takes longer to finish its appointed work and the overall performance of the program will be limited. The programmer must carefully analyze the problem to make sure that the work is evenly distributed among the threads to balance the load across all processors.

■ *Coarse and fine grain threads.* Threads, whether organized by task or data, should do as much work as possible. Do not bother threading a memory copy inside an algorithm when the whole algorithm could be threaded. Always look to find the smallest number of independent threads that can execute the largest tasks. Too many small threads cause performance to be lost in all the overhead of creating and task switching threads.

- *Synchronization.* Threads that run independently requiring little synchronization will be ready to run most often and therefore will result in higher performance. At some point, threads are likely to require some amount of synchronization, but the fewer synchronization points used, the better the performance can be.

- *Minimize memory sharing.* Multiple threads like to share memory, but multiple processors do not. When memory is shared among processors, extra bus transactions are required to flush data out of one processor's cache and load it into the other's cache because a specific memory location can only be in one processor's cache at a time Furthermore, sharing memory usually involves additional synchronization, which can also hurt performance. Sharing as little memory as possible is very desirable.

- *Number of threads.* Optimally, the program would have one ready thread per processor. At run time, your application can query the operating system to determine the number of processors so that your program can create a reasonable number of threads. If your application creates too many threads, efficiency could be lost as the operating system frequently task-switches threads. Too few threads and processors could be sitting idle.

Threading Issues

In addition to all the performance issues and optimization strategies listed in this book, you should be aware of a few unique issues specific to parallel processing, as follows:

- *Thread overhead.* Threads can be expensive if not used carefully. Thread creation should not be performed inside critical loops because the create thread function call is expensive. Furthermore, every task swap costs performance. As the number of threads increases, the amount of time lost due to task switching also increases. Keeping the number of ready threads roughly equal to or slightly greater than the number of processors is optimal.

- *Short loops.* For threads to be useful they must perform a significant amount of work compared to task switching and synchronization overhead. Threading short functions like memory copies is rarely a good idea even if it is easy to program. Focus on the big time-consuming hotspots, not on the smaller individual loops where thread overhead can consume the entire performance benefit.

■ *False sharing.* The false sharing of memory among threads can be expensive due to cache inefficiencies. False sharing occurs when two or more processors are accessing different bytes of memory that happen to be located on the same cache line. Technically, the threads are not sharing the exact same memory location, but because the processor deals with cache line sizes of memory, the bytes end up getting shared anyway. Since multiple processors cannot cache the same line of memory at the same time, the shared cache line is continually sent back and forth between the processors, creating cache misses and potentially huge memory latencies. It is important to make sure that the memory references by the individual threads are to different non-shared cache lines. This principle applies to all cache levels, L1, L2, and when available L3. Keep memory accesses at least 128 bytes apart.

■ *Total memory bandwidth.* Even though the total number of instructions that can be executed by a system increases with each additional processor, the memory bandwidth along with most hardware resources does not increase. All processors must collectively share a fixed memory bandwidth. The Pentium 4 processor has a high memory bandwidth compared with older processors, but it can quickly become an issue for memory intensive applications. The basic idea is that if a single-threaded application is memory bound, multiple threads and processors will not help. Threading helps when the application is compute bound, not memory bound.

■ *Cache efficiency, conflicts, and memory bandwidth.* Good cache efficiency is even more important when using multiple processors since the maximum bus bandwidth remains unchanged. Transferring extra bytes across the bus for whatever reason- memory sharing, conflicts, capacity, compulsory, or unused bytes within a cache line are just a few- uses up the bandwidth of all processors. Be extra sure to double-check memory access patterns and cache efficiency.

■ *Synchronization Overhead.* Rarely are threads totally independent, which forces the program to need some amount communication or synchronization. Synchronization almost always forces one thread to wait for another thread. Waiting threads do no work and therefore reduce the amount of parallelism in your application. Furthermore, the synchronization APIs calls can be expensive. You can reduce synchronization overhead by more effectively decomposing the tasks and data in the application.

■ *Cache ping-pong.* Cache ping-pong is similar to sharing memory. In the fork-join model during transitions from parallel regions to serial regions, memory contained in teamed processors could be flushed out of the workers' processor caches for use by the master thread. In the cases where parallel- to- serial transitions happen frequently, the memory ping-ponging between the master thread on one processor and teams' threads on other processors wastes bus bandwidth and time.

To minimize cache ping-pong, reduce the number of parallel- to-serial transitions and limit the amount of memory shared by the master thread and team threads in the serial portions of your application.

■ *Processor affinity.* Processor affinity describes which processor(s) threads execute on. It is a possible performance issue if a thread jumps back and forth between processors, as shown in Figure 14.3. In the figure, Task 1 runs on both processors, requiring its cache data to also be moved back and forth.

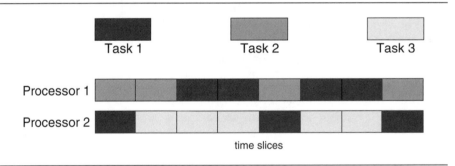

Figure 14.3 Threads Can Jump Back Between Processor Lowering Performance

When threads do not execute on the same processor, cache issues could become a problem. In Win32, the affinity can be set using the SetThreadAffinityMask and SetProcessAffinityMask functions. Unfortunately, OpenMP does not have any pragmas that set the affinity.

The lack of processor affinity does not automatically mean lower performance. Performance is more dependent upon how many total threads and processes are executing and on how well the threads are load-balanced than on which processor executes the code. Testing the application using the benchmark is the only way to be certain whether or not processor affinity, or the lack of it, is creating a performance issue.

■ *Spin-waits versus Operating System waits.* You have many choices for thread synchronization and no one method is useful in all situations. Sometimes calling the operating system for synchronization is best, and other times a simple spin-wait loop is best.

Spin-wait loops are tight loops that repetitively check a memory location waiting for a variable to change before continuing as shown in the following code.

```
while (BufferFull != TRUE)
     ;
```

As long as BufferFull is defined with the keyword volatile, as shown in the following line of code, the compiler continuously loads the value from memory, expecting that the variable eventually is changed by the operating system, a piece of hardware, or a concurrently executing thread.

```
int volatile BufferFull;
```

Unfortunately, spin-wait loops keep the thread active and consuming processing power. If the thread was suspended, a different thread could execute. Therefore, spin-wait loops are only good for short waits expected to last less than the overhead of an operating system call. Additionally, when writing a spin-loop, the PAUSE instruction should be used. See Chapter 13 for details about the PAUSE instruction.

Tools

A whole set of tools are available to assist with parallel programming optimizations and validation. Unfortunately, the tools are evolving too quickly to be helpful inclusions in this book. But, a few important concepts will be around for the long term and those are worth discussing.

The issues that plague all programs like slow algorithms and memory latency also affect parallel programs. Tools like the VTune analyzer and the Microsoft Performance Monitor can be used on multithreaded applications to detect issues like time-based hotspots, hot algorithms, cache misses, branch mispredictions, and task swapping. These issues should be addressed regardless of the number of threads created in an application.

The next optimization step for parallel programs is analyzing how well the application is balanced. A global look at application balancing can be made with the Microsoft Performance Monitor by tracking % Processor Time for each individual processor. This view immediately shows which CPUs are active and which are idle. A more detailed examination of an application's threads can be accomplished using the VTune analyzer's call graph feature and GuideView[†], an OpenMP performance-oriented tool available from KAI Software, a division of Intel Corporation.

Scalability is an important aspect of a parallel program's performance. Usually, the addition of a second processor yields a very good performance increase. But adding an eighth processor realizes little benefit. This decrease is due to many factors like a limited bus bandwidth and additional synchronization. The KAP/Pro Toolset for OpenMP from KAI Software can analyze scalability issues.

Go to the OpenMP Architecture Review Board's Web site to learn more about the current OpenMP performance tools and debuggers.

Key Points

In summary, follow these simple guidelines:

- Let compiler technologies like OpenMP help you add threads to your application. It is easier to write and debug.

- Be careful of memory bandwidth requirements and make sure to avoid sharing memory, falsely sharing memory, and all the cache efficiency issues.

- Keep threads ready by load balancing and using a minimal amount of synchronization.

Part III
DESIGN AND
APPLICATION
OPTIMIZATION

Dessert

Gooey Brownies

Ingredients

½ pound (2 sticks) sweet butter

4 ounces high-quality unsweetened chocolate, preferably 99% unsweetened
Scharffen Berger pure dark chocolate

4 eggs

¾ cup unbleached all-purpose flour

2 teaspoons vanilla extract

1 cup Ghirardelli semi-sweet chocolate chips

Directions

1. Preheat oven to 350°F. Grease a 9 x 13 inch baking pan.
2. Melt butter and chocolate in the microwave and set aside to cool to room temperature.
3. Beat eggs and sugar until thick and lemon-colored. Add vanilla. Fold in cooled chocolate mixture into eggs and sugar mixture. Mix thoroughly.
4. Sift the flour and fold gently into batter, mixing just until blended. Fold in chocolate chips. Avoid adding too many air bubbles.
5. Pour into greased pan and bake for 18-20 minutes for fudge-like brownies or a little longer for cake-like brownies. Check doneness with a toothpick inserted about 1-inch from the side of the pan. As soon as the toothpick comes out clean, the brownies are done. The center will be a little undercooked. Do not overcook!

Chapter 15

Design For Performance

Software optimizations can occur at any time during application development, but the earlier you start, the better. Software architecture-as in the key data structures and buffers, algorithms, and memory access patterns-can make a huge difference in performance and these fundamentals are easy to change early in the development process. Just like building a house, laying a good foundation and testing a few designs saves time and increases quality in the final product. Before any code is written, think about performance and what foundation-laying things can be done to guarantee a high-performance application.

Designing for performance starts with the design of the critical algorithms and movement of the data through the application. You need to select efficient and scalable algorithms that work well within the performance features and instructions of the processor. Data buffers and structures must be designed to be cache friendly and to be able to accommodate access with the SIMD instructions. Good algorithms and data layouts are the foundations of a fast application, and apt use of them can open up many more performance opportunities later on in the development cycle.

Data Movement

Data movement refers to how well data moves into and out of the processor and how many times it does so. Data movement can either limit performance or make it soar. Data movement globally affects an application by controlling everything from the scalability, the instructions that can be used, and the algorithms that will work best. Good data movement means that data flows into the processor caches, is operated on, and flows out of the caches never to be needed again. Your application has poor data movement when data is constantly being reloaded into the caches generating extra cache misses and wasting time.

When designing an application, consider how and when every piece of data is used. Look for predictable patterns of data movement that allow for good cache efficiency while avoiding randomly accessed memory and the cache misses that come along with it.

Dynamically allocated, linked data structures like lists, queues, and trees are a common source of problems with data movement and cache efficiency because memory tends to be spread out instead of in neat cacheable regions. When traversing a linked data structure, the processor loads discontinuous memory that generates cache misses. In the Huffman Encoding example, the following inefficient, dynamically allocated, linked data structure is used.

```
typedef struct tagHuffTreeNode{
    BYTE symbol;
    DWORD freq;
    tagHuffTreeNode *pLeft;
    tagHuffTreeNode *pRight;
    tagHuffTreeNode *pNext;
} HuffTreeNode;
```

The first thing to notice is that this structure is used for both a queue (pNext pointer) and a tree (pLeft and pRight pointers) wasting memory in this application. Secondly, the BYTE declaration at the start of the structure wastes three bytes because the compiler automatically aligns data structures on multiples of four bytes to avoid data alignment issues. So, even though this data structure appears to use 17 bytes, it actually uses 20. But even worse than these superficial issues is the way that the data structure fits in memory when accessed. Figure 15.1 shows a sample tree layout for a very simple Huffman compression tree.

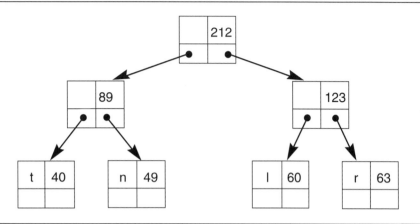

Figure 15.1 Simple Huffman Compression Tree

When traversing the data structure, a new location of memory must be fetched for each node. Ideally, the new location would be on the same cache line, but since the nodes are dynamically allocated the nodes are not guaranteed to be next to each other in memory. Therefore, they probably are not on the same cache line. Jumping around in memory like this causes many cache misses and limits performance. Using less memory by changing the data layout can help reduce the number of cache misses and increase performance. Using two separate data structures, one for the tree and one for the queue, can reduce the amount of memory used. Furthermore, the tree data structure can be improved by overlapping the symbol and pointer elements because they are never used at the same time, as shown in the following improved tree data structure.

```
typedef struct tagHuffTreeNode{
     tagHuffTreeNode *pLeft;
     union {
          BYTE symbol;
          tagHuffTreeNode *pRight;
     };
} HuffTreeNode;
```

A leaf node (a node with a symbol) is identified by a NULL left pointer, which means that a symbol is valid instead of the right pointer. This 8-byte structure reduces the memory requirements by 60 percent, but more importantly, it reduces the number of cache lines by a factor of 8 for the simple tree shown in Figure 15.1. The memory requirements drop enough so that the entire tree can fit on one cache line, if the memory allocation is perfect. This kind of data movement optimization is critical for high performance.

Performance Experiments for Design

You can use performance experiments and prototypes to determine whether the data movement is good or bad in your application. A performance experiment that accesses memory in the same manner as the final application or algorithm, but does not perform any calculations, shows you the maximum speed at which that portion of your application can run. It should be quick and easy to analyze and modify the experiment to improve memory access patterns and performance. Once the optimal pattern is discovered, the calculations can be put in and performance can be monitored to make sure that memory does not become a bottleneck.

When designing data structures keep the following things in mind.

Cache efficiency. Memory that gets transferred across the bus because it is part of a loaded cache line, but never is used, is a huge waste. Find ways to organize data to increase the efficiency of the processor's caches, and as a result, transfer less memory. Refine algorithms and their use of data structures to minimize cache conflicts, cache capacity issues, and wasted memory loads. Think about what the best possible data layout would be, and then try to work towards it, tweaking the algorithm if necessary. Remember, when working with small performance experiments, it will be easy to try a bunch of different data structures to find the one that works best.

Instruction Parallelism. The right data organization, alignment, and padding can make it easy to add instruction parallelism. Make sure to accommodate the requirements of the SIMD instructions and multiple threads by organizing the data and adjusting algorithms when you still can do so easily. Even if you do not plan on using the SIMD instructions or multiple threads, at least consider what the friendliest SIMD format is and move in that direction. Just because you don't specifically use the SIMD instructions does not mean the compiler cannot use them automatically for you. Furthermore, do not overlook the goal of keeping the data dependencies low.

Algorithms

During the design phase, you probably can guess fairly easily which algorithms will be the most costly and which ones will access the majority of memory or, more specifically, incur the most cache misses. These key algorithms could end up using the majority of the computing resources, and therefore they should also consume the majority of the design time optimizations.

Computational complexity, as discussed in Chapter 6, "Algorithms," is the critical starting point. But, right along with selecting an efficient algorithm comes the task of making sure that it fits well within the rest of the application and with the processor's performance features such as the cache and the SIMD instructions. The fastest algorithm is not always the one with the lowest computational complexity. When designing an algorithm or process, consider the following issues:

■ *Always use the most efficient algorithm.* An algorithm's computational complexity makes a huge performance difference and should always be considered a top priority. But algorithms also have memory requirements, instruction requirements, and data dependency issues. Consider the big picture when choosing an algorithm. Look for ways to tweak the current algorithm to get the best possible performance from it before trying a different one. See Chapter 6, "Algorithms" for more details.

■ *Don't be limited by memory access patterns and cache efficiency.* The algorithm mostly dictates memory access patterns and cache efficiency. Examine the memory used by a particular task or algorithm to determine the cache usage. Look for ways to minimize cache misses by changing data structures, reducing the amount of memory used, blocking, or any of the other memory optimizations discussed in Chapter 8, "Memory." If possible, determine whether an algorithm will be called with a warm (data already in the cache) or cold (data needs to be loaded) cache, and whether the data can be left in the cache to be used by a future function, if needed.

■ *Allow room to use the SIMD Instructions.* Analyze the algorithms to determine whether the SIMD instructions can be used. The fastest way to get an extra performance boost is to do more operations at the same time using instruction-level parallelism. If the data is in a SIMD friendly format, you easily can use the Intel C++ Compiler to generate the SIMD instructions automatically or to use the SIMD C++ data types. See Chapter 12, "SIMD" for more details.

■ *Keep data dependencies low.* The Pentium 4 processor only executes code as fast as the data dependencies will allow. Some algorithms have few dependencies while other algorithms are full of them. Choosing an algorithm with few dependencies keeps the performance ceiling high, allowing plenty of room to make a fast application.

■ *Plan to use multiprocessing.* The personal computer industry is on the verge of inexpensive parallel computing with Hyper-Threading technology. A good algorithm should be able to be multithreaded to keep up with hardware improvements and customer demands.

Consider at design time how to decompose the algorithms for parallel execution. Even if the first version of the application is single threaded, it will be easy to improve performance later on with a good foundation. See Chapter 14, "An Introduction to Multiprocessing," for additional details.

■ *Find the bottlenecks and the constrained resources early.* Use the prototypes and performance experiments to identify the location of the bottleneck as soon as possible; it will help to steer you towards making good algorithm decisions. Off motherboard bottlenecks like network access, USB transfer rates, and disk access usually dominate most programs. When bottlenecks are known early, you can plan more easily for the use of threads and non-waited I/O that keeps the processor doing useful things during the wait for these slower resources. Engineering time can be spent designing and improving the actual bottleneck instead of on other non-performance enhancing locations.

Key Points

Keep the following design-time issues in mind:

- Design-time optimizations can have a big impact on performance. Start early!

- Design efficient data structures and buffers before application development to allow for the greatest flexibility laying the performance foundation for your application.

- No substitute exists for a well-chosen highly efficient algorithm that fits well within the data movement of your application and performance features of the processor.

Balinese Grilled Bananas In Coconut Milk Caramel

From The Barbecue! Bible

Ingredients for the Caramel Sauce

2/3 cup palm sugar or firmly packed light brown sugar
2 cups coconut milk
1 cinnamon (3 inches)
1 stalk lemongrass, trimmed and lightly flattened with the side of a cleaver
2 teaspoons cornstarch
1 tablespoon water

Ingredients for the Bananas

6 firm, ripe bananas (each about 6 inches long)
1 cup coconut milk
1 cup granulated sugar
1 quart vanilla ice cream (optional), for serving

Directions

1. Prepare the sauce. Place the sugar in a large, deep, heavy saucepan (preferably nonstick) and melt it over medium heat, stirring constantly with a wooden spoon. (It will take the sugar 2 to 3 minutes to melt.) Continue cooking the sugar until it begins to caramelize (turn brown), 3 to 5 minutes. You're looking for a rich brown color, but not the dark brown of chocolate. Do not overcook, or the sugar will burn and the sauce will be bitter.

2. Immediately remove the pan from the heat and stir in the coconut milk. (Be careful, it will sputter and hiss.) Return the pan to the heat and bring the coconut milk to a boil, stirring to dissolve the sugar. Stir in the cinnamon stick and lemongrass. Reduce the heat and simmer the mixture, uncovered, until thick and richly flavored, about 10 minutes, stirring from time to time to prevent scorching.

3. Dissolve the cornstarch in the water and stir it into the sauce. Simmer for 1 minute; the sauce will thicken even more. Remove the pan from the heat, transfer the sauce to a bowl, and let cool to room temperature. Remove the cinnamon stick and lemongrass with tongs and discard. Cover and refrigerate the sauce until cold.

4. Preheat to grill to high.

5. Peel the bananas. Cut the bananas into quarters on the diagonal. Place the coconut milk and sugar in separate shallow bowls at grillside.

6. When ready to cook, oil the grate. Dip each banana piece first in coconut milk, then the sugar, and place on the hot grate. Grill, turning with tongs, until nicely browned all over, 6 to 8 minutes in all.

7. To serve, arrange the bananas on plates or in bowls and spoon the sauce on top. If serving with ice cream, place scoops of it in the bowls and arrange the bananas on top. Spoon the caramel sauce on top and serve immediately.

Chapter **16**

Putting It Together: Basic Optimizations

With all the knowledge in place, it is time to optimize an application from beginning to end. The optimization process for this application has been split into two chapters. This chapter corresponds to the quick and easy optimizations. Chapter 17 explores more involved optimizations that require some of the source code to be rewritten.

Before you begin optimizing an application, you should know what your end goal is. Most of the time, optimizations will end when a goal, usually expressed in fractions of a second, is met. Other times, you might just want to significantly raise the performance of the application. Basically, you apply the 90/10 rule-gain 90 percent of the maximum performance for only 10 percent of the effort. The goal for this application will be to significant raise the performance.

The Sample Application

The application to be optimized is called RotateBlend, and it is located on the included CD. The RotateBlend application is a simple graphics application that uses bitmap rotation, bilinear filtering, and alpha blending to move a foreground image over a background image. To keep the application simple, the code supports only 32 bits per pixel displays. The application is written in C and consists of the following four source files.

■ app.cpp-All the real work takes place in this source file. The main functions `AppInit`, `AppTerm`, and `AppIdle` are called from `WinMain`. During the app idle time, the `AppIdle` function is called, which in turn calls the rotate, blend, copy, and blit functions to update the screen.

■ bitmap.cpp- The function for loading a 32-bit per pixel bitmap image file from the disk is located in this source file. If the file is a 24 bits per pixel image file, the function converts it to 32 bits, setting the alpha channel to zero.

■ dd.cpp- This file contains a few functions for working with Microsoft DirectDraw[†] functions. Includes initialization, termination, blit, and error handling functions.

■ RotateBlend.cpp- This file contains the `WinMain` function and the Windows message loop.

Two image files are used, one for the background image and one for the foreground image.

The application starts by running through an initialization process in the `AppInit` function that loads the bitmap images into memory, adjusts the client window to be the same size as the background image, and initializes DirectDraw, which is used to display the image. To initialize DirectDraw, a primary surface and an off-screen surface are created with the same dimensions as the background image, a very standard procedure when working with DirectDraw. The off-screen surface is placed in system memory instead of on the graphics card, so that the alpha blending function can read from the destination bitmap (more about this in the next chapter). The resulting combined image will be composed on the off-screen surface then blit'ed to the primary surface to avoid having the user see any partial images being created.

When the initialization is complete, the application uses the system idle time to endlessly move and rotate the position of the foreground image over the background image. The process starts by using `PeekMessage` to detect application idle time, which is when `AppIdle` will be called. A new position and rotation angle for the foreground image is computed to simulate the ball rolling across the background. The foreground image is then rotated by a calculated number of degrees and placed in a temporary buffer by the `Rotate` function. Since the rotation of an image could result in fractional pixel coordinates, bilinear interpolation is performed to improve the image quality, avoiding the need to truncate pixel coordinates.

Once the foreground image is rotated, a write pointer for the off-screen surface is then retrieved from DirectDraw. Using this write pointer, the previous image is erased from the off-screen surface by copying the background to the surface and then the new rotated image is blended onto the surface, using the alpha blending technique, providing the translucency effect. The following code is the `AppIdle` function.

```
void AppIdle (HWND hWnd)
{
        BYTE *pBackBuf;
        DWORD BackBufWidth, BackBufHeight;
        long  BackBufPitch;

        UpdatePositionAndRotation();    // updates FgPos.x and Angle

        // rotates pFgBmp by Angle radians and
        // places result in pRotatedImage
        Rotate(pRotatedImage, FgBmpPitch,
               pFgBmp, FgBmpPitch,
               FgBmpWidth, FgBmpHeight, Angle);

        // retrieve a write pointer to the
        // off-screen surface from DirectDraw
        HRESULT dd_RetVal = dd_LockSurface(&pBackBuf,
               &BackBufWidth, &BackBufHeight, &BackBufPitch);
        if(dd_RetVal != DD_OK)
               return;
        // erase the old image by copying the
        // pBkgBmp to the off-screen surface
        MemCopyRect(pBackBuf, BackBufPitch,
               (BYTE*)pBkgBmp, BkgBmpPitch,
               BkgBmpWidth*4, BkgBmpHeight);

        // calculate the offset of the upper left pixel of
        // the foreground image on the off-screen surface
        DWORD *pBallPosOnSurface = (DWORD*)(pBackBuf +
               FgPos.x*4 + FgPos.y*BackBufPitch);

        // blend the rotated foreground image onto the background
        // note: the blend process reads from the destination
        AlphaBlend32to32((DWORD *)pBallPosOnSurface, BackBufPitch,
               pRotatedImage, FgBmpPitch, FgBmpWidth, FgBmpHeight);

        dd_UnlockSurface(pBackBuf);

        // copy the off-screen surface to the visible client window
        dd_BltBackToPrimaryFull(hWnd);
}
```

The process repeats indefinitely until the application is closed and the memory is freed. Figure 16.1 is a block diagram showing the sequence of actions taken by the application.

Initialization

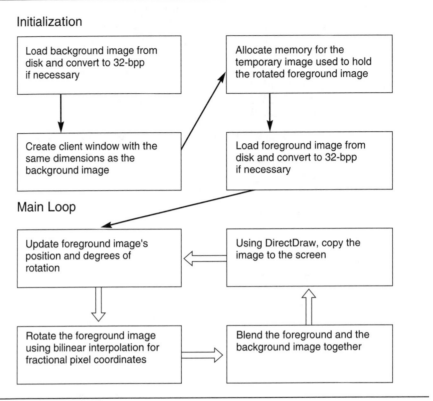

Figure 16.1 Block Diagram of the RotateBlend Sample Application

The application uses four memory buffers as shown in Figure 16.2.

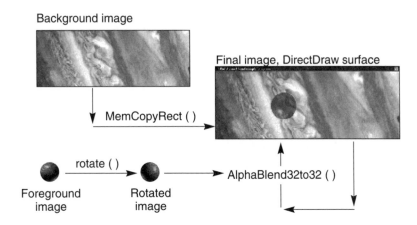

Figure 16.2 Four Memory Buffers Used by the RotateBlend Application

You should be able to open the `RotateBlend` application located on the CD, compile it, and run it. The output in Figure 16.3 should appear. Make sure to have your graphics card in 32 bits per pixel mode.

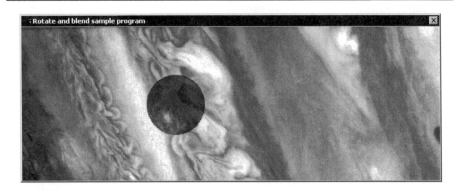

Figure 16.3 Sample Output of the RotateBlend Application

The ball in the foreground rotates around its center as it moves left and right, giving it the appearance of rolling.

Quick Review of the Algorithms

Bilinear pixel interpolation, alpha blending, and image rotation are used in this sample application. Since the optimizations focus on these algorithms, it is important for you to have an understanding of how they work.

Bilinear Pixel Interpolation

Linear interpolation in both the X and Y directions (called bilinear interpolation) can be used to improve image quality when fractional pixels are required as in image resizing and rotation algorithms. Figure 16.4 shows the foreground image after rotation with and without bilinear interpolation.

No interpolation   Bilinear interpolation

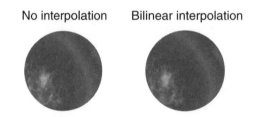

Figure 16.4 Bilinear Interpolation Improves Image Quality

The basic idea of interpolation is to generate an interpolated pixel instead of the nearest integer match. The pixel at (1.25, 2.25) is a combination of the four pixels located at (1,2), (2,2), (1, 3), and (2,3) as shown in Figure 16.5, not just pixel (1,2).

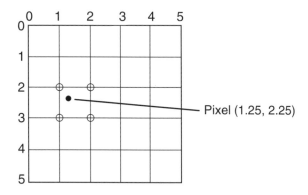

Figure 16.5 Pixel at (1.25, 2.25) is a Combination of the Four Pixels
Surrounding It

By inspection, it is easy to see that the pixel at (1.25, 2.25) is mostly
pixel (1, 2) because that is the closest pixel, but the other three pixels
still contribute some amount of color information. If the pixel were exactly in the middle like (1.5, 1.5), it would be 25 percent of each of the
four surrounding pixels. The algorithm starts by removing the integer
portion of the pixel location, leaving just the fractional part.

```
float x, y; // requested pixel (e.g. 1.25, 2.25)
float dx = x - (int)x; // decimal portion (.25)
float dy = y - (int)y; // decimal portion (.25)
```

Combinations of the fractional portions now multiply the four surrounding pixels as shown in Figure 16.6.

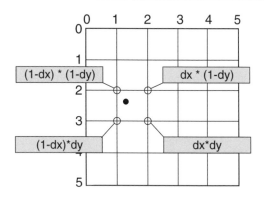

Figure 16.6 Multipliers for the Four Surrounding Pixels

The math shown in Figure 16.6 has to be performed on each of the four individual color components separately. The following code is the portion of the `Rotate` function that computes the bilinear interpolated value for the blue color component.

```
float fx = fSrcX - dwSrcX;
float fy = fSrcY - dwSrcY;

// blue interpolation
DWORD TopLeftBlue     = *pTopLeft     & 0xff;
DWORD TopRightBlue    = *pTopRight    & 0xff;
DWORD BottomLeftBlue  = *pBottomLeft  & 0xff;
DWORD BottomRightBlue = *pBottomRight & 0xff;
float blueFP = TopLeftBlue     * (1.0-fx) * (1.0-fy) +
               TopRightBlue    *      fx  * (1.0-fy) +
               BottomLeftBlue  * (1.0-fx) *       fy +
               BottomRightBlue *      fx  *       fy;
DWORD  blue_value = (DWORD)(blueFP + 0.5);
```

Alpha Blending

Translucency is accomplished by blending two source pixels to produce a destination pixel where the destination pixel also could be one of the source pixels. The amount of translucency is defined by either a global alpha value that is applied to the whole image or a per pixel alpha value that is applied on each individual pixel. When using a per pixel alpha value, it is placed in the highest 8 bits of the 32-bit pixel, as shown in Figure 16.7.

31 24	23 16	15 8	7 0
alpha	red	green	blue

Figure 16.7 4-bytes per Pixel (32 bpp)

This application uses the destination pixel as one of the source pixels and a per pixel alpha value. The general alpha blending formula uses a floating-point alpha value in the range of zero to one.

$$Pixel_{blend} = Pixel_1 \cdot \alpha + Pixel_2 \cdot (1 - \alpha)$$

Since this application uses 1-byte integer alpha values, the following integer-based formula is used.

$$Pixel_{blend} = \frac{Pixel_1 \cdot \alpha + Pixel_2 \cdot (255 - \alpha)}{256}$$

The division by 256 at the end, which is not present in the floating-point version, scales the result back to the range of one unsigned byte. The alpha blending math is done on each of the three color components individually, as shown in Figure 16.8.

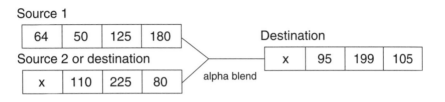

Figure 16.8 Sample Alpha-blended Pixel

Image Rotation

Image rotation through angle φ about the origin is mathematically defined as:

$$x' = x \cdot \cos\phi - y \cdot \sin\phi$$

$$y' = x \cdot \sin\phi + y \cdot \cos\phi$$

The only problem with this formula is that the foreground bitmap is not centered on the origin and the application uses an integer coordinate system not a floating-point one. You can easily get around the origin problem by subtracting half the width and height from the values for x and y, effectively centering the bitmap over the origin.

The floating-point coordinate system issue is overcome by reversing the formula. So instead of calculating the location of source pixel (x, y) in the destination bitmap, you reverse the formula to calculate the source pixel for every destination pixel. Since the coordinates of the source pixel are unlikely to be integers, bilinear interpolation is used to retrieve an approximation of the pixel. The pseudo-source code follows.

```
for (int y=-height/2; y<height/2; y++)
{
    for (int x=-width/2; x<width/2; x++)
    {
        float fSrcX = x*cos(angle) - y*sin(angle);
        float fSrcY = y*sin(angle) + y*cos(angle);

        fSrcX += width / 2;
        fSrcY += height / 2;

        Dest_Pixel(x,y) = BilinearInterpolate(fSrcX, fSrcY)
    }
}
```

Let The Optimizations Begin

With the basic idea of how the application works, the image buffers in use, and an understanding of how the three algorithms work together, it is now time to start optimizing. Step one is to make sure that the application can be compiled using the optimization switches and that the binary code can be executed.

Throughout the remainder of this chapter and the next chapter, every code change is contained in a separate file that is indicated by the filename in the **[bold brackets]**. All the files are located on the CD-ROM and the changed files can be swapped in the Visual C++ project for compilation, execution, and optimizations.

Compilation

Open the project and make sure to Set Active Configuration, as shown in Figure 16.9, to Release build; doing so turns on the optimization switches.

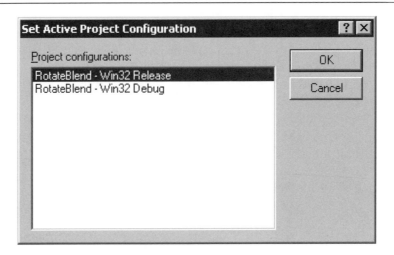

Figure 16.9 Always Do Performance Analysis on a Build with Compiler
Optimizations Enabled

The next step is to turn on Debug information by modifying the Project Settings for the Release Build, as shown in Figure 16.10. Debug information is used by the VTune analyzer to display function names and source code.

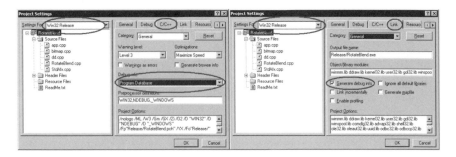

Figure 16.10 Generate Debug Symbols in the Release Build

Once compiled, you should be able to execute the application and see the output shown back in Figure 16.3.

The Benchmark

The first step when optimizing an application is to create the benchmark you can use to detect performance changes. See Chapter 2, "The Benchmark" for details. For this application, the benchmark should measure the speed of the entire screen refresh routines, which include the rotation, bilinear interpolation, and alpha blending algorithms. Excluded from the benchmark are the initialization routines, which load the bitmaps and perform memory allocation, because they only run once at the very start of the application and do not consume much time as viewed by the user.

The amount of time it takes to complete the processing for one entire frame can be measured using one of the timing tools discussed in Chapter 3, "Performance Tools." For this example, the Windows multimedia timer was chosen because it is easy to use and the frame time is expected to be less than one second, which is appropriate for this timer.

The frame time in milliseconds can be displayed in the title bar by adding the following code to the beginning and end of the `AppIdle` function. The use of the windows multimedia timer requires including mmsystem.h and linking with winmm.lib. The file **[appA.cpp]** located on the included CD uses these lines to display the frame time.

```
// at the beginning of AppIdle
    DWORD StartTime, ElapTime;
    StartTime = timeGetTime();
    ...
// at the end of AppIdle
    ElapTime = timeGetTime() - StartTime;
    char WinTitle[80];
    wsprintf(WinTitle, "%d ", ElapTime);
    SetWindowText(hWnd, WinTitle);
```

When running the application, the frame time switches between 0 and 10 milliseconds,[1] indicating that this counter is not precise enough and a different, higher precision time must be used.

A more accurate timer is the processor's clock ticks counter, and you can switch the code to use it by simply replacing the calls to timeGetTime with the execution of RDTSC as shown in the following code sample.

```
// at the beginning of AppIdle
    DWORD StartTime, ElapTime;
    _asm {
        RDTSC
        mov StartTime, eax
    }
    ...
// at the end of AppIdle
    _asm {
        RDTSC
        sub eax, StartTime
        mov ElapTime, eax
    }
    char WinTitle[80];
    wsprintf(WinTitle, "%d ", ElapTime);
    SetWindowText(hWnd, WinTitle);
```

The file **[appB.cpp]** located on the included CD, contains these lines of code used to display the elapsed time in clock ticks on the title bar. But unfortunately, the value varies greatly, making it very difficult to read. Transient effects like operating system tasks, display synchronization with the vertical blank interval, and many other things are contributing to the variability. At this point, displaying just the fastest frame time is a good solution because it is very easy to implement and still represents

---

[1] Timing information and performance analysis has been conducted on the author's computer that contains a 1.4 GHz Pentium 4 processor. Your results will vary.

the speed of the software. Adding a `MinElapsedTime` variable is very easy as shown in the next code sample.

```
// at the end of AppIdle
static DWORD MinElapsedTime = 0xffffffff;
if (MinElapsedTime > ElapTime)
{
    MinElapsedTime = ElapTime;
    char WinTitle[80];
    wsprintf(WinTitle, "%d ", MinElapsedTime);
    SetWindowText(hWnd, WinTitle);
}
```

These lines of code have been added to the [appC.cpp] file. After a couple of seconds, the minimum time stops changing and settles on about 10,300,000 clocks- on this author's computer.

At this point, you need to stop and think about this number and what it means. On a computer that contains a 1.4 GHz Pentium 4 processor, the number is 10,300,000 / 1,400,000,000 = 0.007 seconds = 7 ms per frame time or about 136 frames per second. To double-check the validity of the number, you could take a measurement with a physical stopwatch. Using a stopwatch, it takes the ball about 2.4 seconds to travel from the left side of the screen to the right side. Since the background is 720 pixels wide, the ball is 104 pixels wide, and the ball moves 2 pixels per frame, 308 frames are required to move the ball from the left side to the right. Creating 308 frames in 2.4 seconds means the update rate is 308/2.4=128 frames per second, which is in line with the results obtained using clock ticks.

An interesting experiment at this stage is to measure the performance of the application without compiler optimizations. About 32,000,000 clocks are used per frame time or roughly three times slower than the version with the optimizing compiler.

Locate the Hotspots

After the benchmark is in place, it is time to use a performance analyzer to find the hotspots. The expected result is that some combination of the rotate with bilinear interpolation and alpha blend functions will be the hotspot. Figure 16.11 shows the results of time-based sampling using the VTune analyzer.

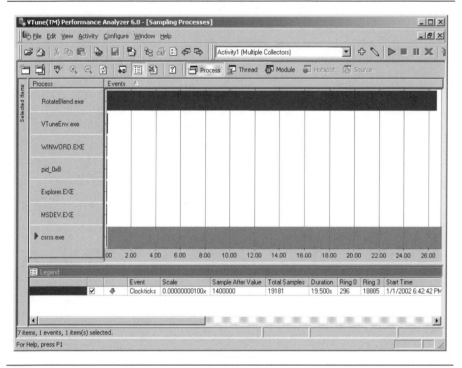

Figure 16.11 Time-based Sampling Results

The results show that RotateBlend.exe consumes almost all the time. By drilling down on the RotateBlend.exe bar, the hotspots within Rotate-Blend.exe are located, as shown in Figure 16.12.

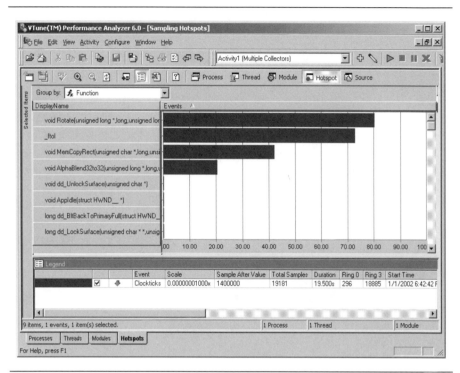

Figure 16.12 Hotspots in Application RotateBlend.exe

The graph shows that four functions dominate the time consumed by this application. The functions `Rotate` and `_ftol` consume most of the time, followed by `MemCopyRect` and `AlphaBlend32to32`.

Removing Calls To _ftol

Removing the calls to `_ftol` results in a quick and easy performance increase. From Chapter 11, "Floating-Point," you might remember that the compiler calls `_ftol` every time a floating-point number is cast to an integer. Even though this function is not the largest hotspot, it should be fixed first because the fix is so easy and should result in a large performance boost, and because the call is usually unnecessary. By inspection, `_ftol` is called six times in the `Rotate` function and four of the calls perform rounding. With only two lines of assembly language, the four calls that round floating-point to integer numbers can be optimized. The following code shows you the optimization.

```
// replace the current C float to int conversion
BYTE  alpha_value = (BYTE)(alphaFP + 0.5);
// with the following quick assembly language
_asm {
      fld alphaFP
      fistp alpha_value
}
```

In the file, **[appD.cpp]**, this change is made four times, once in each of the places where the color components are converted to integers. After the change is made, you can run the benchmark again to see if there was an improvement. The minimum frame time now is about 9,200,000 clocks, or about 1,100,000 clocks faster per frame time, which is about 10 percent faster than the original. Not bad for four changes and about five minutes worth of work!

Back to the VTune analyzer, shown in Figure 16.13, to determine what changed.

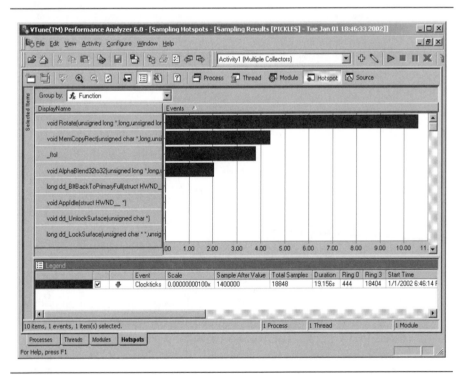

Figure 16.13 Sampling After Removal of Four Calls to _ftol

The amount of time for _ftol has dropped dramatically, but calls to that function are still not gone altogether. Call graph analysis can show all the places where _ftol is being called and the resulting graph is shown in Figure 16.14. Remember, call graph analysis requires linking with the /fixed:no option. See Chapter 3, "Tools" for details.

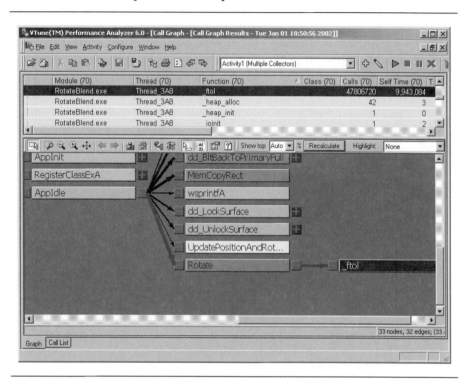

Figure 16.14 Call Graph Analysis to Determine all the Locations That Call _ftol

The call graph shows that only the Rotate function calls _ftol. The last two locations that do float-to-integer conversions use truncation, which requires the control word to change. To minimize the costly operation of changing the control word, you can change it once as you enter the function and restore the original value as you exit the function, simply by inserting the following two lines in the Rotate function. See Chapter 11, "Floating Point" for details.

```
// on entry
WORD OldCtrlWord = Changex87FPToTrunc();
// before exiting
RestoreFP(OldCtrlWord);
```

The same two lines of assembly language that you used previously to do the four color conversions also can be used here for these remaining two. However, changing the control word affects all floating-point to integer conversions, so the color conversions that used to be rounded now become truncated. However, the difference between rounding and truncation is negligibly small for color components, so you would use truncation because it is convenient and fast.

The file [appE.cpp] changes the floating-point control register and uses assembly language to convert all the floating-point numbers to integers. The speed is now about 8,500,000 clock ticks per frame, or a drop of 1,800,000 clocks per frame, which is equal to about a 20 percent performance increase. A quick double check with the VTune analyzer, shown in Figure 16.15, shows that no calls are made to _ftol, which achieves our goal.

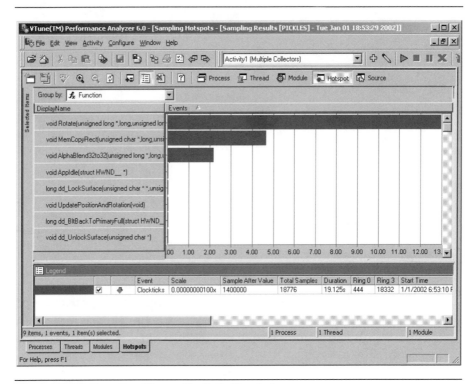

Figure 16.15 Sampling Shows No Calls To _ftol

Let's stop to think about this optimization. We removed six calls per loop to _ftol and it saved 1,800,000 clocks per frame. The foreground bitmap is 104 x 104 pixels = 10,816 total pixels, which means the original code contained 6*10,816 = 64,896 calls to _ftol each frame, accounting for roughly 1,800,000 / 64,893 ~ 28 clocks that were consumed by _ftol in this application.

Algorithm Issues

By looking at the sampling results in Figure 16.15, it is obvious that Rotate consumes a huge portion of time, which is not surprising since it does so much work. But to see MemCopyRect consuming almost half as much time as Rotate is a little unexpected, and you should investigate it as another potential area for quick and easy performance improvement.

A quick search of the code shows that MemCopyRect is called in only one place and is used to copy the background to the surface, basically erasing the previous image of the ball. The functionality is required, because without it, the previous image of the ball would be visible. But the program need not update the whole screen, just the dirty region. You can add a few lines of code to AppIdle to have that function remember the location of the ball on the previous frame so that a smaller region can be redrawn. Just before the position is moved, right at the start of the function, the foreground position is saved with the following code.

```
POINT LastPosition = FgPos; // save the last position
UpdatePositionAndRotation();
```

The call to MemCopyRect is then modified to copy over only the last position of the ball. The sole problem is that the whole background image is never copied to the surface, just the strip where the ball travels. Adding some code in the AppInit function to copy the background for the initial condition solves this problem. The file **[appF.cpp]** on the included CD contains all these changes.

Running the benchmark shows us that the frame time is now down to 7,200,000 clock ticks or 3,100,000 clocks faster than the original version. Sampling using the VTune analyzer should confirm that MemCopyRect now consumes much less time. Figure 16.16 shows the sampling results.

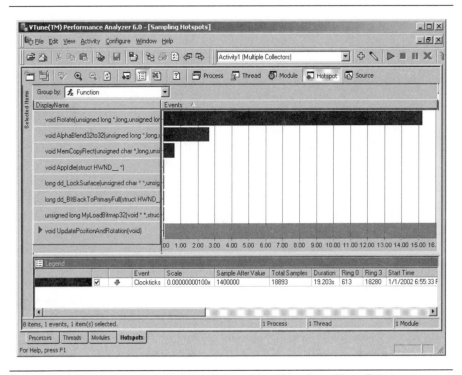

Figure 16.16 Sampling Results After Calling MemCopyRect More Efficiently

The VTune analyzer sampling shows that `Rotate` is taking almost all the time followed by `AlphaBlend32to32` and then `MemCopyRect`.

Investigation and Thought

Now that all the quick and easy optimizations are out of the way, it is time to focus on improving the `Rotate` function. A quick look at the source code for the `Rotate` function reveals that a few performance issues might be present.

■ *Branch mispredictions:* The two loops and one conditional branch could be generating branch mispredictions. However, the two loops count up in order, making them predictable and therefore unlikely to be a performance issue. The `if` statement is also fairly well-behaved, or at least not random, because it is conditional on a simple calculation which consistently increases in value. So, the `if` statement is unlikely to be a performance issue, which leads to the conclusion that branch mispredictions are not a problem. You can verify this conclusion using the VTune analyzer.

■ *Slow instructions*: Calls to sine and cosine are made on every pixel. Hopefully, the compiler will see that the calls are invariant and only call the functions once. An examination of the compiler-produced assembly code could double-check how many times sine and cosine are executed. Aside from trigonometry, the function does not use any long latency instructions- the function executes a bunch of multiplies, shifts, and bitwise AND operations none of which consume very much time. So, the trigonometry functions might be contributing to a performance loss, which can be proven by looking at the compiler-produced assembly code.

■ *Good blend of instructions:* The `Rotate` function does a horrible job of using a variety of different instructions. Most instructions are floating-point multiplies and shifts. Changing the blend of instructions will probably result in a significant performance improvement.

■ *Memory access:* Four pixels are read at the beginning of the loop and one pixel is written at the end, hardly a memory hog compared to all the shifts and multiplies. However, cache capacity misses are occurring because the pixels written by the `Rotate` function are immediately read by the `AlphaBlend32to32` function, and the cache is too small to hold all of the memory. Three 104x104 32-bit buffers are used for both functions, totaling about 128Kb. Merging the `AlphaBlend32to32` and `Rotate` functions and removing the intermediate temporary buffer used to hold the rotated image reduces the memory requirements and the number of cache misses.

■ *Data dependencies:* The same set of calculations occurs on each of the four individual color components, so it would make sense that the data dependencies would be low if the compiler interleaves the operations. The number of multiplies, not the data dependencies, is probably hurting this application.

One or more of these issues is causing this application to run slowly. To determine what to do next, you must seek out those issues costing the most time. A combination of performance experiments and trial-and-error recoding will help you determine which issues to optimize.

Performance Experiments

Running performance experiments by slightly changing the code, temporarily, makes it easy to determine what to do next. The first experiment will be to see how expensive the calls to sine and cosine are. The quickest way to run the experiment is to assume a constant angle and not call sine or cosine. The easiest angle to choose is zero because the value of the sine function is 0 and cosine is 1 as shown in the following code.

```
// Original code
fSrcX = (float)(width /2.0 + x*cos(angle) - y*sin(angle));
fSrcY = (float)(height/2.0 + x*sin(angle) + y*cos(angle));
// Performance experiment, assume angle is zero
float fSrcX = (float)(width /2.0 + x);
float fSrcY = (float)(height/2.0 + y);
```

These lines are changed in **[appG.cpp]**. The performance of this code is 6,900,000 clocks per frame time, which is 300,000 clocks faster. So it looks like sine and cosine are getting called for every pixel. You can easily fix the sine and cosine issue by adding two variables at the beginning of the function, then using them inside the loop.

```
// call sine and cosine only once
float CosAngle = cos(angle);
float SinAngle = sin(angle);
// use constant values for sine and cosine
fSrcX = (float)(width /2.0 + x*CosAngle - y*SinAngle);
fSrcY = (float)(height/2.0 + x*SinAngle + y*CosAngle);
```

The file **[appH.cpp]** contains the optimization to call sine and cosine only once per frame. The performance of the application is now 7,100,000 clocks so it looks like the four multiplies, an addition, and subtraction costs 200,000 clocks for 10,816 pixels, or about 18 clocks per pixel, which is roughly in line with the latency and throughput expectations calculated using Table 6.2 in Chapter 6. This information is also evidence that too many multiplies and shifts are being executed because the code is limited by roughly the full multiply latency that is caused by data dependencies or the lack of an available execution port. Since data dependencies are unlikely to be an issue in this function, the issue must be with available execution ports. Using a better blend or fewer instructions will improve performance and make better use of all the execution ports.

Removing Work

Since the `Rotate` function executes so many multiply operations, reducing the amount of them will probably make a big difference. The easiest sequence of multiplies that can be removed are the fx*fy calculations because they don't require many changes to the code. It is possible to calculate the combinations of multiples once and use the result four times. The four calculations required are:

```
float TopLeft = (1.0f-fx) * (1.0f-fy);
float TopRight = fx * (1.0f-fy);
float BottomLeft = (1.0f-fx) * fy;
float BottomRight = fx * fy;
```

Swapping the order of the calculations can improve performance even more, as shown in the following four lines of code.

```
float BottomRight = fx * fy;
float TopLeft = 1.0f -fx - fy + BottomRight;
float TopRight = fx - BottomRight;
float BottomLeft = fy - BottomRight;
```

In the file [appI.cpp] this simplification is used four times to replace 32 multiplies with 17.

The performance is now 6,500,000 clocks or 600,000 clocks faster than the previous version and 3,800,000 clocks faster than the original.

Additional calculations that can be easily removed are the shifts and bitwise ANDs that are used to isolate one of the color components. If the pixels were accessed by bytes, it might be faster. The basic idea is to convert the code from shifts and bitwise ANDs to BYTE accesses, as shown below.

```
// original code
TopLeftRed = ((*pTopLeft) >> 16) & 0xff;
// using byte access
TopLeftRed = pTopLeft[2];
```

This simplification is performed for each of the four color components in [appJ.cpp]. The performance is now 5,500,000 clocks per frame time.

With all the recent changes, the function seems a little hard to read due to all the excess local variables. In the file [appK.cpp], the code is rearranged and simplified making it easier to read, and doing so, unexpectedly improves performance another 400,000 clocks- and one frame time is now 5,100,000 clocks.

Calling Functions Differently

At this point, the VTune analyzer can be used to determine the best next step. Time-based sampling shows that the modules RotateBlend.exe and DirectDraw (ddraw.dll) are consuming nearly all the total time as shown in Figure 16.17.

Since DirectDraw is consuming two-thirds of the total time and we just optimized RotateBlend.exe, you might profit from spending a little optimization time working on improving DirectDraw, to see if some easy performance might be gained there.

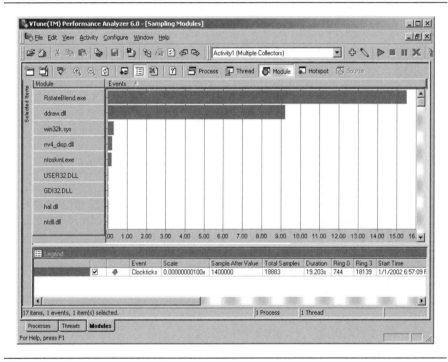

Figure 16.17 DirectDraw is Now Consuming Half the Total Time

DirectDraw is being used to copy the bitmap to the screen. Since source code is not available for DirectDraw, optimizations are limited to either calling the function differently or using a different function.

The DirectDraw pixel blit function takes a rectangle that defines the region to copy, and right now the application is refreshing the whole region. If the call were modified so that only the dirty rectangle was copied, less work would be done which should result in higher performance.

The dirty rectangle is the union of the old and new foreground image locations that is calculated by the following lines of code.

```
RECT DirtyRect;
DirtyRect.left   = min(LastPos.x, FgPos.x);
DirtyRect.top    = min(LastPos.y, FgPos.y);
DirtyRect.right  = max(LastPos.x, FgPos.x) + FgBmpWidth;
DirtyRect.bottom = max(LastPos.y, FgPos.y) + FgBmpHeight;
```

In the file [appL.cpp], the call to the DirectDraw blit function is modified to use the dirty rectangle region instead of the whole client window, causing the performance to improve to 3,300,000 clocks per frame. However, the screen repaints incorrectly because the whole window is never painted. A quick change to the Window's message loop to capture the WM_PAINT message and update the whole screen is all that you need do to fix this bug. The files [appM.cpp, RotateBlendA.cpp] on the included CD contain these changes. The performance stays the same at 3,300,000 as expected because these changes only occur when windows are moved and repositioned, which happens infrequently.

Summary of Optimizations

A few key optimizations have been made and the application is now more than three times faster. These optimizations have been quick and easy, requiring just a few source code changes. Table 16.1 reviews all the changes that have been made to the indicated sample files.

Table 16.1 Summary of Basic Optimizations

Description of Optimization	Files Effected	Clocks Per Frame	Performance Improvement from Original
Original application	app.cpp	Unknown	
Benchmark using the timeGetTime timer	appA.cpp	Variable	Unknown
Benchmark using the RDTSC timer	appB.cpp	Variable	Unkown
Benchmark using minimum time of RDTSC	appC.cpp	10,300,000	Original measurement
Remove four floating-point to integer conversions	appD.cpp	9,200,000	1.1
Remove remaining two more floating-point to integer conversions	appE.cpp	8,500,000	1.2
Dirty rectangle copy to remove previous foreground image	appF.cpp	7,200,000	1.4
Performance experiment to remove calls to sine and cosine	appG.cpp	6,900,000	Experiment only
Call sine and cosine once per frame	appH.cpp	7,100,000	1.5
Simplify and remove multiplies for the fx*fy calculation in the bilinear interpolation algorithm	appI.cpp	6,500,000	1.6
Use BYTE pointers instead of SHIFT/AND operations	appJ.cpp	5,500,000	1.9
Rearrange code for better readability, unexpected improvement	appK.cpp	5,100,000	2.0
Repaint only the dirty rectangle, not the whole client window	appL.cpp	3,300,000	Introduces a bug
Fix repaint bug	appM.cpp RotateBlendA.cpp	3,300,000	3.1

Key Points

When optimizing an application, keep the following things in mind:

■ Always use the benchmark to verify performance improvements and degradations.

■ Use performance experiments and performance tools like the VTune analyzer to determine what optimizations make sense to do next.

■ Try to find the cheap and easy performance improvements before working on the more difficult ones.

Very-berry Mixed-berry Cobbler

Ingredients
8 pints total of blueberries, raspberries, and blackberries. Pat dry.
1½ cup sugar
8 tablespoons (1 stick) cold unsalted butter
½ cup all-purpose flour
½ teaspoon baking powder
Pinch salt
1 egg
1 tablespoon vanilla extract

Directions
1. Preheat oven to 375°F.
2. Toss the fruit with 1 cup of sugar, and spread it in a lightly buttered 9-inch square baking dish.
3. Mix the flour, baking powder, salt, and ½ cup sugar in a food processor. Cut the butter into bits, place in food processor, and pulse a few times until the mixture is blended, but still granular. Add the egg and vanilla and pulse two or three times more to mix.
4. Drop this mixture in small clumps on the fruit; do not spread it out. Bake until golden yellow and just starting to brown, 35 to 45 minutes. Serve immediately with ice cream.

Chapter 17

Putting It Together: More Optimizations

In the last chapter, the optimization efforts resulted in the application running about three times faster. The optimizations started by creating an easy to run benchmark and then using the benchmark with the VTune analyzer to help identify things to optimize. The top few hotspots were discovered, and some quick and easy optimizations were made to those areas. With the "low-hanging" fruit all gone, optimizations now focus on the more time-consuming optimizations.

With the easy-to-run benchmark and the VTune analyzer in hand, you can continue optimizing.

Additional Analysis

Using time-based sampling with the VTune analyzer, a significant hotspot can be spotted in the RotateBlend.exe application, as shown in Figure 17.1.

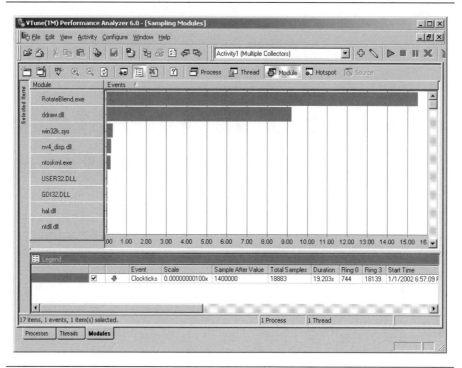

Figure 17.1 Time-based Sampling Module View

Drilling down to RotateBlend.exe, shown in Figure 17.2, shows you that the function Rotate is still consuming the majority of time followed by AlphaBlend32to32, at roughly one third as much time, and MemCopyRect, at about one-twelfth of the time.

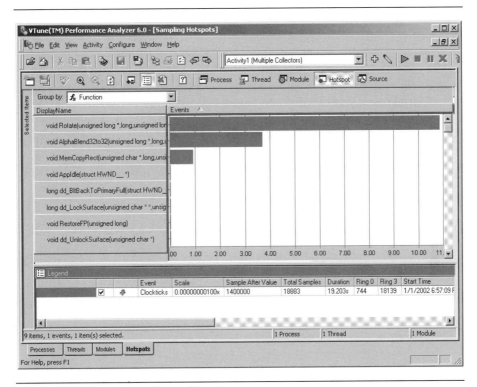

Figure 17.2 Hotspots in RotateBlend.exe

At this point, two optimizations make sense.

■ Merge the `Rotate` and the `AlphaBlend32to32` functions, in an attempt to reduce the number of cache misses. Merging the two functions also adds the benefit of saving memory because the intermediate buffer used for the rotated foreground image is not necessary.

■ Use SIMD technology in the `Rotate` function to reduce the number of instructions used by the function.

The most promising optimization is probably merging the two functions because excess cache misses are occurring and merging the two functions removes them. Furthermore, cache misses typically hurt performance more than a bunch of multiplies, which is what using the SIMD instructions would address.

Before making the change, you should conduct a performance experiment to verify the cache miss hypothesis. By removing the read cache misses from the `AlphaBlend32to32` function, you can determine the performance loss due to them. The `AlphaBlend32to32` function reads a source pixel, extracts the alpha channel, and compares it to 0, 255, or some other value. Your performance experiment should at least avoid reading from the source to remove all the redundant cache misses, and it should test the performance of the three ranges of alpha values 0, 1-254, and 255. Listed below are the four versions of the code, the original line and the three new experimentation lines.

```
DWORD sColor=pSrc[col];    // original line of code
DWORD sColor=0x00123456;   // alpha of zero (does nothing)
DWORD sColor=0x80123456;   // alpha of 1/2 scale (blends)
DWORD sColor=0xff123456;   // alpha of 255 (always copies)
```

The performance of the four different versions is listed in Table 17.1.

Table 17.1 Performance Experiments Results

Experiment	Description of Calculations	Clocks Per Frame
Original	Read source, blends, and writes	3,300,000
Alpha = 128	Constant source, blends and writes	2,800,000
Alpha = 255	Constant source, no blends, writes	2,680,000
Alpha = 0	Constant source, no blends, no writes	2,550,000

Table 17.1 indicates that 500,000 clocks are used to read the source and incur a cache miss (the difference between the original code and the alpha=128 code) and 130,000 clocks are used writing to the destination (the difference between the alpha=0 code and the alpha=255 code). This result indicates that the cache misses for reading the source are costly and should be optimized. Furthermore, these results show that about 2,550,000 clocks are being used by the rest of the application, which is mostly the Rotate function, proven by the time-based sampling results in Figure 17.2.

The performance experiments show that merging the functions, `AlphaBlend32to32` and `Rotate` with the goal of reducing the number of cache misses, will improve application performance. Additionally, merging the two functions is quicker and easier than converting the functions to use the SIMD instructions. So, it makes sense to merge the functions first, then use the SIMD instructions on the merged function, which will include the calculations for rotation, bilinear interpolation, and alpha blending.

Writing a Specialized Merged Function

In the file **[appN.cpp]** located on the included CD, the two functions `Rotate` and `AlphaBlend32to32` have been merged into one, called `RotateAndAlphaBlend`, replacing two general-purpose functions with one specialized function. Using the combined function, the performance of the application improves to 3,200,000 clocks per frame- not a huge improvement, but since it is an improvement and it will open up additional optimizations, it will be kept. Sampling the application again, shown in Figure 17.3, shows that the new merged function, `RotateAndAlphaBlend`, is consuming almost all the time, but that two functions, `RotateAndAlphaBlend` and `MemCopyRect`, share the majority of L1 cache misses.

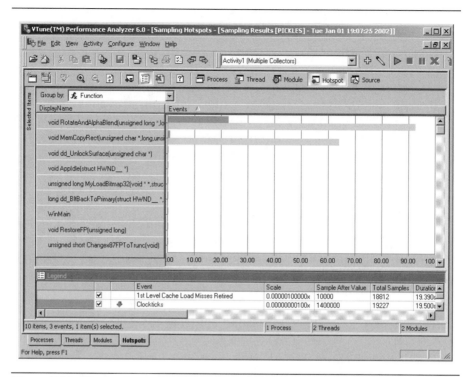

Figure 17.3 Clockticks and L1 Cache Misses in RotateAndBlend.exe

Together, `MemCopyRect` and `RotateAndAlphaBlend` generate the majority of the L1 cache misses but only `RotateAndAlphaBlend` consumes a significant amount of time. Therefore, the L1 cache misses are not the primary reason that `RotateAndAlphaBlend` is slow, because if that were the cause, `MemCopyRect` would also be slow. With this in mind, only branch mis-predictions and the amount and type of instructions used can be causing a performance issue because the function does little else.

Using the VTune analyzer, the branch mis-prediction possibility can be tested. Figure 17.4 shows the sampling results of branches retired and mis-predicted branches.

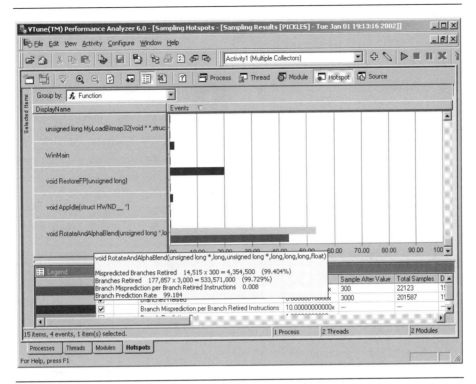

Figure 17.4 Branch Analysis

The VTune analyzer says that the mis-prediction rate is about 1 in 100 branches, which is very low and not worth changing.

With branch prediction eliminated from the list of possible causes for lost performance, only the instructions, both the amount and types, can be causing the performance problems. The best solution for instruction-related performance issues is to switch to using the SIMD instructions because fewer instructions are executed to perform the same amount of work. Since the data type is single-precision floating-point, the 16-byte, single-precision, floating-point Streaming SIMD Extensions will be used with the Intel C++ Compiler.

Using SIMD Technology

Using the Streaming SIMD Extensions requires a rewrite of the function. Either the intrinsics or assembly language must be used to access the SIMD instructions because they contain the functionality needed to implement this function. But the intrinsics should be used because they are easier to write than assembly language, and take advantage Intel C++ Compiler's advanced code-scheduling optimizations for the Pentium 4 processor. Switching to the Intel C++ Compiler is as easy as checking a box in the Compiler Selection Tool. See Chapter 3, "Performance Tools," for details.

To start the rewrite, it is easiest to consider the format of the data at the beginning and end of the algorithm and to work your way towards the middle.

The goal is to have one 4-byte value at the end of the function that contains the four individual color components (alpha, red, green, and blue). The inputs are a 4-byte source pixel and a 4-byte destination pixel to blend together, as shown in Figure 17.5.

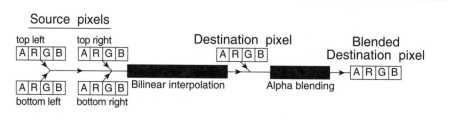

Figure 17.5 Basic Idea to Convert to SIMD Technology

At first glance, it might seem like two pixels can be loaded (e.g. top left and top right) at the same time, because the pixels are next to each other in memory. But since only 4-byte data alignment is guaranteed, only one 4-byte pixel should be loaded at a time.

The algorithm begins by loading a pixel and converting it to four single-precision floating-point values as shown in Figure 17.6.

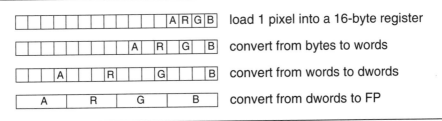

Figure 17.6 Steps to Convert a Pixel to SIMD Single-precision Floating Point

Repeating this conversion four times expands all four pixels to single-precision floating-point. Four variables can be loaded with the fx*fy combinations for the pixel multipliers, as shown in Figure 17.7.

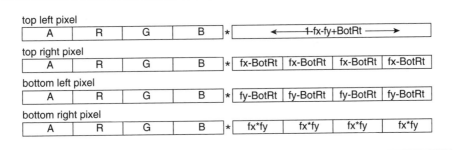

Figure 17.7 The Four Multiplies for the Four Pixels

Executing four multiply operations then adding the results together completes the bilinear interpolation. Converting the result back to integers gets the data ready for the alpha blend. The test for alpha channel equal to 0 or 255, which avoids the blend, is skipped because the extra cost for the test is probably greater than just doing the work. The destination pixel is converted to double words followed by the blend operation. The complete listing of the new function follows and is located in the file [appO.cpp], which you can find on the included CD.

```
void RotateAndAlphaBlend (DWORD *pDst, long DPitch,
                          DWORD *pSrc, long SPitch,
                          long width, long  height, float angle)
{
    WORD OldCtrlWord;
    DPitch /= sizeof(DWORD);
    SPitch /= sizeof(DWORD);
    float CosAngle = (float)cos(angle);
    float SinAngle = (float)sin(angle);
    __m128i zeros = _mm_setzero_si128();
    __m128i Sub255 = _mm_set_epi32(0xff,0xff, 0xff, 0xff);

    for (int y=-height/2; y<height/2; y++)
    {
        for (int x=-width/2; x<width/2; x++)
        {
            long dwSrcX, dwSrcY;
            float fSrcX = width /2.0f + x*CosAngle - y*SinAngle;
            float fSrcY = height/2.0f + x*SinAngle + y*CosAngle;

            // When using the Intel C++ compiler and /QxW this
            // conversion does not call _ftol.
            // It uses the SSE2 instruction
            dwSrcX = (int)fSrcX;
            dwSrcY = (int)fSrcY;
            if (dwSrcX > 0 && dwSrcY > 0 &&
                dwSrcX < width-1 && dwSrcY < height-1)
            {
                DWORD *pTopPixels, *pBottomPixels;
                pTopPixels    = pSrc + dwSrcY * SPitch + dwSrcX;
                pBottomPixels = pTopPixels + SPitch;
                float fx = fSrcX - (float)dwSrcX;
                float fy = fSrcY - (float)dwSrcY;

                float BottomRight = fx * fy;
                float TopLeft     = 1.0f - fx - fy + BottomRight;
                float TopRight    = fx - BottomRight;
                float BottomLeft  = fy - BottomRight;

                // expand each byte to single-precision floating-point
                __m128i iTopLeftPixel     = _mm_unpacklo_epi8(
                    _mm_cvtsi32_si128(*pTopPixels), zeros);
                __m128i iTopRightPixel    = _mm_unpacklo_epi8(
                    _mm_cvtsi32_si128(*pTopPixels+1), zeros);
                __m128i iBottomLeftPixel  = _mm_unpacklo_epi8(
                    _mm_cvtsi32_si128(*pBottomPixels), zeros);
                __m128i iBottomRightPixel = _mm_unpacklo_epi8(
                    _mm_cvtsi32_si128(*pBottomPixels+1), zeros);
```

```
        __m128 FpTopLeftPixel     = _mm_cvtepi32_ps(
               _mm_unpacklo_epi16(iTopLeftPixel, zeros));
        __m128 FpTopRightPixel    = _mm_cvtepi32_ps(
               _mm_unpacklo_epi16(iTopRightPixel, zeros));
        __m128 FpBottomLeftPixel  = _mm_cvtepi32_ps(
               _mm_unpacklo_epi16(iBottomLeftPixel, zeros));
        __m128 FpBottomRightPixel = _mm_cvtepi32_ps(
               _mm_unpacklo_epi16(iBottomRightPixel, zeros));

        // load the destination pixel
        __m128i dColor = _mm_cvtsi32_si128(pDst[x+width/2]);

        // load the multipliers
        __m128 TopLeftMultiplier   = _mm_load_ps1(&TopLeft);
        __m128 TopRightMultiplier  = _mm_load_ps1(&TopRight);
        __m128 BottomLeftMultiplier=_mm_load_ps1(&BottomLeft);
        __m128 BottomRightMultiplier =
                    _mm_load_ps1(&BottomRight);

        // do the multiplies
        FpTopLeftPixel =
               _mm_mul_ps(FpTopLeftPixel, TopLeftMultiplier);
        FpTopRightPixel =
               _mm_mul_ps(FpTopRightPixel, TopRightMultiplier);
        FpBottomLeftPixel =
        _mm_mul_ps(FpBottomLeftPixel, BottomLeftMultiplier);
        FpBottomRightPixel =
        _mm_mul_ps(FpBottomRightPixel,BottomRightMultiplier);

        // do the additions
        __m128 pixel;
        pixel = _mm_add_ps(FpTopLeftPixel, FpTopRightPixel);
        pixel = _mm_add_ps(FpBottomLeftPixel, pixel);
        pixel = _mm_add_ps(FpBottomRightPixel, pixel);

        // iPixel has the color values in 32-bit integers
        __m128i iPixel = _mm_cvtps_epi32(pixel);

        dColor = _mm_unpacklo_epi8(dColor, zeros);
        dColor = _mm_unpacklo_epi16(dColor, zeros);
        __m128i sAlpha = _mm_shuffle_epi32(iPixel, 0xff);
        __m128i dAlpha = _mm_sub_epi32(Sub255, sAlpha);
        iPixel = _mm_mullo_epi16(iPixel, sAlpha);
        dColor = _mm_mullo_epi16(dColor, dAlpha);
        iPixel = _mm_add_epi32(iPixel, dColor);
        iPixel = _mm_srli_epi32(iPixel, 8);
        iPixel = _mm_packs_epi32(iPixel, zeros);
        iPixel = _mm_packus_epi16(iPixel, zeros);
        pDst[x+width/2] = _mm_cvtsi128_si32(iPixel);
      }

    }
    pDst += DPitch;
  }
}
```

The performance of the application using the new function is 2,200,000 clocks per frame, which is 1,000,000 clocks per frame faster than the previous version and more than 8,000,000 clocks per frame faster than the original version.

More Analysis, Reduce MemCopyRect

Running the VTune analyzer again reveals that MemCopyRect is now consuming about one third of the total time, as shown in Figure 17.8.

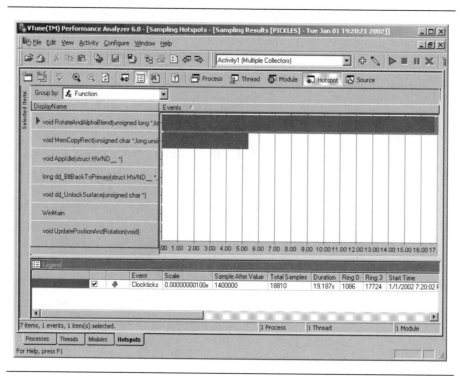

Figure 17.8 MemCopyRect is Now Consuming Some Time

It would be great once again to find something easy that reduces the MemCopyRect time. MemCopyRect is being used to remove the image of the old ball, which is not completely necessary; only the area that will not be overdrawn by the current ball needs to be redrawn, as shown in Figure 17.9.

Ball moves from here to here

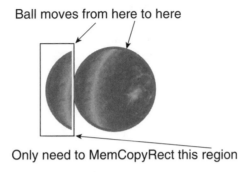

Only need to MemCopyRect this region

Figure 17.9 A Smaller Dirty Rectangle Can Be Redrawn

This optimization requires that the RotateAndAlphaBlend function does not read from the destination because it may have dirty pixels and instead needs to read from the original source.

Changing the RotateAndAlphaBlend function to accept three pointers, two source pointers and one destination pointer, plus changing the call to MemCopyRect to update the smaller region improves performance even more down to 1,500,000 clocks per frame. The code changes are contained in the **[appP.cpp]** file located on the included CD.

Running the VTune analyzer again shows a dramatic drop in the amount of time for MemCopyRect, as shown in Figure 17.10. A performance boost from quick and easy "low-hanging fruit" is always welcome.

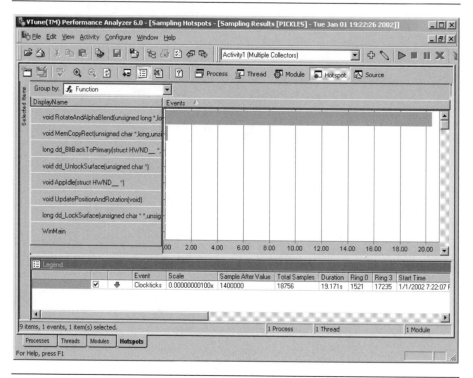

Figure 17.10 Calling MemCopy with Less Work

Pick a Different Algorithm

With the performance of the application now more than six times faster than the original, the ball appears to blur as it moves. Surely, bilinear filtering is no longer required because you can't even see the image improvement since the ball is moving so fast. Using integer truncation instead of bilinear interpolation is a great way to get even more performance since any image quality issues are obscured in the motion blur.

Removing all the bilinear interpolation code, the code is greatly simplified and performance is now down to 930,000 clocks per frame. See file [appQ.cpp] for these code changes.

Improving the Algorithm

With bilinear interpolation gone and just the rotation and alpha blending left, it is time to run the VTune analyzer again to determine what to do next. Figure 17.11 shows that the `RotateAndAlphaBlend` function is still a very time consuming function.

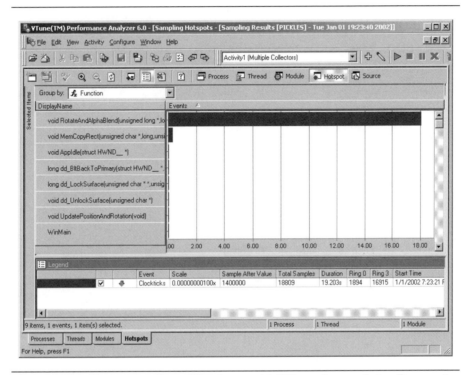

Figure 17.11 Hotspots in RotateBlend.exe with Bilinear Interpolation Removed

Again, the types and quantity of instructions used and the cache misses are the only possible performance issues because the function does little else. Trying to reduce the number of instructions requires re-thinking the algorithm and the way that it is implemented. A mathematical simplification can be used to reduce the number of operations, as shown in Equation 17.1.

$$\frac{SA + D(255 - A)}{256} = \frac{SA + 255D - DA}{256} = \frac{A(S - D)}{256} + D$$

Equation 17.1 Simplification of the Alpha Blending Formula

After making this change to the algorithm, the performance degrades and goes back up to 1,100,000 clocks per frame, which is totally unexpected and needs to be investigated. You can see the changes in file [appR.cpp].

Examining the data dependencies shows that both versions are full of them. Figure 17.12 is a diagram of the data dependencies for the two versions of the equation.

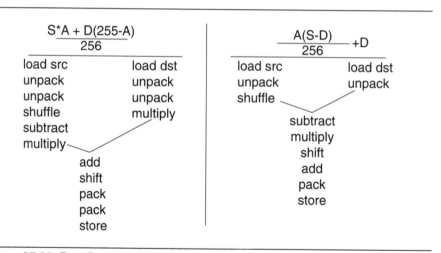

Figure 17.12 Data Dependencies for Both Equations

It appears that the simplified version on the right has a slightly shorter data dependency chain, so it should be faster, but it isn't. At this point, the assumption is that the compiler is somehow optimizing the instruction sequence on the left more than the one on the right. Whatever the reason, it is better to undo the change, keep this simplification on hand for a possible future use, and look for a different optimization.

Pre-calculating Values

Going back to the original alpha blending formula, shown below in Equation 17.2, a good optimization would be to pre-calculate S*A/256 and 255-A.

$$\frac{SA + D(255 - A)}{256}$$

Equation 17.2 Standard Alpha Blending Formula

The algorithm would then use the formulas shown in Equation 17.3

$$S_{precalc} + \frac{DA_{precalc}}{256}, S_{precalc} = \frac{SA}{256}, A_{precalc} = 255 - A$$

Equation 17.3 Alpha Blending Formula Using Pre-calculated Values

The following code pre-calculates the two values and is inserted in the `AppIdle` function.

```
// pre-calculate foreground bitmap values
// store s*a/256, change alpha to 255-a
for (i=0; i<FgBmpWidth*FgBmpHeight; i++)
{
    BYTE *pClrBmp=(BYTE *)&(pFgBmp[i]);
    DWORD alpha=pClrBmp[3];
    pClrBmp[0]=(BYTE)((DWORD)(pClrBmp[0]) * alpha / 256);
    pClrBmp[1]=(BYTE)((DWORD)(pClrBmp[1]) * alpha / 256);
    pClrBmp[2]=(BYTE)((DWORD)(pClrBmp[2]) * alpha / 256);
    pClrBmp[3]=255-alpha;
}
```

Then, the alpha blending code in the `RotateAndAlphaBlend` function code is changed to the following.

```
__m128i SrcPixel = _mm_unpacklo_epi8(
        _mm_cvtsi32_si128(*pPixel), zeros);
__m128i DstPixel = _mm_unpacklo_epi8(
        _mm_cvtsi32_si128(pSrc2[x+width/2]), zeros);
__m128i SrcAlpha = _mm_shufflelo_epi16(SrcPixel, 0xff);
DstPixel = _mm_mullo_epi16(DstPixel, SrcAlpha);
DstPixel = _mm_srli_epi16(DstPixel, 8);
SrcPixel = _mm_add_epi8(SrcPixel, DstPixel);
```

```
SrcPixel = _mm_packus_epi16(SrcPixel, zeros);
pDst[x+width/2] = _mm_cvtsi128_si32(SrcPixel);
```

This change to the alpha blending code is made in [appS.cpp], located on the CD, and the performance is 910,000 clocks per frame making it ten times faster than the original.

Write-Combining Memory

Once the pixels are blended, the graphics card takes over and displays them in the client window. Since the processor does not read the blended pixels again, ideally the pixels would not be written into the processor's caches. This improvement is achieved by using write-combining memory or the non-temporal move instructions (MOVNT). By changing the application to store pixels directly on the graphics card, which is configured as write-combining memory by the device driver, the pixels do not pollute the processor's caches and performance should improve.

From a performance perspective, the graphics card's frame buffer is write-only memory; reading from the graphics card functionally works but at a huge performance loss. During the course of optimizations, this application changed from blending a source pixel with the destination pixel, which requires reading from the destination, to blending two source pixels and only writing to the destination. So this application now meets the criteria of never reading from the frame buffer on the graphics card and can be safely switched to using the graphics card directly.

Before changing the application, use the VTune analyzer to track WC writes so that you can observe the change. Sampling on the event counter All WC from the processor shows that DirectDraw is actively using write combining memory, as shown in Figure 17.13.

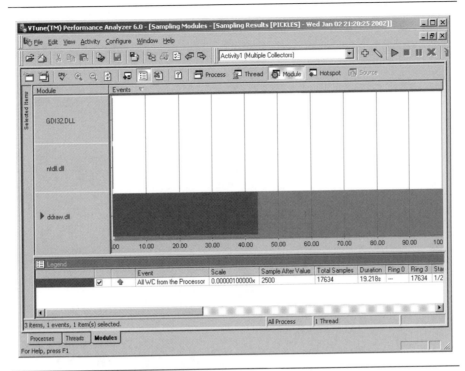

Figure 17.13 Module Hotspots for Write-Combining Memory Stores

DirectDraw uses the write-combining memory when copying from the off-screen surface in main memory to the frame buffer on the graphics card. If the application could draw directly on the graphics card's frame buffer, DirectDraw would not have to execute the copy, and performance would be improved. The change to make the application write to the frame buffer is made when creating an off-screen surface using DirectDraw. Currently, the application requests a system memory off-screen surface in the dd_Init function as shown in the following code sample.

```
ddsd.ddsCaps.dwCaps = DDSCAPS_OFFSCREENPLAIN |
DDSCAPS_SYSTEMMEMORY;
```

DirectDraw will automatically place the surface on the graphics card if the system memory flag is removed. File [ddA.cpp] has the flag removed from the create off-screen surface function call. The performance of the application improves to 760,000 clocks per frame. The VTune analyzer now shows that WC writes are occurring in RotateBlend.exe application in the RotateAndAlphaBlend and MemCopyRect functions, as shown in Figure 17.14.

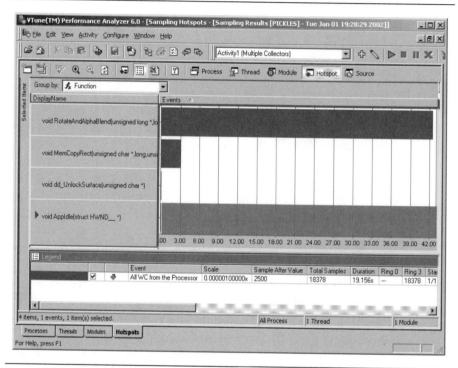

Figure 17.14 WC Hotspots in the RotateBlend.exe Application

All of the WC writes have moved from DirectDraw to Rotate-Blend.exe, confirming that DirectDraw is no longer copying memory from an off-screen buffer in system memory to one on the graphics card and that this application is now using the non-temporal write buffers.

In cases where the operating system, device driver, or DirectDraw-as in this case- has not set the memory type, the streaming-store instructions would have to be used.

More Analysis, Remove Multiplies

Hotspot analysis now shows two regions of time being consumed in the `RotateAndAlphaBlend` function, as shown in the source code view in Figure 17.15.

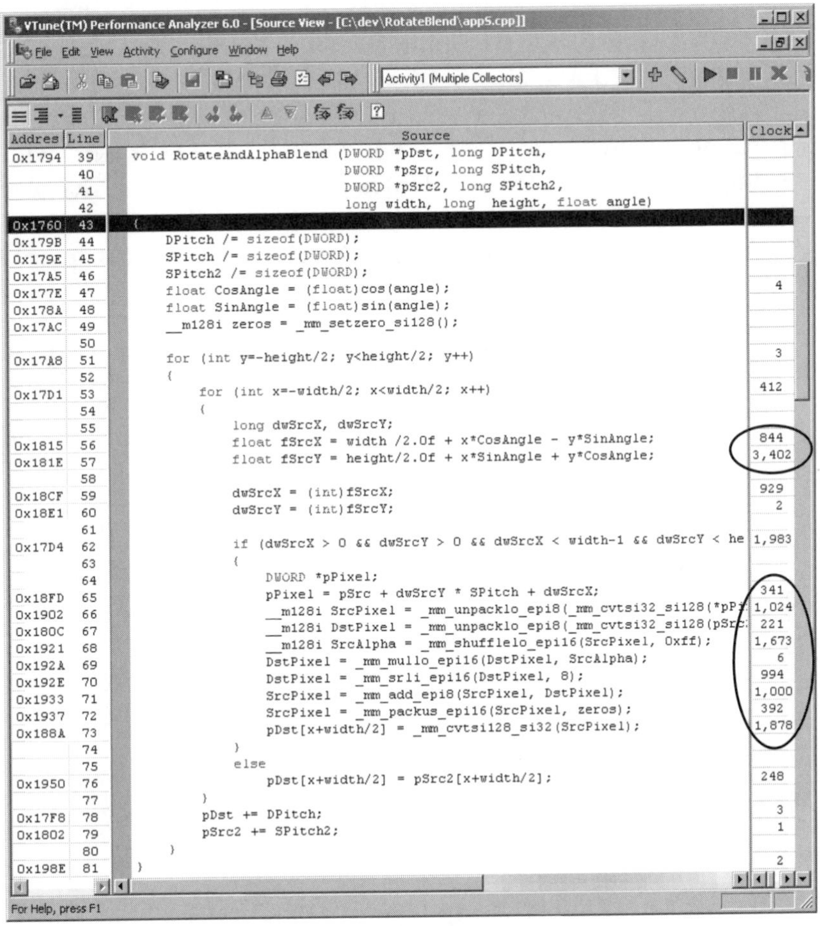

Figure 17.15 Two Hotspot Regions in RotateAndAlphaBlend

The two regions correspond to the calculation of the rotated pixel and the alpha blend. Surprisingly, the two regions look like they consume a similar amount of time, which means that the rotation calculation is taking longer than expected. Every time through the loop, the following lines of code are executed to calculate the rotated pixel location.

```
fSrcX = width /2.0f + x*CosAngle - y*SinAngle;
fSrcY = height/2.0f + x*SinAngle + y*CosAngle;
```

The code uses four multiplies, but it can be simplified to use just two additions if the value of fSrcX increases by CosAngle and fSrcY increases by SinAngle every time through the loop. Moving the multiplications before the inner loop and replacing them with additions improves performance to 375,000 clocks per frame. The changes are in file [**appT.cpp**]. The hotspots profile for the RotateAndAlphaBlend function now shows that most of the time is spent alpha blending, as show in Figure 17.16.

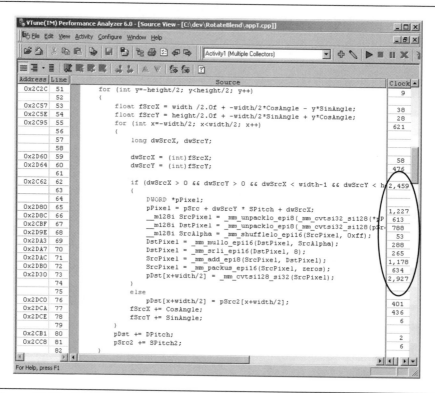

Figure 17.16 Hotspots in RotateAndAlphaBlend After Improving Rotation Calculation

Knowing When to Stop Optimizing

Optimizations should end when the performance goals have been met. Performance goals usually are expressed in terms of the benchmark, so for this application, faster than 500,000 clocks per frame would be an example of a performance goal. For this application, the performance has significantly increased, which was the goal. Whether you stop when a benchmark-based goal is met or when you achieve significant improvements, the speed-of-light calculation can help determine what performance goals to set in the first place and when to stop optimizing because of diminishing returns.

Approximating the minimum required work by focusing on the critical operations computes the speed-of-light for a specific algorithm or application. This application's minimum required work is rotation, reading two source pixels, blending them, and writing the blended pixel to the frame buffer. Simplifying that work down to just reading two pixels, adding them together, and writing the result provides a good approximation of the maximum speed even though it would not be functionally the same. The speed-of-light for this application is calculated at 210,000 clocks per frame with the code contained in the file [appU.cpp]. The number is too slow because not all pixels need to be written to the destination, only the pixels that have a non-zero alpha value, and the number is too fast because the real alpha blending calculation has many more data dependencies than just one addition. However, even with these limitations, the number is still valuable. A fairly accurate statement can be made that the maximum performance will be around 200,000 clocks without other algorithmic changes.

Knowing that the speed of light is 200,000 clocks per frame, which is 175,000 clocks per frame faster than the current implementation, means that additional performance improvements can be made, if desired. Further optimizations would focus on optimizing the RotateAndAlphaBlend function because it is now consuming almost 100% of the total application time. Optimizations would deal with changing the function to use less memory, to cause fewer cache misses, to avoid the if statement inside the loop, to use simpler calculations, or finding additional work to do in parallel.

Summary of Optimizations

This application has undergone many optimizations and is now about 25 times faster than the original. Table 17.2 is a list of the optimizations made in this chapter.

Table 17.2 Summary of Optimizations

Description of Optimization	Files Effected	Clocks Per Frame	Performance Improvement from Starting Point in this Chapter
Starting point	apM.cpp	3,300,000	Baseline
Merge rotate and blend functions	appN.cpp	3,200,000	1.03
Use SIMD instruction	appO.cpp	2,200,000	1.5
Dirty rectangle memory copy, do not read from destination, use 2 source pointers	appP.cpp	1,500,000	2.2
Remove bilinear interpolation	appQ.cpp	930,000	3.5
Simplify equation	appR.cpp	1,100,000	Performance regression, failed attempt.
Precalculate values	appS.cpp	910,000	3.6
Switch to off-screen surface	ddA.cpp	760,000	4.3
Change rotate calculation from four multiplies to two additions	appT.cpp	375,000	8.8
Speed-of-light performance experiment	appU.cpp	200,000	Experiment only.

Key Points

When optimizing an application, remember the following key points:
- Performance regressions do occur. Changing one thing at a time and constantly using the benchmark makes it easy to catch the regressions quickly.
- There is no such thing as the fastest code.

References

Publications

Intel Corporation, *IA-32 Intel Architecture Software Developer's Manual, Volume 1: Basic Architecture*, Order number 245470.

Intel Corporation, *IA-32 Intel Architecture Software Developer's Manual, Volume 2: Instruction Set Reference*, Order number 245471.

Intel Corporation, *IA-32 Intel Architecture Software Developer's Manual, Volume 3: System Programming Guide*, Order number 245472.

Intel Corporation, Application Note AP-485, *Intel Processor Identification and the CPUID Instruction*, Order number: 241618.

Intel Corporation, *Intel Pentium 4 and Intel Xeon Processor Optimization Reference Manual*, Order number: 248966.

Intel Corporation, *Intel Architecture Optimization Reference Manual*, Order number: 245127.

Intel Corporation, *Using Spin-Loops on Intel Pentium4 Processor and Intel Xeon Processor*, Order number: 248674.

Parallel Programming in OpenMP by Chandra, Menon, Dagum, Kohr, Maydan, and McDonald.

Web Sites

OpenMP Architecture Review Board's Web site,
http://www.OpenMP.org

Intel Software Development Products Web site,
http://developer.intel.com/software/products/

Index

32-bit Intel architecture. *See* Intel
    32-bit architecture

A

algorithms
    alpha blending, 222-23, 259-60
    bubble sort, 61, 62
    choice of instructions, 62-66
    creating in RotateBlend example,
      220-23
    design issues, 211-12
    detecting issues, 69-71
    elementary school example, 64
    Euclid's, 65-66
    image rotation, 223
    issues in RotateBlend example,
      233-34
    memory requirements, 68-69
    O-notation analysis, 61
    overview, 61
    quicksort, 61-62
    and SIMD instructions, 211-12
alpha blending algorithm, 222-23,
    259-60

app.cpp file, 215-16
AppInit function, 216
applications. *See also* optimizations
    causes of inconsistent execution,
      40-41
    finding page misses, 103-5
    optimization pitfalls, 4-6
    optimization process overview,
      6-7
    RotateBlend example, 215-66
architecture, 32-bit. *See* Intel 32-bit
    architecture
assembly language
    converting floating-point
      numbers to integers with
      truncation, 154-56
    inline, 26
    methods for using SIMD
      instructions, 162
    need for, 5-6
automatic vectorization, 23, 24, 163
automobile fuel economy example,
    13

B

bandwidth, 199

benchmarks
   complete coverage attribute, 12
   creating for RotateBlend
      example, 225- 27
   easy-to-run attribute, 11
   exercise in creating, 14
   industry standard, 10
   list of attributes, 10- 13
   measure elapsed time attribute,
      12
   off-the-shelf, 10
   overview, 6, 9- 10
   precision attribute, 12
   quality assurance and testing
      attribute, 13
   repeatable attribute, 10- 11
   representative attribute, 11
   verifiable attribute, 12
   writing programs, 10

bilinear pixel interpolation algorithm,
   220- 22, 256, 257

bitmap.cpp file, 216

branch prediction, 52, 53

branches
   call and return, 81
   conditional, 73- 75, 80
   and indirect calls, 81
   and jump tables, 81
   mis-predicted, 75, 76- 80, 234
   optimizing, 81- 86
   predicting order of instructions,
      52, 53
   removing by doing extra work,
      85- 86
   removing inside loops, 124- 25
   removing with CMOV
      instruction, 82- 83
   removing with masks, 83- 84

   removing with min/max
      instructions, 84- 85
   types, 80- 81
   unconditional, 73- 75, 81

bubble sort algorithm, 61, 62

bus bandwidth, 199

C

C/C++ languages. *See also* Intel C++
   Compiler
   class libraries and SIMD data
      types, 24- 25
   method for using SIMD
      instructions, 163

C++ compilers. *See* Intel C++
   Compiler

cache conflicts, 98, 99- 100, 110- 11

cache efficiency, 100, 109- 10, 199,
   208, 210

cache lines, 93, 199, 210

cache loads, 98- 100, 109, 111

cache misses, 41, 42, 69, 98- 100,
   106- 7, 109, 186

cache ping-pong, 200

caches, 56, 91- 93, 96. *See also* L1
   cache; L2 cache

call graph analysis, 31- 32, 44, 69, 70

call/return branches, 81

capacity cache misses, 98- 99, 111

Clockticks counter, 30

CMOV instruction, 82- 83

Compiler Selection Tool, 19, 20

compilers. *See also* Intel C++
   Compiler
   and data alignment, 102
   and debugging process, 5
   overview, 19
   and RotateBlend example,
      224- 25

compulsory cache misses, 98, 109

concurrency, and parallel programming, 192-93

conditional branches, 73-75, 80

conflicts. *See* cache conflicts

cpu_dispatch keyword, 22-23

CPUID assembly instruction, 22

cpu_specific keyword, 22-23

D

data, misaligned, 101-2

data alignment, 100-102

data dependencies
    and instruction parallelism, 66-68
    keeping low, 55, 212
    and loops, 68, 119, 125-26
    overview, 54
    in RotateBlend example, 235

data movement, 208-10

data parallelism, 192, 193

data structures
    design considerations, 210-11
    linked, 208-9
    optimization example, 113-14
    traversing, 208-9

data types. *See also* floating-point numbers
    integer, 25, 152, 157, 166-67, 185
    proper alignment, 101
    SIMD, 24-25

dd.cpp file, 216

debugging *vs.* compiler optimization, 5

denormal numbers, 144, 147

direct bit manipulation, 157

divide-by-zero exceptions, 144

double-precision floating-point numbers, 25, 148, 149, 150, 151, 152, 165-66, 168

E

elementary school algorithm example, 64

Empty MMX State (EMMS) instructions, 166-67

Euclid's Algorithm, 65-66

event counters, 187

exceptions
    Application Error dialog box, 146, 147
    and denormal numbers, 144, 147
    detecting, 145-46
    inexact-result, 144
    invalid operation, 144
    numeric overflow, 144
    numeric underflow, 144
    stack overflow, 144
    stack underflow, 144

execution ports, 53-54, 130

F

fast-food restaurant analogy, 49-51

flag stalls, 189

floating-point numbers
    Application Error dialog box, 146, 147
    converting to integer values, 152-57, 185
    detecting exceptions, 145-46
    double-extended precision, 148, 149, 150, 165-66
    double-precision, 25, 148, 149, 150, 151, 152, 165-66, 168
    and flush-to-zero mode, 147
    global calculation precision, 148
    list of exceptions, 144
    manipulation tricks, 157, 158
    and numeric exceptions, 144-47
    overview, 143
    precision in, 144, 148-51

floating-point numbers (continued)
   and SIMD instructions, 147, 151, 152, 165-66, 167, 168
   single-precision, 25, 148, 149, 150, 151, 152, 165-66, 167
flush-to-zero mode, 147
Fortran compilers, 19
_ftol function, removing calls, 153, 229-33
functional blocks
   fast-food restaurant analogy, 49-51
   instruction execution stage, 53-55
   instruction fetch and decode stage, 52-53
   instruction retirement stage, 55
   instruction stage overview, 48-49
   overview, 47, 48, 49
   Pentium 4 processor, 47, 48-55
   Pentium III processor, 182
functions
   improving on sscanf, 136-37
   optimization example without performance analyzer, 112-13
   optimizing system calls, 135-36

G

Gantt charts, instruction execution with and without data dependencies, 66-68
global calculation precision, 148. *See also* floating-point numbers

H

high-level thread libraries, 193, 194-97
hotspots
   detecting, 43-45
   inconsistent execution, 40-41
   locating in RotateBlend example, 228-29, 243-47, 263-64
   overview, 6, 39-40
   slow operation overview, 129-41
   and threading, 197, 198-99
   time-consuming, 77-78
   types of activity, 41-42
   in VTune Performance Analyzer, 40
HUFF.EXE file
   create benchmark exercise, 14
   mis-predicted branches, 76-80
   VTune analyzer call graph results, 69
Huffman Encoding example, 208, 209
Hyper-Threading technology, 181, 191, 197

I

IA-32 Intel architecture. *See* Intel 32-bit architecture
image rotation algorithm, 223
indirect calls, 81
inexact-result exceptions, 144
inline assembly language, 26
instruction latency, 62, 63, 64, 130
instruction-level parallelism, 191, 192, 210
instruction pool, 48, 52, 54, 89
instruction throughput, 63, 64, 130
instructions
   algorithm implementation, 62-66
   fast-food restaurant analogy, 49-51
   fetch and decode stage, 52-53
   Pentium 4 processor execution stages, 48-55
   prefetch, 94-95, 110, 186-87

instructions (continued)

reasons for being slow, 130- 31

retirement stage, 55

in RotateBlend example, 235

serializing, 131

SIMD, 23- 26

instrumentation profilers

Microsoft Visual C++ Profiler, 34

overview, 28

vs. sampling profilers, 35

VTune Performance Analyzer,
29- 33

integer data type

converting floating-point
numbers to, 152- 57, 185

and SIMD, 25, 166- 67

Intel 32-bit architecture, 179, 180- 81

Intel C++ Compiler

-Qrcd command-line switch, 154

and automatic vectorization, 23,
24, 163

and inline assembly language, 26

methods for using SIMD
instructions, 23- 26

optimization features, 27

optimization options, 21, 22

optimizing for specific
processors, 21- 22

PAUSE instruction, 189

processor dispatch feature, 22-
23

selecting, 19, 20

support for intrinsics, 26

writing functions specific to one
processor, 22- 23

Intel Fortran compilers, 19

Intel VTune Performance Analyzer.
See VTune Performance Analyzer

interprocedural optimizations, 27

intrinsics, 26, 162

invalid operation exceptions, 144

invariant work, 123- 24

iteration dependencies, 125- 26

I32vec4 data type, 25

J-L

jump tables, 81

L1 cache

finding misses, 106- 7

overview, 91- 92

Pentium 4 processor, 91- 94, 186

Pentium III processor, 182- 83,
186

role in performance
improvement, 93- 94, 96

L2 cache, 91, 92, 93, 94

latency

and algorithm selection, 64

and instruction performance, 63

overview, 62, 130

problems when long, 130

libraries, thread, 193, 194- 97

linked data structures, 208- 9

Linux compilers, 19

load balancing, 193, 197

lookup tables

keeping small, 131

optimization example, 132- 34

organizing, 131

overview, 131

storing calculations, 132

loops

advantages and disadvantages,
118

common problems, 118- 19

and data dependencies, 68, 119,
125- 26

as hotspots, 117- 18

invariant branches, 124- 25

invariant work, 123- 24

iteration dependencies, 125- 26

loops (continued)
optimizing by unrolling example, 122
overhead, 118
overview, 117
and parallelism, 119
removing branches inside, 124-25
spin-wait, 201
unrolling, 27, 119-22
low-level thread libraries, 193, 194

M

main memory, 91
masks, creating, 83-84
matrix multiplication, 169-71
memory. *See also* L1 cache; L2 cache
access in RotateBlend example, 235
address dependencies, 126-27
algorithm requirements, 68-69
cache efficiency, 100
cache loads, 98-100, 109, 111
detecting problems, 102-9
false sharing, 199
finding page misses, 103-5
fixing problems, 109-14
main, 91
non-temporal writes, 96-97, 110
overview, 89, 90-97
and Pentium 4 processor, 56, 89, 91-94
performance experiments, 107-9
performance issues, 97-102
processor cache overview, 91-93
processor steps in executing loops, 89-90
sharing, 198
spatial locality, 92
temporal locality, 93
using less, 109
virtual, 91
write-combining, 96-97
MFC (Microsoft Foundation Class), 194
micro-operations (µOps), 52, 53, 54, 55
Microsoft Foundation Class (MFC), 194
Microsoft Performance Monitor, 28-29, 202
Microsoft Visual C++, 19
Microsoft Visual C++ Profiler, 34
mis-predicted branches, 75, 76-80, 234
misaligned data, 101-2
MMX technology, and SIMD, 161, 166-67
multiprocessing. *See also* parallel programming
and algorithm design, 212
illustrated, 191
overview, 191-92
and thread execution, 200-201
ways to execute instructions, 191

N

NetBurst micro-architecture, 181
Newton-Raphson Method, 168
non-temporal instructions, 96-97, 110
numeric overflow exceptions, 144
numeric underflow exceptions, 144

O

O-notation analysis, 61
OpenMP threads, 193, 194-97
µOps (micro-operations), 52, 53, 54, 55

optimizations. *See also* applications
  interprocedural, 27
  knowing when to stop, 265
  pitfalls, 4-6
  process overview, 6-7
  processor-specific, 21-23,
    179-89
  profile-guided, 27
  role of benchmarks, 9-10
  role of processor architecture, 6,
    47-48
  RotateBlend example, 224-66
optimizing compilers. *See* compilers;
  Intel C++ Compiler

P

P6 micro-architecture, 181
page faults, 91
page misses, 103-5
page swapping, 91, 103
parallel programming. *See also*
  multiprocessing
  and concurrency, 192-93
  illustrated, 191
  and multiple threads, 192-93
  scalability issue, 202
  task parallelism *vs.* data
    parallelism, 192-93
  threading issues, 198-201
  tools for optimizations and
    validation, 202
parallelism
  data, 192, 193
  instruction-level, 191, 192, 210
  task, 192-93
PAUSE instruction, 189
Pentium 4 processor
  fast-food restaurant analogy,
    49-51

floating-point control register,
  185
functional blocks, 47, 48-55
instruction execution stage,
  53-55
instruction fetch and decode
  stage, 52-53
instruction retirement stage, 55
instruction stage overview, 48-
  49
L1 cache, 91-94, 186
and memory, 56, 89, 91-94, 186
memory prefetch, 186-87
optimizing Intel C++ Compiler
  for, 21
partial flag stall, 189
partial register issue, 188
PAUSE instruction, 189
sampling processor events, 187
steps in executing loops, 89-90
and Streaming SIMD Extensions,
  21
Pentium III processor
  floating-point control register,
    185
  functional blocks, 182
  instruction decoding, 183-84
  instruction latencies, 184
  instruction set, 185
  L1 cache, 182-83, 186
  optimizing Intel C++ Compiler
    for, 21
  partial register stalls, 187-88
  sampling processor events, 187
PERFMON.EXE file. *See* Microsoft
  Performance Monitor
performance. *See also* optimizations
  designing for, 207, 210-11
  when to test, 4, 207
Performance Monitor, 28-29, 202

performance tools
    and benchmarks, 9-10
    optimizing compilers, 19-27
    software profilers, 28-35
    timing mechanisms, 17-19
    tips for using, 36
ports, execution, 53-54, 130
POSIX threads, 193
precision, in floating-point math, 144, 148-51, 152, 165-66, 167, 168
prefetch instructions, 94-95, 110, 186-87
processor dispatch, 22-23
processor-specific optimizations, 21-23, 179-89
processors. *See also* Pentium 4 processor; Pentium III processor
    data alignment, 100-102
    optimization overview, 179, 180-81
    optimizing Intel C++ Compiler for, 21-22
    original Pentium processor execution pipeline, 47-48
    relationship of architecture to optimization, 47-48
    role of architects in program optimization, 6
    sampling events, 187
    writing compiler functions specific to, 22-23
profile-guided optimizations, 27. *See also* software profilers
profilers
    instrumentation *vs.* sampling, 35
    Intel VTune Performance Analyzer, 29-33
    Microsoft Performance Monitor, 28-29
    Microsoft Visual C++ Profiler, 34
    overview, 28

Q-R

quicksort algorithm, 61-62
recipes
    Ahi Tuna Burger, 116
    Balinese Grilled Bananas In Coconut Milk Caramel, 214
    Cheese and Basil Risotto, 46
    Chicken Monterey, 190
    Chili Party Chili, 72
    Crab-licious Crab Cakes, 16
    Creamy Baked Mac and Cheese, 128
    Gooey Brownies, 206
    Green Meatloaf, 60
    Not-Your-Kid's Grilled Cheese Sandwich, 142
    Patriotic Potato and Bean Salad, 8
    Pizza, 160
    Sandmans' Sweet and Sour Meatballs, 38
    Shrimp Stir-Fry, 178
    Turkey Lasagna, 88
    Very-berry Mixed-berry Cobbler, 242
    Winter Squash and Apple Soup, 2
reciprocal square root function, 158
register stalls, 187-88
restaurant analogy, 49-51
RotateBlend example
    algorithm issues, 233-34
    application overview, 215-19
    block diagram, 218
    calling functions differently, 238-39
    compiling, 224-25
    creating algorithms, 220-23
    creating benchmark, 225-27

RotateBlend example (continued)
  improving Rotate function, 234- 35
  locating hotspots, 228- 29, 243- 47, 263- 64
  memory buffers, 219
  optimizations, 224- 66
  performance experiments, 236
  removing work, 237
  still more analysis, 254- 56
  summary of optimizations, 239- 40, 266
  using Streaming SIMD Extensions in, 250- 53
  writing merged function for, 247- 49
RotateBlend.cpp file, 216
rounding, in floating-point-to-integer conversion, 27, 152- 57

S
sampling profilers
  Microsoft Performance Monitor, 28- 29
  overview, 28
  vs. instrumentation profilers, 35
  VTune Performance Analyzer, 29- 33
scalability, 202
scalar-SIMD floating-point operations, 152
serializing instructions, 131
sets, cache line, 93
sharing memory, 198
SIMD convert, in floating-point-to-integer conversions, 157
SIMD data types, 24- 25
SIMD (single-instruction multiple-data) feature
  and algorithms, 211- 12
  and buffer size, 166

  and C/C++ language, 23- 26
  compatibility with x87 FPU calculations, 165- 66
  and data alignment, 164- 65
  data organization and layout, 169- 76
  double-precision floating-point, 151, 152, 165- 66, 168
  execution model diagram, 161
  function example, 163- 64
  history, 161, 162
  integer, 25, 166- 67
  matrix multiplication example, 169- 71
  optimizing functions example, 172- 76
  overview, 161
  RotateBlend example use, 250- 53
  setting computations to zero, 147
  single-precision floating-point, 151, 152, 165- 66, 167
  ways to use instructions, 162- 64
  when to use, 176
single-instruction multiple-data feature. *See* SIMD (single-instruction multiple-data) feature
single-precision floating-point numbers, 148, 149, 150, 151, 152, 165- 66, 167
slow operations. *See also* hotspots
  overview, 129
  reasons for slow instructions, 130- 31
  role of data dependencies, 130
  role of lookup tables, 131- 34
  in RotateBlend example Rotate function, 235
  strategies for functions, 134- 37
  system idle loop problem, 137- 41

software profilers
  instrumentation *vs.* sampling, 35
  Intel VTune Performance
    Analyzer, 29- 33
  Microsoft Performance Monitor,
    28- 29
  Microsoft Visual C++ Profiler, 34
  overview, 28
source code analysis, 33
spatial locality, 92
spin-wait loops, 201
split loads, 101
split stores, 101
square root function, 158
SSE. *See* Streaming SIMD Extensions
  (SSE)
stack overflow exceptions, 144
stack underflow exceptions, 144
stopwatch programs, 17- 18
Streaming SIMD Extensions (SSE), 21,
  166, 167, 168
strip mining, 98
synchronizing threads, 198, 199- 200,
  201
system calls, 134- 37
system idle loops
  detecting, 138
  optimizing, 139- 41
  overview, 137- 38

T

task parallelism, 192- 93
temporal locality, 93
threads
  categories of APIs, 193, 194
  coarse *vs.* fine grain, 197
  false sharing of memory, 199
  and hotspots, 197, 198- 99
  load balancing, 197
    low-level *vs.* high-level libraries,
      193, 194
    multithreaded program
      strategies, 192- 93
    optimum number, 198
    overhead, 198
    parallel processing issues,
      198- 201
    processor affinity, 200
    role in converting programs to
      multiprocessing, 197- 98
    synchronization, 198, 199- 200,
      201
throughput, 63, 64, 130
TIMEC.EXE file, 17- 18
timing tools
  function calls, 18- 19
  overview, 17- 19
  stopwatch programs, 17- 18
  TIMEC.EXE file, 17- 18
trace-cache buffer, 52, 91

U

U-V pairing, 48
unconditional branches, 73- 75, 81
unknown store address blocking, 127
unrolling loops, 27, 119- 22
_USE_INTEL_COMPILER macro, 19,
  20

V

vectorization, automatic, 23, 24, 163
virtual memory, 91
Visual C++, 19, 34
VTune Performance Analyzer
  call graph analysis, 31- 32, 44, 69
  Counter Monitor feature, 104- 5
  hotspot examples, 42
  identifying floating-point to
    integer truncations, 153
  identifying hotspots, 40

VTune Performance Analyzer
(continued)
  locating hotspots in RotateBlend
    example, 228- 29, 243- 47,
    263- 64
  overview, 29
  and parallel programming issues,
    202
  sampling processor events, 187
  as sampling profiler, 29- 31
  source code analysis, 33

  using time-based sampling to
    find additional hotspot in
    RotateBlend application,
    243- 47

W

ways, cache line, 93
Win32 API, 193, 194
worksharing, 195
write-combining (WC) memory,
    96- 97, 260- 62